DISABILITY &
DIVERSITY

An Introduction

EDITED BY
PHIL SMITH

REVISED PRINTING

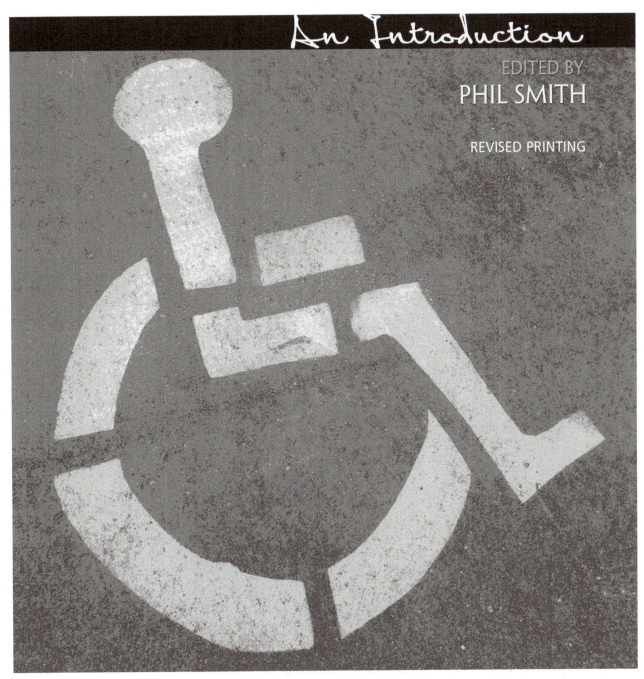

Kendall Hunt
publishing company

Cover image provided by the author.

Kendall Hunt
publishing company

www.kendallhunt.com
Send all inquiries to:
4050 Westmark Drive
Dubuque, IA 52004-1840

Contents

SECTION 4   How Does Disability Intersect with Other Social Identities?   207

SECTION 5   How Do We Imagine a Society in Which People with Disabilities
Are a Part of All Communities?   223

Acknowledgments

Editing a book means that LOTS of people have their hands on lots of parts of the resulting book. I won't be able to talk about everyone's contribution—but I'll try to cover some. The faculty of Eastern Michigan University's Department of Special Education planned and implemented this book as part of a process to substantially revise SPGN 251, originally an introduction to special education. They (and others) wrote the book that is in your hands now. Without their hard and careful work, this book would never have appeared.

Rhonda Kraai led the team effort to revise SPGN 251. Her organizational work, and attention to detail, are all over the course, and this book.

Students think that professors do the heavy lifting in the teaching-learning biz. The truth is that without students, faculty would be in nowhere's-ville. Thanks to all the students (at EMU and elsewhere) that I've worked with for the past 30+ years. Some have made a critical mark on my thinking and writing: Jacob, Scooter, Christie Routel, Michael Peacock, and Pamela Colton come to mind. More recently, Jason DeCamiillis, Kevin Dorn, Bill Massey, Megan Hoorn, Sarah Mueller, Katie Stanton, and Rachel Lewandowski have poked, prodded, questioned, and answered. Y'all are the real teachers.

The work of colleagues—some at other universities, some unaffiliated scholars—helped make this book happen, too. Liat Ben-Moshe, Emily Titon, Zach Richter, and Ibby Grace deserve note.

Finally, thanks to Rilla and Sara, for the reasons you both know.

Introduction

Phil Smith

Through our interactions with those who have disabilities, we stand to learn valuable lessons that will lead us to greater appreciation of diversity in all of its forms. (Van der Klift & Kunc 2002, p. 28)

This book is about the social and cultural diversity of the United States. It seeks to understand what that means, and how it plays out, by exploring disability in the United States. To do that means asking a bunch of questions: What is disability? What kinds of disabilities are there? How is disability created and maintained in U.S. culture? How does disability intersect with other social identities? And, finally, how do we—can we—imagine a society in which people with disabilities are a part of all communities? *Disability & Diversity: An Introduction* will explore these questions, and more.

The chapter authors of this book, all highly acclaimed experts in the fields of disability and education, offer insights into what it means to have a disability in twenty-first-century America. They outline the history of disability; how disability is defined, and who defines it; who benefits from disability labels; and what teachers and other professionals can do to change how we think about disability, and how people with disabilities fit into our society. User-friendly, easy to read and understand, *Disability & Diversity* will also challenge what it is you think you know about being normal, having a disability, and living in a diverse, democratic society.

The authors of this text are varied, and so are their values, opinions, and thinking. They don't always agree with each other—and that lack of agreement is reflected in the chapters you'll read here. That's not a bad thing, for several reasons. First, you'll be exposed to a diverse set of styles and ideas, so that you can begin to think about what your own ideas, values, and opinions are. You'll also begin to get an idea for the variety of ideas, values, and opinions that make up the fields of education, special education, disability studies, and the disability rights movement, and start to understand what concepts are in contention. You'll also get a feel for how professionals, scholars, practitioners, and theorists engage with one another when they disagree about a particular issue or idea. And you'll start to understand that there is no single way of understanding, of knowing, the world, and the cultures that people make and inhabit.

I'd like to say that this book will provide you with answers to questions about disability, and diversity, in U.S. society and culture. But as I think about that, maybe providing you with answers is not such a great idea. Probably providing you with questions, or at least an opportunity to ask your own questions, is a better purpose for this book. Answers are always final, done, and finished, and this book shouldn't be a final thing. It should be a starting point, a place for your own growth and learning.

As you read this book, take some time to reflect and take stock. What is *your* experience and understanding of disbility? What values, opinions, and ideas have shaped how *you* think about disability? What is *your* cultural background? What is *your* social identity, and how did you acquire it? How has that impacted *your* life? Do *you* want to push back against the way you've been brought up to think about and understand disability? What will that mean for *your* life, work, and relationships? What kind of community and culture do *you* want to live in? What will *you* do to make that happen?

Challenge yourself. Don't just accept at face value what you read here. Challenge the writing that is within this book. Argue with it. And then go do something about it. Don't just talk; do. Put into action what you learn from this book, these authors. The intersection between theory and action (some people call that praxis)—that's where the *real* learning happens.

So, after you read this book, go make stuff happen. Now. By tomorrow's breakfast, at the latest.

Section 1

What Is Disability?

Chapter 1

What Is Disability?

Phil Smith

Defining disability is a complicated thing—it's not an easy task. Oh, I suppose it could be done quickly, to say that it represents "the atypical, the out-of-step, the underfooted" (Linton 2006, 3). It "hints at something missing either fiscally, physically, mentally or legally" (Goodley 2011, 1). It "is a social enigma" (Berger 2013, 1). Some see it as whatever is different from the norm. Others see disability as being natural, that what is normal is a spectrum, an essential variety, rather than seeing disability, or normal, as one, single, simple thing.

Image © ankudi, 2014. Used under license from Shutterstock, Inc.

One scholar defines disability as "the product of social injustice" (Siebers 2008, 3). More fully, it is "a cultural and minority identity … an elastic social category both subject to social control and capable of effecting social change" (Siebers 2008, 4).

I could define disability in numbers: statistically, some say that very nearly 20% of American people who are over five years of age, and not living in an institution, have a disability (Goodley 2011). Other researchers suggest that the number of Americans with a disability is a bit larger than that, at 22% (Centers for Disease Control and Prevention 2011). Still other researchers, basing their findings on survey results, suggest that the number is approximately 30% of Americans (U.S. Department of Health and Human Services 2008).

These definitions are important, and useful but they seem—not enough. They're not complicated enough; that is, they don't seem to capture everything that we mean by the concept of disability (sometimes, simplicity isn't a good thing; sometimes, it's better to complexify rather than to simplify, to completely and fully understand an idea or concept. Maybe, rather than trying to define disability itself, it would be helpful to describe how we look at disability.

Image © Hannah Ensor, 2014. Used under license from Shutterstock, Inc.

A Note About Language

People with disabilities have been called all kinds of things, for a very long time. Idiots, feeble-minded, crazy, mad, cripples, handicapped—these are all words that have been used to describe people with disabilities. Recently, people in the United States have started to be more intentional about the language they use when they refer to people with disabilities. Folks have begun to use what is called "person-first language," describing the person literally first, and then talking about the disability. So instead of saying, "Bob is an autistic person," people now say, "Bob is a friend of mine with autism." Such language is more respectful of the person.

For example,

Instead of saying	Say this, instead
the handicapped, the disabled	people with disabilities
the blind	people who are blind; people who are visually impaired
suffers a hearing impairment; hearing impaired	people who are deaf; people who are hard of hearing; the Deaf
afflicted by MS	people who have multiple sclerosis
CP victim	people with cerebral palsy
retarded; mentally defective; slow	people with developmental disabilities
confined to a wheelchair; wheelchair bound	people who use a wheelchair; wheelchair user
dumb; mute	unable to speak; non-verbal
fit	seizure
courageous	successful; productive
cripple; lame	people with mobility impairments
mental; crazy; psycho; nutcase	people with mental illness; psychiatric survivors (Vermont Developmental Disabilities Council 2007)

(Vermont Development Disabilities Council 2007)

Recently, a movement to end the use of the R-word (retard, retarded, retardation) has begun. The generally acceptable phrase is intellectual disabilities, used now by the national American Association of Intellectual and Developmental Disabilities. The R-word has been eliminated from all documents and language used by the U.S. government.

To make things more complicated, people with disabilities have taken to using "disability-first" language, to highlight their social identity as disabled people. It's a way for them to identify with and gain solidarity from a social group that gives them strength and power in the world. Writer, activist, and scholar Simi Linton puts it this way: "I identify as a member of the minority group—disabled people—and that is a strong influence on my cultural make-up, who I am, and the way that I think" (2006, 118). It also is a way for them to point toward the fact that disability is not something that is part of them, is not part of their mind or body, but is something imposed on them by society. In effect, they seek to highlight the fact that what disables them is not some part of themselves, but what society does to them. People without disabilities sometimes use euphemisms for disabilities and disabled people: vertically challenged, differently abled, handi-capable, special needs, physically and mentally challenged. People with disabilities generally reject these terms: "virtually no disabled person uses these cute phrases … [They are] silly and scoffed at … Only by using direct terminology … will people think about what it means to be disabled …" (Shapiro 1993, 33). People with disabilities talk about themselves in ways that sometimes seem crude, but to them are a way to reclaim their identity and culture: crips, gimps, and blinks. They sometimes refer to people without disabilities as walkies, a.b.'s (able-bodied's), or TAB's (Temporarily Able-Bodied's) (Shapiro 1993). Just like terms adopted by other identity groups that reclaim identity, use of such words by people without disabilities may seem insensitive and oppressive.

All of this leads us to think about and discuss models of disability.

What's a Model?

There are two main ways of understanding disability—they're called models of disability. A model, of course, is not the real thing—like a model airplane or model car—it's a depiction of what the real airplane or car is, something like what the real thing is, but not a precise copy of the real thing. A model is kind of a way to talk about the real thing when the real thing is pretty complicated, or big, or hard to understand. That's something to bear in mind, though, when talking about models (whether of disability, or anything else)—while they can be useful in coming to understand a particular idea or concept, they are imprecise and incomplete replicas, rather than precise and exact copies. While they may share common features with the original, they are not the thing itself.

The Medical Model of Disabilities

The first model of disability is the medical model—some have called it an essentialist model (Berger 2013). The medical model says that people with disabilities have something about their bodies or minds that is broken, something that needs to be fixed. Within the medical model, disability is something that is within people—they "have" it. Disability is seen as being something that is real, measurable, describable, identifiable. The medical model of disability says that you can say that there is a specific and real difference within an individual, and that professionals can describe what it is, and where it is, and how it operates, in people's minds and bodies.

And, from a medical model perspective, because people with disabilities are seen as being not right, or broken, ways of fixing them have been developed: "fixing or curing the disability becomes the primary focus" (Baglieri and Shapiro 2012, 16). Special education is one way of doing that; so is rehabilitation; and so is mental health treatment. Implied in the medical model of disability is that there are people without disabilities (probably MOST people don't have disabilities, from the medical model perspective). The medical model asserts that disability is about individuals. It describes different kinds of disabilities, and finds the commonalities among those different kinds of disabilities (for example, people with Down syndrome often have intellectual disabilities—the medical model would say that is a key, perhaps even defining feature, of Down syndrome).

Many people with disabilities are critical of the medical model, because they don't feel like they are broken. They say that their disabilities are defining features of who they are, how they are, in the world. Many would argue that they could not imagine having their disability removed from them—fixed, if you will—it's a part of their essence, their identity, who they see themselves as being.

Here, the medical model of disability is usually thought of as a single thing, as one particular model. That's probably not really true—there are probably multiple medical models. But most disability theorists talk about the medical model as a single model, a single way of understanding and describing disability.

When people with disabilities and their allies criticize the medical model of disability, they don't (at least usually) mean to be critical of the field of medicine, or at least all of it. When they have the flu, they still go to the doctor; if they have appendicitis, they still go to the hospital. It's not about the field of medicine, per se, that they're criticizing. Rather, they're criticizing the way that people think about and understand the idea of disability—the notion that people are broken, need to be fixed, and that there are ways of fixing them.

Social Models of Disabilities

The other kind of model of disability is the social model. Here, disability theorists talk about multiple social models of disability, because there are a number of different kinds. But they all have some common features. Generally, social models see disability, at least in part, as being socially constructed. That is, disability is portrayed as being something that is created by society, or culture, rather than being something that is real and in people's minds and bodies.

This is kind of a tough idea to wrap your head around, the notion that disability—or many other things, for that matter—is socially constructed. We think of things like disability (or race, or gender, or even something like wilderness) as being things that are real and definable. But folks who think that ideas like disability are socially constructed have a different frame of reference.

Here's an example of how disability is socially constructed. Take the idea of intellectual disability (we used to call it the "R" word, but now most people with disabilities and their allies see the "R" word as being something like a swear word, so we don't use that term anymore—and get pretty upset when people who don't know better, or who don't think about the impact of their language on others, use it). One of the key definitions of intellectual disability has to do with the measure of intelligence, which is referred to as IQ, or intelligence quotient. The so-called normal IQ is 100. People are said to have an intellectual disability if they have an IQ of 70 or below (we'll talk more later about IQ, intelligence, and intellectual disability—this is the short version here).

So the question is: why 70? Why not 85? Or 55? Or 115, for that matter? Well, statisticians would come up with some fancy reason why it needs to be 70 (70, it turns out, is two standard deviations below the mean—but don't worry about that, at least for now), but the real reason is: just, well, just because.

Essentially, what it boils down to, is some folks in the fields of statistics, intelligence, and supporting people with disabilities, got together and decided that the right number was 70. In fact—and this is sort of the kicker—the number didn't always used to be 70. Within the last 60 years—in 1959—it was decided that the IQ number at which people were said to have an intellectual disability was 85. For a bunch of reasons (not least to do with the fact that the higher number of 85 meant that more people were labeled as having an intellectual disability, but also because of the number of people with intellectual disabilities who were from racial minorities), the decision was made to lower the number from 85 to 70—in 1973, just forty years ago. Heck, for that matter, the idea of representing intelligence as a number, one that we might call IQ, wasn't invented until the early 1900s. Up until then, no one had thought that it was important to quantify intelligence (more about that later, too).

The point is that the IQ cutoff score for intellectual disability could be changed (and was) because people decided that it needed to be changed, to resolve or address or deal with some perceived issue or concern. So that intellectual disability, rather than being some real thing inside people, is something created by people in a social context—in other words, it is socially constructed. Other specific disability categories are similarly socially constructed—who does and doesn't have a learning disability; who does and doesn't have cerebral palsy; who is or isn't on the autism spectrum—these are all examples of ways that disability is socially constructed.

Another feature shared among the several kinds of social models of disability is where the attribute of disability is said to lie. The medical model of disability would say that the disability lies in the bodies and minds of people so labeled. Social models of disability would say that the attribute of disability lies in society, rather than in people. That is, because disability is constructed by society, that's where it sits. One implication of this is that disability categories can be changed or modified by society.

An important implication of the site of disability being in society has to do with institutions. The work that modern, and especially Western, societies do for and with the individual people who make up those societies is accomplished through social institutions. Sometimes, institutions are real bricks-and-mortar entities. Sometimes, social institutions are the set of processes, behaviors, attitudes, and ideas needed to accomplish some important social function or goal. The spiritual needs of a particular society, for example, might be dealt with through religious institutions. The need to equitably exchange goods and services in a capitalist society might be accomplished through financial institutions. And so on.

In this way, the needs and desires of people with disabilities (and those said not to have disabilities, too) are accomplished through a variety of social institutions. Understanding the kinds of social institutions that impact people with disabilities, and the ways in which they respond to the needs of both people with disabilities and the larger society, then, is an important focus of theorists, researchers, activists, and thinkers looking at disability from a social model perspective.

For example, some folks in the disability world, looking at capitalist societies, see disability as having an industrial component. That is, they would argue that the whole notion of disability arose to meet the needs of an increasingly industrialist society. And, they would assert, the needs of people with disabilities are dealt with or resolved by disability industry, designed to create financial wealth and gain for some by meeting the needs of people with disabilities. In so doing, disability categories, and the services required to address those categories, are created in order to enhance financial wealth (mostly for people without disability labels). So, the thinking goes, one can understand and analyze the way disability plays out in industrial, capitalist societies by understanding and exploring the interplay between capital, industry, and disability.

There are different kinds of social models of disability. The minority model of disability understands disabled people as being part of a social minority, experiencing life in many of the same ways that other social minorities experience life (often, for example, minorities experience oppression, violence, abuse, and poverty).

Another kind of social model separates disability from impairment. Impairment is described as the actual physical, cognitive, or other difference in people's bodies and minds. Disability is portrayed, in this kind of social model, as the social construction that people with impairments experience. This kind of social model is one frequently held by people in England and Europe, and is formally codified in United Nations' projects and language. Some social models do not separate disability and impairment, seeing them both as being socially and culturally constructed.

Questions for Discussion

▶ What is disability? What does it look like? What does it sound like? What is the opposite of disability (is that normal)? If you were walking down the street, how would you know if someone had a disability? Or could you? Who defines what a disability is—who gets to say who has a disability and who doesn't?

▶ Down syndrome, geneticists and medical experts say, is the result of a chromosomal abnormality, called Trisomy 21. That is, there is a difference in the twenty-first human chromosome that results in what we call Down syndrome. Given this genetic (and very real) difference, is Down syndrome a socially constructed disability category? How? Why? Are ALL specific disability categories socially constructed? Why or why not?

▶ How was the notion of disability created by the coming of industrialism? What does the idea of a disability industry mean, and what are its implications for both people with and without disabilities? Who benefits from such a disability industry? Understanding that people with disabilities in the United States are vastly un- and under-employed, as well as extremely impoverished, what does that tell us about the place of people with disabilities in U.S. society, and their role in it, in both individual and structural ways?

Chapter 2

A Short History of Disability

Phil Smith

"...disabled people [are] significant actors in history..." (Baynton 2005, 562)

Prehistory and Disability

Disability has always been a part of us—part of the human condition. Archaeologists have found evidence of disability from the historical past—from the time before written records—as well as how people with disabilities were treated. A Neanderthal man, who died 45,000 years ago at age 50, had disabilities that would have required substantial support for him to live. A teenage boy with a developmental disability lived 10,000 years ago, and would have needed tremendous amounts of support to live so long. Another young man, with spina bifida, lived to the age of 15 years old—7,500 years ago. The buried 4,000-year-old remains of a young man discovered in Vietnam reveal that he had a developmental disability, and that he was cared for by his family and community throughout his life (Gorman 2012). Disability has been a part of what it means to be human for as long as there have been humans. And communities and families provided support and care for their loved ones, giving a clear indication that the discrimination and oppression of people with disabilities is a relatively modern, perhaps wholly European, phenomenon.

Disability in Indigenous North American Cultures

The incredibly diverse and numerous cultures indigenous to North America, and to what we now call the United States, generally had a much different understanding of the place of people in culture and community, and of the meaning of disability, than of the white European cultures that arrived there in the fifteenth and six-teenth centuries. Speaking generally—because the cultures native to North America are remarkably varied—these peoples believed that each person had a gift to share. They also saw deeper connections between an individual's body, spirit, and mind; individual and community; and people and environment, than did their white, European conquerors. The meaning of disability as we know it today was much different for peoples of the North American First Nations cultures—often, it reflected a perceived imbalance with other parts of the person. At other times, what we might now characterize as disability—psychiatric disability, for example—was understood as a gift, a perception of the world to be revered and shared rather than stigmatized. It mattered less to North American indigenous cultures about what individuals *couldn't* do, and more about what they contrib-uted to the common good of the community (Nielsen 2012). These differences in how varied cultures under-stood and viewed what we have come to call disability have much to teach our own culture.

Disability in the Early United States

Early white settlers to North America gave little notice to bodies that were physically different. Because of medical knowledge of the time, and the relative difficulty of life, many people had bodies that varied from the norm—severe injuries were not uncommon; and injuries that we would not think twice about became severe because of the kind of treatment (and its lack) available at the time. Still, because people with disabilities were able to do the work needed to stay alive in the New World, they were not seen as unusual or different. People who *were* marked as different by the early colonists were people with psychiatric or intellectual disabilities, referred to, in the language of the time, as "distracted persons" and "idiots." They (as well as those with significant developmental impairments) were felt to have disabilities because they were not able to contribute their labor toward the well-being of their family and community (Nielsen 2012).

Those who were marked as having disabilities in the colonies were sometimes at risk of not being allowed into colonial America. Others were deported back to the European countries from which they came (Shapiro 1993). In some ways, the cultural signals sent by the colonialists were mixed.

Many influential, historical figures or their family members in what would become the United States were felt to have psychiatric or intellectual disabilities: the wife of Patrick Henry; the sister of Thomas Jefferson; James Otis; and the wife of Cotton Mather are examples. Early law in Massachusetts, Rhode Island, and elsewhere, protected them from being punished for infractions, because it was felt they could not understand what they did—they were "considered innocent and harmless and in need of protection" (Nielsen 2012, 23). At least one who helped draft the constitution, Gouverneur Morris from New York, was missing a leg. And Stephen Hopkins, who signed the Declaration of Independence, had cerebral palsy (Shapiro 1993).

Deaf people did come to what would be the United States—one fisherman settled on the island of Martha's Vineyard in 1694. Deafness was widespread on the island, because of genetic heritage and intermarriage, and almost everyone used sign language, even those who could hear. Deaf and hearing citizens were fully included in the culture of the island. Although the last Deaf resident died in 1952, older islanders continued to use sign language into the 1980s. In the rest of the country, up through the present, there remained huge conflicts between proponents of oralism (teaching people with hearing impairments to communicate through speech, advocated by Alexander Graham Bell) and the use of American Sign Language (resulting in what became Deaf culture, advocated by Thomas Gallaudet) (Shapiro 1993).

In the period leading up to the Revolutionary war, families were primarily responsible for the care and support of people with disabilities, and so most lived at home. For those families that were not able to provide appropriate support, local communities—towns and villages—were responsible. In the early 1700s almshouses, poor houses, or workhouses were created in the colonies. There, people who were "lunatic" or "idiots," and too difficult for families to care for, were forcibly confined (Nielsen 2012).

In this same time period, African slaves began to be brought to North America. The racist beliefs so foundational to the culture of the colonies (and our own country now) meant that all African slaves were perceived to be abnormal in mind and body. Those who encouraged the slave trade drew on the language of disability as a rationale for why being a slave was actually better for Africans than their former, miserable existence. Ableism and racism worked hand in hand to create and support slavery in what would become the United States of America (Nielsen 2012). In the same way, women were perceived as less human, less able, and less intelligent, than white, middle- and upper-class men. People of color and women were all seen as being not normal (Nocella 2012).

At the time of the American Revolution, and the creation of the United States, there was much discussion about who could and could not be a citizen—who could and could not vote. It was taken for granted that African slaves, people of the native indigenous cultures, women of whatever race, and people with disabilities were unfit to govern themselves, never mind participate in the governance of their communities, the States, or the country (Nielsen 2012).

Disability was used, strategically and intentionally, as a rationale for excluding not just people with disabilities, but also women and people with minority status in the United States, from the rights and responsibilities of those given citizenship, typically only white, middle- and upper-class men. Negative disabling characteristics were ascribed to all others: "irrationality, excessive emotionality, physical weakness ... supposed tendencies to feeble-mindedness, mental illness, deafness, blindness, and other disabilities" (Baynton 2013, 17). Ableism, racism, and sexism were built into the very core of what it meant to be a citizen, into the fabric of law, government, and culture of the United States (Nielsen 2012).

The Revolutionary War resulted in numerous casualties, some with significant disabilities. Because war veterans were seen as heroes, the new federal government and the states provided funding for their care and support. Hospitals were established for their care, some as early as 1798. These became the system that we now know as the Veteran's Administration, which was established in 1922 (Shapiro 1993).

Into the 1800s

Almshouses in the cities, and poor farms in more rural settings, continued to be settings where people with disabilities lived in the 1800s. One activist, Dorothea Dix, set about reforming this system, where conditions were often squalid at best. Partly as a result of her activism, states started to take over these institutions in the 1840s. Proposed federal legislation in 1852 to help fund these facilities was vetoed by President Franklin Pierce (Shapiro 1993).

After the Revolutionary War, what defined disability was being able to work. Those who could not were deemed to have a disability. Because some in American society at the time were felt to be unable to do at least some kinds of work, they became associated with disability—these included women (whether white or African American who were free), Native Americans, and slaves. African Americans, whether free or enslaved, were understood to be physically and intellectually incompetent. That owners of slaves inflicted on them much harm so as to cause actual physical disability can also not be denied. Slavery, as an institution, was felt by those who supported it as a just solution for those considered less than human (Nielsen 2012).

Institutions for people with disabilities developed in the early 1800s in the United States, and began spreading throughout the country, beginning in the Northeast and then spreading south and west. At the same time, coupled with expansion of medicine as a profession, understanding of disability as something supernatural or theological shifted to seeing disability as a biological phenomenon (Nielsen 2012).

Much of the development of institutions for people with disabilities was done privately, but had a wide impact. Thomas Gallaudet (for whom Gallaudet University, the premier Deaf university in the world, was named), established a school for the deaf in 1817, in Hartford. Samuel Howe opened a school for the blind in 1832—it would later be called the Perkins School. Howe also opened a school to teach students with intellectual disabilities in 1848 (Nielsen 2012; Shapiro 1993).

The Civil War also resulted in numerous, severe casualties, which brought again to the forefront the necessity for caring for injured veterans. The number and severity of their injuries placed a huge financial burden on the newly reunited states, some of it taken on by the states themselves (Shapiro 1993). In addition to physical injuries, soldiers returning from the war also experienced psychiatric disabilities. Substantial progress was made on developing adaptive technology for disabled veterans (Nielsen 2012).

The federal government took on a more active role supporting veterans after World War 1, as well as others with disabilities. The Veterans Bureau was established in 1921, and other rehabilitation programs were set up in 1918 and 1920. Following World War II, federal rehabilitation programs expanded again (Shapiro 1993).

In the later part of the 1800s, into the early twentieth century, institutionalization of people with disabilities increased substantially. In the South, these institutions were segregated by race (Nielsen 2012).

Hiding and Eliminating Disability

In some ways, the history of disability in the United States during the end of the nineteenth century and the early part of the twentieth century was a history of invisibility, or at least making disability invisible. It was a time when much work was done to hide or eliminate disability from the public sphere and consciousness. At times, this was done overtly, by the enactment of so-called ugly laws, in which people with disabilities were forbidden to appear in public spaces (Nielsen 2012).

Perhaps one of the best examples of the ways in which everyone in North American culture conspired to hide disability is the story of President Franklin D. Roosevelt, who played a major role in bringing the country through the Great Depression and World War II. Roosevelt was a person with a disability—he contracted polio and used a wheelchair. Yet "he was never seen in public, nor photographed in private, in his wheelchair" (Shapiro 1993, 62). Even after his death, and into the twenty-first century, portrayals of Roosevelt as a disabled man met with great controversy. It was only after much disagreement that a statue of Roosevelt sitting in a wheelchair was placed just outside the official Roosevelt memorial in Washington DC.

Another President, Woodrow Wilson, had dyslexia, which would have a powerful impact on his work. But he also experienced an apparent stroke during his second term, one kept hidden from the public and even his own Cabinet for some time. Because of the disabilities that resulted from the stroke, he was in large measure unable to fulfill his responsibilities as President—yet almost no one at the time knew about it, and few do today.

Development of the ideology of eugenicism in the late 1800s meant that many cultural and political leaders worked actively to eliminate disability, and people with disabilities, both in the United States and around the world. The word eugenics was created in 1883 by naturalist Frances Galton, cousin to Charles Darwin. The word comes from "eu", which means good, and "gen", which has the meaning of being born, or produced. Galton's idea was to take the ideas of Darwin's survival-of-the-fittest conception of evolution, and apply it to human, social activity. This meant supporting the progeny of people seen as morally good, and doing away with human lineages that were seen as morally bad (Smith 2008). Eugenics has been described as "the belief that the way to improve society is through better human breeding practices so that only those with 'positive' hereditary traits reproduce" (Nielsen 2012, 101).

Eugenicist thinking and work was based in racism, classism, and sexism. People seen by eugenicists as being morally good were white, middle- or upper-class, and men. People who were morally bad were non-white, impoverished, lower-class, and, more often than not, not male. Eugenicists developed statistically-based tests to sort those who were morally good from morally bad—modern IQ tests are one result (given where they came from, we should not be surprised that IQ tests are often described as being culturally and racially biased) (Smith 2008). Immigrants were scrutinized closely to determine whether they were "likely to become a public charge" (according to federal law), and were rejected if they had bodily anomalies, appeared to be homosexual, or were from impoverished, minority racial and ethnic backgrounds (Nielsen 2012).

As a result of the eugenicist's efforts, well over 100,000 people in the United States were forcibly (sometimes without their knowledge) sterilized. Over thirty states required forced sterilization; Michigan, for example, forcibly sterilized 3,786 people between 1907 and 1937. The Supreme Court determined, in *Buck v. Bell*, that these forced sterilization laws were constitutional under the Constitution, a decision that has never, to this date, been overturned. Carrie Buck, for whom the court decision is named, was a white, impoverished woman who had a child out of wedlock—for which she was institutionalized and forcibly sterilized (Nielsen 2012).

Laws were enacted that prevented certain groups from marrying (some of these laws were still on the books into the latter part of the twentieth century). Widespread institutionalization of people with disabilities was enacted, nation-wide. People were institutionalized for being an unwed mother, or for having epilepsy (Smith 2008). The institutionalization of people with disabilities continues to the present-day around the United States.

Some in Europe were very attracted to the ideas and practices of eugenicists in the United States. They invited important eugenicists to speak, and their writing had a huge impact on social policy in Europe in the early twentieth century. One group that was greatly affected by U.S. eugenicist thinking was the Nazis in Germany. They were so taken with this work, that they used it to eliminate Jews, Gypsies, gay people, and other groups of people without disabilities throughout Europe (Smith 2008).

In essence, what we have come to call the Holocaust was created by the thinking of U.S. eugenicists. And the practices used in the Holocaust itself were developed by practicing on people with disabilities, who were systematically killed in death camps developed for their elimination, in what was called the T-4 program, so-called for its address on Tiergartenstrasse in Berlin. The Nazis learned the techniques for killing millions of people by the experiments they developed in the Disability Holocaust, in which as many as half a million disabled people were killed. Hundreds of thousands of others were forcibly sterilized. The disability Holocaust resulted in the elimination of an entire generation of Deaf people in Europe.

In spite of these moves to eliminate and hide people with disabilities, some still rose to prominence. One was Helen Keller. Though renowned as a disabled woman, and for the story about her education (which often portrays the heroine of the story as her teacher, rather than Keller herself), Keller didn't see herself as being at the forefront of advancing the place of people with disabilities—she saw her primary legacy being a result of her work as a socialist, a feminist, a labor rights activist, a pacifist, and a writer.

The legacy of the eugenics movement continues to this day. Special education itself is founded in deeply eugenicist beliefs and practices, including reliance on IQ and other standardized text procedures. In the 1990s, over 400 book-length works were written supporting and describing eugenicist ideology. In the first few years of the twenty-first century, almost that number of books were written on the same topic. Some argue that much genetic and human genome research is eugenicist. Eugenics is far from dead in our culture (Smith 2008).

The 1950s and 1960s

At the end of the 1940s and into the 1950s, parents of people with disabilities began to engage in significant advocacy work. Many worked to get their children out of institutions. Others tried to convince schools to include their children, especially those with significant disabilities, into regular schools. Some gave up after being rebuffed many times, and set up their own schools, some in church basements. The organizations sponsoring these activities became groups that continue to this day. One, The Association for Retarded Children, became the Arc (no longer an acronym), still a force to be reckoned with. The movement to include children with disabilities in schools gained new energy with the Supreme Court *Brown vs. Board of Education* decision in 1954. Although focused on racial integration, it was also used to enable the inclusion of disabled children (Shapiro 1993).

In 1966, comedian and actor Jerry Lewis took over a Labor Day telethon raising money for the Muscular Dystrophy Association. He raised billions of dollars for research about muscular dystrophy, supporting what came to be called "Jerry's kids." But people with disabilities saw his efforts as having a negative impact, creating and supporting negative stereotypes about people with disabilities, and criticized his involvement and the telethon for many years (Shapiro 1993). They described ways in which Lewis created a "poster child" image for people with disabilities. Lewis finally stopped hosting the telethon in 2010.

The Beginning of the Disability Rights Movement in the United States

Image © Dirk Ercken, 2014. Used under license from Shutterstock, Inc.

The Disability Rights Movement (DRM) and the independent living movement began in Berkeley, California, at the University of California at Berkeley, when a man named Ed Roberts started taking classes there in 1962.

At the age of fourteen, in 1953, Roberts contracted polio, which left him almost completely paralyzed. He was able to move only his head—he was unable to breathe on his own. He survived because he used an "iron lung," a large device in which he lay, and that helped him breathe (Shapiro 1993).

Although at times extremely depressed (he tried to commit suicide by not eating), he finished high school, at first taking classes by telephone, then in a wheelchair. He completed two years of study at a community college. He applied to UC-Berkeley, but was at first denied. He was also denied funding from the California Department of Rehabilitation, which refused to pay for his education. Roberts fought back, obtained the funding he needed, found a place on campus where he could live with his iron lung (in the student infirmary, a building called Cowell), and started classes. Necessary personal attendant services were paid for through state funding (Nielsen 2012; Shapiro 1993).

Roberts engaged in all that college students did in the early '60s: experimented with drugs, drank too much, and fell in love. His drive for independent living led him to adopt an early motorized wheelchair. He finished an undergraduate and masters degree, and started a doctoral program. By the late '60s, he and a group of students with significant disabilities lived together in Cowell—they called themselves the Rolling Quads. They fought hard for their rights, including access to the community. Their advocacy forced the city of Berkeley to put in curb cuts, letting them get off of campus on their own (Shapiro 1993).

Some in the Rolling Quads wanted to live on their own, independently, away from Cowell. Roberts, with a counselor from his community college, helped establish a program that would support disabled students, with federal funding. The Physically Disabled Students Program (PDSP) established an office on campus, and began finding apartments that would allow for independent living. They set up a workshop to repair and modify wheelchairs, and provided advocacy when needed, for students with significant disabilities. Full- and part-time disabled people staffed the project, allowing many students with disabilities to come to Berkeley (Shapiro 1993).

In the early 1970s, Roberts and others at the PDSP set up the first Center for Independent Living (CIL), to provide the same kind of supports for people not going to college in Berkeley. Run by people with disabilities, with little funding, the CIL saw disability as an issue of civil rights. Roberts served as director for a year and a half, then became the state director of the Department of Rehabilitation (the same one that had initially denied him funding to attend college) in 1975. In that role, he completely reformed the department, expanding funding, ensuring greater flexibility (Shapiro 1993).

Disability activism began to move from supporting disabled people in practical ways, to taking on political goals. This move toward increasingly political work was supported when Judy Heumann, who contracted polio as a baby, and had become a disability activist when she was refused a license to teach school because of her disability, came to the CIL first as deputy director, and then as director (Nielsen 2012; Shapiro 1993).

Legislation for the Civil Rights of Disabled People

One of the most important federal laws supporting the rights of people with disabilities happened almost by accident. The Rehabilitation Act of 1973, signed into law by Richard Nixon, was designed to provide funding to support rehabilitation efforts. But tacked on at the very end, almost as an afterthought, was a part of the law that was to take on huge importance for disabled people. Section 504 of the Rehabilitation Act "made it illegal for any ... institution or activity that received federal funding to discriminate against anyone" (Shapiro 1993, 65) because of disability. This included almost all schools, universities, and federal contractors.

President Ford's and Carter's administrations recognized how far-reaching and expensive this legislation would be, and stalled the implementation of regulations required by it. In 1977, disability activists, fed up with the stalling, organized a protest in Washington, DC, in which they occupied the office of the Secretary of Health, Education, and Welfare (HEW) overnight (Shapiro 1993).

Another protest, led by Judy Heumann of the CIL in San Francisco, lasted twenty-five days, and drew widespread national attention, when they took over the state HEW office. Ed Roberts, in his role as California Director of Rehabilitation, announced his approval and support of the action. Officials responded by cutting off food, telephone, and attendant services. Food and other support was provided by other radical and civil rights groups. When HEW representatives suggested that they wanted to water down the regulations, Heumann, Roberts, and others attacked their ideas. HEW finally backed down, and enacted the regulations. At the same time, it also enacted regulations for P.L. 94-142 (the law that would become the Individuals with Disabilities Education Improvement Act), which it had also been stonewalling for several years (Nielsen 2012; Shapiro 1993).

Following these victories, though the DRM experienced setbacks, it also achieved success. The independent living movement spread widely, and CIL's cropped up all over the country (Shapiro 1993).

In 1988, disability activists began pushing for the development of additional civil rights protection. Robert Burgdorf, Jr., attorney for the President Ronald Reagan-appointed National Council on the Handicapped, and Justin Dart, Jr., a member of the Council, began the process of writing potential legislation. They gained allies in Senators Tom Harkin and Edward Kennedy, who rewrote their initial work under the President George Bush administration. Their law, the Americans with Disabilities Act (ADA), was passed and signed on July 26, 1991—a day that continues to be celebrated by disability advocates around the country (Shapiro 1993). Although its initial vision has been blunted by subsequent court decisions, it remains an international model for the rights of people with disabilities.

Deaf Culture, Deaf Rights

In 1988, Deaf students at Gallaudet University rose up to urge the university to hire a Deaf President. In the history of the university, it had always been led by hearing people. As Deaf people began to recognize themselves as a culture (and not a disability), students at Gallaudet felt that only a Deaf person could truly understand their experience and identity. When the latest hearing president resigned in 1987, they felt it was time. Two of the three candidates were Deaf; but the one hearing candidate, Elisabeth Zinser, was selected, in March of 1988. Students were outraged, and protested with marches and speeches. They effectively closed down the school. The Board of Trustees resisted their demands, but students fought back, keeping the incumbent, Zinser, off the campus (Shapiro 1993).

Students brought the issue to Congress, which provided federal funding to Gallaudet. After a week of protests, Zinser resigned, and the Board of Trustees elected I. King Jordan, dean of the college of arts and sciences, very popular—and Deaf. The Board also elected a new Board chair, again, a Deaf person (Nielsen 2012; Shapiro 1993).

Advocating for Transportation Equality—and Beyond

Wade Blank, a nondisabled man who had worked to support people with disabilities, helped a number of disabled people escape from nursing homes. They formed a community, and in 1983 established an organization focused on making public transportation accessible in their hometown of Denver, Colorado. They called the organization ADAPT, which originally stood for American Disabled for Accessible Public Transit, used nonviolent direct action protest tactics, reminiscent of other civil rights movements. Some of their strategies included blocking buses from moving, and then crawling up the bus stairs, as well as chaining themselves to buses to prevent them from moving. Their crawl up the steps to the U.S. capitol sent a powerful message to legislators about the importance of the ADA to disabled people. After seven years of struggle, with passage of the ADA, accessible transit was required nationwide.

Blank died in the early 1990s. People with disabilities, like Bob Kafka, assumed leadership roles. Their focus has shifted from transportation to a wide range of issues, including abolishing the bias toward institutionalization in disability funding. Their focus on direct action remains strong, however, and their attention to issues has grown from a focus on local concerns to national ones. They remain a powerful force in the DRM, with participation from disabled people from around the United States.

Another influential—and controversial—DRM organization has been the focus of two extraordinary disabled people, Stephen Drake and Diane Coleman. For many years, they have fought against physician-assisted suicide, which often targets people with disabilities, through their loosely knit organization, Not Dead Yet. Their advocacy, nationally and internationally, has had a powerful influence on philosophy and legislation—yet laws permitting physician-assisted suicide, and the euthanasia of infants with disabilities, continue to exist.

Kim Nielsen, in her book about the history of disability in the United States:

> U.S. disability history is not only the history of people with disabilities. Whether one's life is shaped by able-bodiedness and the economic and legal advantages that issue from that, or by the economic and legal implications of disability's long-stigmatized past, disability, both as lived reality and as concept, impacts us all...The story of the U.S. nation is a contested, sometimes vicious, sometimes gloriously marvelous story of creating a national home. People with disabilities have been and will continue to be an integral part of that story. (2012, 182–183)

And the story is not yet finished.

Questions for Discussion

► Were you taught this kind of history in your history classes? Why or why not? Who benefits from NOT being taught this history?

Chapter 3

Perceptions of Disability

Phil Smith

Throughout history, and into the twenty-first century, people with disabilities have been understood or perceived in different ways. For the most part, people with disabilities have been seen as deviant—not just merely not-normal, without any particular moral value or judgment placed on them, but perceived as being actively malevolent, bad, and evil. The different ways of perceiving people with disabilities sometimes predominated in various time periods in history. Sometimes, these different ways of perceiving people occur at the same point in time. Such portrayals contribute to stereotypic perceptions of disability and disabled people, and to the stigma attached to them.

Wolfensberger's Outline of the Perceptions of People with Disabilities

Wolf Wolfensberger (1975), an important thinker and theorist particularly in the area of intellectual disabilities, outlined the various ways that people with disabilities have been perceived. He did this in order to understand the different ways that social institutions (and the culture in general) responded to people with disabilities in different points in time.

1. Perceived as *sick*. People with disabilities are understood as being literally diseased or ill. The dominant culture responds to people through a medical model, by treating people. Typically, "such a conceptualization often results in pursuit of treatment hoped to result in cure; on the other hand, unless a "cure" is seen as likely, the management atmosphere is often permeated with hopelessness…" (Wolfensberger 1975, 7).

2. Perceived as a *subhuman organism.* Literally, people are seen as being less than human, sometimes even less than animal: "unconsciously perceived or even consciously labeled as subhuman, as animal-like, or even as vegetables" or "vegetative" (Wolfensberger 1975, 7). As such, rights and privileges commonly given or ascribed to all people are denied them. They are "perceived as being potentially assaultive, destructive, and lacking in self-direction and constructive purpose" (8–9). Given this model, people were typically institutionalized in segregated settings without so-called treatment or opportunity: they are not "expected to learn or develop appreciably, or their growth potential is seen as so small as to be irrelevant..." (10). They lack rights to privacy, property, communication, or individuality.

Image © margouillat photo, 2014. Used under license from Shutterstock, Inc.

3. Perceived as a *menace.* As a menace, individual people with disabilities "might be perceived as being a menace individually because of alleged propensities toward various crimes against persons and property; or he/she might be perceived collectively as a social menace because of alleged contribution to social disorganization and genetic decline" (Wolfensberger 1975, 13). Given this perception, social responses are similar to those as when people with disabilities are seen as subhuman organisms.

Image © ostill, 2014. Used under license from Shutterstock, Inc.

4. Perceived as an *object of pity.* People with disabilities are frequently pitied, seen to be suffering because of their disability (and resulting position in society). Because of this, efforts must be made to relieve that suffering. But the pitied person is not conscious of their difference, and "is seen as 'an eternal child' who 'never grows'" (Wolfensberger 1975, 13). And people with disabilities who are pitied are not held accountable for their condition or the acts in which they engage—they don't know any better, the way that sometimes children or animals are seen as not knowing what it is that they do.

Image © Arcady, 2014. Used under license from Shutterstock, Inc.

5. Perceived as a *burden of charity*. Wolfensberger referred to this perception as arising from a "cold" or "sour" charity—a person with a disability, in this view, is seen "as a kept object of (public) charity…seen as entitled to food and shelter, but not to anything interpretable as luxuries, frills, and extras" (Wolfensberger 1975, 14). People with disabilities "are expected to be grateful, and to work as much as possible for his 'keep'" (14).

Image © Leremy, 2014. Used under license from Shutterstock, Inc.

6. Perceived as a *holy innocent*. In this view, people with disabilities "have occasionally been perceived as the special children of God. As such, they are usually seen as incapable of committing evil voluntarily, and consequently may be considered to be living saints. It may be believed that they have been sent by God for some special purpose" (Wolfensberger, 1975, 14–15). Often, that purpose is seen to be to instruct those without disabilities in patience and goodwill.

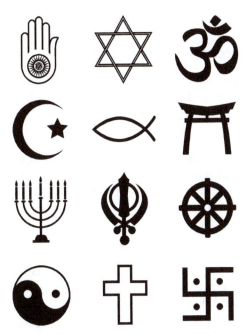

Image © Jane Rix, 2014. Used under license from Shutterstock, Inc.

7.   Perceived as a *developing individual.* This is probably the most positive and progressive perception of those described by Wolfensberger. Here, people with disabilities are felt to be capable of learning and growth, and reaching their maximum potential. They are seen to be individuals, with individual needs, wishes, dreams, and desires, and able to take on responsibility. They are deserving of civil and human rights, rights identified as those common to all people.

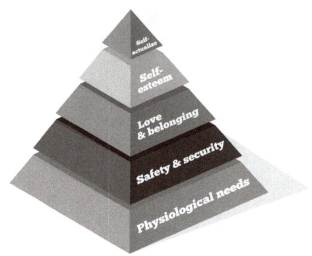

Image © Vitezslav Valka, 2014. Used under license from Shutterstock, Inc.

Barnes' Outline of the Perceptions of People with Disabilities

Barnes has been an influential researcher, activist, and theorist in British disability studies arenas. In 1992, he described the ways that people with disabilities are portrayed, this time in media presentations, including television, film, and print media. His descriptions were based on a wide review of medial portrayals of disabled people.

1.   The disabled person is portrayed as *pitiable and pathetic.* In these portrayals, people with disabilities are portrayed as objects of pity so that "the non-disabled public can feel bountiful" and "to depict another character's goodness and sensitivity" (Barnes 1992)—the other character usually being a person without a disability. This kind of portrayal is as much about extolling the virtues of non-disabled people as it is about portraying disabled people as objects of pity. Such portrayals are often bathed in over-sentimentality.

2.   The disabled person is portrayed as *an object of violence.* It is certain that people with disabilities experience higher levels of violence and abuse in their lives than do those without disabilities (P. Smith 2001). Yet media portrayals of people with disabilities as objects of violence, "besides contributing to and underlining the mistaken belief that disabled people are totally helpless and dependent such imagery helps perpetuate this violence" (Barnes 1992).

3.   The disabled person is portrayed as *sinister and evil.* Portrayals of people with disabilities as sinister and evil are widespread and pernicious in multiple media formats. Stretching back thousands of years, such portraits of people continue into the present, across literature, film, and art; "such disturbing imagery is grossly inaccurate and does much harm" (Barnes 1992).

4.   The disabled person is portrayed as *atmosphere or curio.* In such portrayals, people with disabilities serve to create or support an atmosphere, typically of intense menace, and support the perception of disabled people as being curiosities. In this latter context, people with disabilities have been exhibited as freaks of nature, often heightened by portraying them in ways seen as menacing or sinister (Barnes 1992).

5. The disabled person is portrayed as *super cripple*. In the stereotyped portrait of disabled people as super-crips, "the disabled person is assigned super human almost magical abilities. Blind people are portrayed as visionaries with a sixth sense or extremely sensitive hearing. Alternatively, disabled individuals, especially children, are praised excessively for relatively ordinary achievements" (Barnes 1992). This kind of portrait is particularly pervasive in advertisements for charity.

6. The disabled person is portrayed as *an object of ridicule*. People with disabilities have been ridiculed for millennia, laughed at for their incapacity and lack of understanding, including self-understanding. Such portraits continue into the present time (Barnes 1992).

7. The disabled person is portrayed as *their own worst and only enemy*. In this stereotype, people with disabilities are described "as self pitiers who could overcome their difficulties if they would stop feeling sorry for themselves, think positively and rise to 'the challenge'" (Barnes 1992). If they would only get out of their own way, it is felt, they would overcome adversity and return to normality. This kind of portrayal is a kind of "blame the victim" argument—people with disabilities are responsible for the hardships that they experience, not institutionalized ableism, a culture of normality, or the actions of individual people without disabilities.

8. The disabled person is portrayed as a *burden*. As Barnes points out, "this stereotype is connected to the view that disabled people are helpless and must be 'cared' for by non-disabled people. It fails to recognize that with appropriate support disabled people are able to achieve the same level of autonomy and independence as non-disabled people. It comes from the notion that disabled people's needs are profoundly different to those of the non-disabled community and that meeting those needs is an unacceptable drain on society's resources" (1992). Again, such an understanding is the result of pervasive, institutionalized ableism.

9. The disabled person is portrayed as *sexually abnormal*. Such portraits are endemic in a variety of media throughout the ages, and continue to today. It should be pointed out that many of these portrayals focus on men with disabilities, and their perceived impotence, with little attention paid to the sexual experience of women with disabilities. When women with disabilities are portrayed, they are represented as asexual. The underlying presumption is that "disabled people are sexually dead and therefore their lives are not worth living" (Barnes 1992).

10. The disabled person is portrayed as *incapable of participating fully in community life*. This portrayal of people with disabilities is as much about what is left out of their depiction as what is included: disabled people are rarely shown as integral and productive members of the community; as students, as teachers, as part of the workforce, or as parents. The absence of such portrayals feeds the notion that disabled people are inferior human beings who should be segregated" (Barnes 1992). When people with disabilities are portrayed in the media, they are very clearly represented as being lesser-than the higher status people without disabilities.

11. The disabled person is portrayed as *normal*. This kind of representation is one that is relatively recent in media portrayals of people with disabilities. Barnes points out that while such portrayals are useful in creating understandings of disabled people as successfully included in the common social fabric, one danger is that, in doing so, ways in which they experience discrimination and oppression are downplayed, reducing the chances of addressing such issues.

Questions for Discussion

▶ Have you looked at or understood people with disabilities in any of these ways? Why or why not?

▶ Are there other ways in which people with disabilities are or have been represented?

▶ Can you think of examples of ways in which people with disabilities have been represented in these ways in paintings, literature, film, television, magazines, or…?

Chapter 4

Defining Ableism

Phil Smith and Ruth Salles

What is ableism? Ableism is an ideology, which can be defined as a set of ideas and values in a culture. More formally (and in a little more complicated language), ideology is "the production of sense and meaning. It can be described as a way of viewing the world, a complex of ideas, various types of social practices, rituals, and representations *that we tend to accept as natural and as common sense*" (McLaren 2009, 69). Ableism, as an ideology, creates, supports, and permits the oppression, persecution, and discrimination of people who are said to have disabilities, by people who believe that they do not have disabilities, by what I've called "the dominant, normate culture" (P. Smith 2010, 8)—more about that in a bit. Ableism

> reflect[s] a fear of, an aversion to, or discrimination or prejudice against people with disabilities… Like racism, sexism, or homophobia, ableism is directed at individuals and built into social structures; it is lived out purposefully, accidentally, and unknowingly. (Nielsen 2012, xvi)

People who do not have disabilities create these ideas and values—this ideology—sometimes consciously, sometimes unconsciously. In its unconscious form, ableism is "invisible to most people, even though it constitutes an overarching regime that structures the lives of people with disabilities" (Berger 2013, 15).

The ideology of ableism, just like the ideology of racism, creates the category of people with disabilities in order to support and advance the well-being of those without disabilities. It creates what we think of as the idea of Normal, or being Normal. It does that by creating the Other—in this case, people with disabilities. People who think of themselves as Normal do so in relationship to people who are not normal—who have disabilities. They look at people with disabilities, and think to themselves, "Well, that's not me; I don't have a disability. I'm normal." In so doing, the ideology of ableism says that the right way to do things, to be in the world, is to be able-bodied (and able-minded). The ideology of ableism—the system of ideas and values in our culture about disability—advances the social, economic, and cultural goals of the Normal, of the normative. Whatever is outside of the Normal—what might be described as the Other—is bad, evil, wrong, crazy, broken, and sick.

Culture is one of those ideas that we throw around a lot but don't always define. It is the "set of practices, ideologies, and values from which different groups draw to make sense of the world… cultural questions help us understand who has power and how it is reproduced and manifested…" (McLaren 2009, 65). In our society, the Normal—represented by people who are said not to have disabilities—are the dominant group in our culture. This "*dominant culture* refers to social practices and representations that *affirm the central values, interests, and concerns of the social class in control of the material and symbolic wealth of society*" (McLaren 2009, 65). They are in charge of what's what in terms of disability, in much the same way that whites represent the dominant group in terms of race, or men in terms of gender, or the middle class and rich in terms of class, or heterosexuals in terms of sexuality, and so forth.

Image courtesy of author

NOW THE FOUR OF YOU, FOR OUR PURPOSES HERE, ARE DIFFERENT FROM THE REST OF US. YOUR DIFFERENCES MAKE LIFE MORE CHALLENGING FOR YOU BECAUSE, ALTHOUGH WE RECOGNIZE THAT YOU HAVE SOME CHALLENGES THAT WE DON'T, WE PREFER TO LET SLEEPING DOGS LIE. IN OTHER WORDS, THERE'S WAY MORE OF US THAN THERE ARE OF YOU SO THE MAJORITY RULES. WE CAN'T BE INCONVENIENCED BY MAKING LIFE MORE ENJOYABLE, MORE ACCESSIBLE TO YOU.

YOU FIVE ARE SLIGHTLY BETTER OFF THAN TONY AND HIS GROUP, BUT WHAT SETS YOU APART FROM THEM IS THAT YOUR DIFFERENCES ARE LESS OBVIOUS. SO WE, THE MAJORITY, ARE WILLING TO ACCOMODATE YOU TO SOME EXTENT, WHICH MAKES US FEEL EVEN BETTER ABOUT OURSELVES. YOUR QUALITY OF LIFE IS MUCH EASIER TO MAINTAIN BECAUSE YOU'RE NOT QUITE AS DIFFERENT FROM US AS TONY'S GROUP IS. BUT WE STILL LOOK AT YOU AS DIFFERENT AND LABEL YOU AS DISABLED.

THE REST OF US ARE ALL ABLE-BODIED INDIVIDUALS. WE CAN DO MOST OF WHAT WE'D LIKE TO DO MOST OF THE TIME. THIS MEANS WE REPRESENT THE IDEA OF ABLEISM. WE OCCASIONALLY MAKE ACCOMODATIONS FOR INDIVIDUALS WHO LIVE WITH "CHALLENGES", BUT IN A LOT OF CASES WE ABLEISTS HAVE CREATED THOSE CHALLENGES BECAUSE WE ARE TOO FOCUSED ON OUR OWN ABILITIES TO THINK OF OTHERS WHO HAVE ABILITIES THAT DIFFER FROM OUR OWN. ANY QUESTIONS NOW?

People without disabilities—along with the other dominant groups that I've mentioned—make the rules, the laws, the expected ways of doing things in our culture. These groups form what is known as a cultural hegemony in our society: "the social, cultural, ideological, or economic influence exerted by a dominant group" (Merriam-Webster Online Dictionary 2013). They hold the power in U.S. society (really, globally as well)—they have control of what happens (and what doesn't happen), who gets ahead and doesn't get ahead. They express the dominant ideologies of our culture, controlling the ideas we think about, the books we read, what gets shown on television or at the movies, the music we listen to, where we live or don't live, the foods we eat—just about everything you can imagine.

This hegemony plays out in such a way that "the powerful win the consent of those who are oppressed, with the oppressed unknowingly participating in their own oppression" (McLaren 2009, 67). So, in the context of people with disabilities, this means that they often participate in their own oppression without knowing it. They may accept their oppression and marginalization without realizing it: "that's just the way things are." In many ways, the same process works for people in the dominant culture (the Normal). They may oppress and marginalize without realizing that they are doing so.

Put another way, the ideology of ableism is not (or at least not always) a conscious thing, just like the ideology of racism is not always a conscious thing. It's not as if most people go wandering around thinking, "I'm racist," or, "I'm ableist." Most people don't do things that are intentionally racist, or intentionally sexist, heterosexist, and ageist. Most people don't do things that are intentionally harmful to others because of their marital status, religion, or other individual identities. But ableism, like racism or sexism, is institutionalized in our society. It's built into the very fabric of our social institutions, our cultural values, how we see the world. And so people without disabilities often can't help being ableist, even when they think they aren't.

Which is not to say that people are totally free from being overtly and clearly ableist. Sometimes, people engage in acts that are simply

> crude bigotry, such as that of a private New Jersey zoo owner who refused to admit children with retardation [sic] to the Monkey House, claiming they scared his chimpanzees … a New Jersey restaurant owner to ask a woman with cerebral palsy to leave because her different appearance was disturbing other diners … an airline employee in New York to throw a sixty-six-year-old double amputee on a baggage dolly … a gang of New Jersey high school athletes allegedly raped a mildly retarded [sic] classmate with a baseball bat … three volunteer ambulance rescuers allegedly pummeled to death a homeless man with retardation [sic] in the back of their ambulance because he annoyed them … (Shapiro 1993, 25)

Simi Linton is a disabled woman, author, and scholar. She uses a wheelchair to get around, and sometimes has trouble getting into buildings or rooms or other spaces, or using spaces in particular ways, because they are not accessible to her as a wheelchair user. Over time, she began to realize

> steps or the width of a doorway were results of decisions made by people who didn't have my best interests in mind. The decisions they made were a sorting system: we let some in, we keep *you* out. (Linton 2006, 114).

It's not as if those decisions were always conscious or intentional: "We don't want people who use wheelchairs to use this particular building, so we'll make the entrance only available by climbing a set of stairs." The designers or architects or builders just failed to take into account the desire and need of people using wheelchairs to get into a particular building. But the impact, the outcome, is the same: people with wheelchairs can't get in. In effect, they've been sorted into a group of people who can't—aren't allowed to—get into the building. To some extent, it doesn't matter what the intent of the designers of a particular building (or curriculum, or whatever) is: if it keeps people with disabilities from being able to use the facility (or to be able to learn, or grow, or access whatever social institution they want to access), they have been effectively discriminated against if their needs are not taken into account when the facility (or curriculum, or whatever) was designed or created.

Privilege

People who are white, for example, don't see the ways that their skin color allows them to do things, say things, act in particular ways—ways that are denied to people with different skin color (or ethnic background). This is called privilege—the right or ability to act in particular ways (usually without being aware of doing so)—a right that is denied to others on the basis of race, in this case. So whites have privilege in lots of ways in our culture, because of their race.

In regards to ableism, people who are perceived to be normal—that are not perceived as having a disability—have privilege based on their perceived ability. They (we) take for granted that they can go wherever they want, have physical access to buildings, rooms, and other facilities, without worrying about whether their wheelchair can get into them. Buildings are designed with stairs, to be used by "walkies" (folks who walk to get around, a word used by people who use wheelchairs to get around), something that people who walk take for granted. When buildings are so designed, they privilege people who use their legs to move around, and deny access to people who use wheelchairs, who can't use stairs, or get through revolving doors, or access restrooms with narrow stalls.

Institutionalized Ableism

Ableism is embedded in the very fabric of our culture; it is part of our social and cultural institutions. In other words, it has become institutionalized in our society. Simi Linton describes it this way:

> It wouldn't be possible to set disabled people apart and steal the candy right out of our mouths if people weren't instructed to do it. There is no single primer from which to learn such behaviors, no established decree that sets our place in the social order—it is in our drinking water. Written into works of fiction, religious texts, newspapers, art, drama, film, the annals of history, and, yes, the academic curriculum are the terms of the contract. Beliefs about disabled people, our worth and potential, are inscribed in these texts. (2006, 137)

Linton isn't suggesting that people intentionally and consciously instruct each other about how to discriminate against people with disabilities, or that they write textbooks about how to do that. But she is saying that the artifacts that our culture uses to communicate about itself to itself have ableism embedded in them. And one way to understand how disability plays out in our culture is to look at those texts—novels, film, history, theater—to analyze what disability means to us all.

Agency

So, some groups in our society are dominant, and hegemonic. Other groups experience oppression and discrimination. In terms of ableism, people without disabilities are in the dominant role in our society, and people with disabilities are oppressed and discriminated against. This is not to say that people with disabilities don't speak back to this oppression and discrimination, don't fight it. They are not submissive (or at least not always) about their role in society. Nor is it true that all people without disabilities, all the time, assume the role of dominator and oppressor, harming people with disabilities with and through their actions, speech, and ideology. This is because individual members of any society have what is called agency, the ability and willingness of individual people to act of their own free will. A person's individual agency allows them to make choices on their own, choices that may be contrary to the dominant, and dominating, ideology of a particular culture.

Some people choose to exert their agency in ways that work against the dominant ideology of ableism, to work against it in personal and collective terms. To do so is a difficult act, or set of acts, because the ideology of ableism is so pervasive, so controlling, and so dominant in our culture. To see outside what we understand as Normal and disabled, to work against ableism in one's own life, and the lives of others, is an incredibly demanding proposition. It takes tremendous courage to talk back and speak against what everyone else assumes—*knows*, without even having to think about it—is the right way to do things. The same is true, of course, for those who exert agency to speak back against the dominant ideology in terms of race, gender, sexuality, class, or ethnicity—again, in personal and political terms. And although it is difficult, even dangerous to do so, it is possible.

Chapter 5

What Is Disability Studies?

Phil Smith

Much of the thinking and writing in this book is founded in the ideas, theories, values, and research of the relatively new academic field of disability studies. So it seems important to ask the question, what is disability studies?

Maybe it seems a bit too obvious, but I'll say it anyway: disability studies is, perhaps most importantly, about disability. But it is also about not-disability. That is, it is, at least in part, the values and ideas (ideologies) in a society that create disability, and, by so doing, create the normal. So disability studies is also about normality—what it is, who it serves, who benefits from it, and how it operates (P. Smith 2004).

Secondly, and also importantly, it is interdisciplinary (Berger 2013; Goodley 2011; P. Smith 2010). It doesn't look at disability from one perspective, one vantage point, through one lens. It looks at disability from many perspectives—sometimes from many perspectives all at the same time (multi-disciplinary); sometimes crossing perspectives (transdisciplinary). People who do disability studies work know and believe that it's impossible to understand something as complex as disability from one way of looking at things. They (we) know that it will require looking at disability from many different disciplines in order to unpack its complexity. And so it is that disability studies scholars are sociologists, historians, actors, literary scholars, artists, educators, dancers, photographers, psychologists, sculptors, environmentalists, painters, geographers, poets, filmmakers … The list goes on and on and on and on.

Generally, disability studies assumes that disability is aligned with the social models of disability (Gabel 2005). As a field of study, it works to "place the problems of disability in society" and sees disability "as a cultural and political phenomenon" (Goodley 2011, xi). Such a perspective places it in direct opposition to the medical model of disability (Baglieri & Shapiro 2012; P. Smith 2010).

Disability studies "focuses on the power relationships in society between and among people with disabilities, the struggles for acceptance, self-advocacy, and finding a place within society" (Nocella, Bentley, & Duncan 2012, xv). Like much critical scholarship that looks at social and cultural issues, disability studies looks at power as it relates to disability: who has it, who doesn't, and who benefits from it. Disability studies is also interested in the ways that disabled people seek to speak for themselves (instead of being spoken for), and the social roles that they play in our culture. Disability studies scholars understand that people with disabilities "are systematically oppressed and marginalized" (P. Smith 2010, 8).

Image © Dusit, 2014. Used under license from Shutterstock, Inc.

As a result of this exploration of the role of power in and around disability, many disability studies scholars find themselves in alignment with critical theory and pedagogy, which focus on understanding power in society and culture. But critical theory is not some tower-of-academia, armchair, purely theoretical and philosophical exploration of power: it actively and intentionally works "to empower the powerless and transform existing social inequalities and injustices" (McLaren 2007, 186). Critical theory tries "to confront the injustice of a particular society or public sphere within the society"; it is "a transformative endeavor"; and critical theorists "announce their partisanship in the struggle for a better world" (Kincheloe, McLaren, & Steinberg 2012, 16). Critical pedagogy is the way that critical theory is played out in schools. As a field, it

> "asks how and why knowledge gets constructed the way it does, and how and why some constructions of reality are legitimated and celebrated by the dominant culture while others clearly are not. Critical pedagogy asks how our everyday commonsense understandings—our social constructions or "subjectivities"—get produced and lived out. In other words, what are the *social functions* of knowledge? The crucial factor here is that some forms of knowledge have more power and legitimacy than others. For instance, in many schools in the United States, science and math curricula are favored over the liberal arts. This can be explained by the link between the needs of big business to compete in world markets and the imperatives of the new reform movement to bring "excellence" back to the schools. Certain types of knowledge legitimate certain gender, class, and racial interests. Whose interests does this knowledge serve? Who gets excluded as a result? Who is marginalized?" (McLaren 2009, 63–64)

So critical disability studies looks at these questions and ideas specifically as they relate to disability. Critical pedagogists use the term praxis to describe their combination of theory and practice as a way to take action in the world (Freire 1971).

Disability studies is an activist field because of its history. It began in the disability rights movement, which seeks to address wrongs in society that cause harm—discrimination and oppression—to people with disabilities. Disability studies grew out of that movement, as people with disabilities sought reasons for why society enacts that harm on the bodies and minds of people seen to be different, and labeled as deviant. As they begin to understand the place of disability within an ableist society, disability studies scholars act on their knowledge, changing themselves and society.

One thing that disability studies is *not* is special education (P. Smith 2010). Far from it. Most disability studies scholars are critical of special education, not supportive of it: "special education is not a solution to the 'problem' of disability; it *is* the problem" (Linton 2006, 161). The kind of work that disability studies scholars engage in seeks "to expose the mythology of 'special' in education" (Ware 2006, 271). Disability studies, as it explores education, is very much in alignment with inclusive education, seeing itself as "the antithesis of special education" (Underwood 2008, 2).

Much of special education is in alignment with the medical model of disability, seeking to fix people. Disability studies is opposed to this—it

> does not treat disease or disability, hoping to cure or avoid them; it studies the social meanings, symbols, and stigmas attached to disability identity and asks how they relate to enforced systems of exclusion and oppression… (Siebers 2008, 3)

In fact, some disability studies scholars see special education *as* "the medical model as practiced in schools" (Baglieri & Shapiro 2012, 15). Most disability studies scholars are extremely critical of the foundations of, suppositions inherent in, and work of, special education (P. Smith 2010).

Questions for Discussion

▶ What do you think about this idea of disability studies? Does it make sense?

▶ How would you imagine that scholars would explore disability in the arts, literature, education, medicine, chemistry, or … ?

Section 2

What Kinds of Disabilities Are There?

Chapter 6

Physical Disability

Ann Orr

What do you think when you see me?

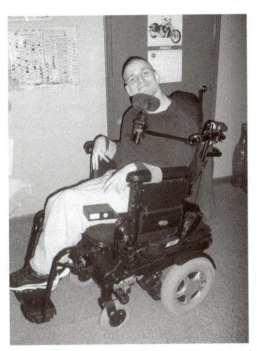

Figure 1   Kenny Haran, Assistive Technology Designer and EMU Presenter
Image courtesy of author

Do you see me or my chair?
Do you see me or my disability?
Would you be nervous to talk to me?
Do you think I am intelligent?

Physical Disability: Definitions

"A physical disability is any impairment which limits the physical function of one or more limbs or fine or gross motor ability. Other physical disabilities include impairments which limit other facets of daily living, such as respiratory disorders and epilepsy." (Wikipedia 2012)

"…any physiological disorder or condition, cosmetic disfigurement, or anatomical loss affecting one or more of the following body systems: neurological, musculoskeletal, special sense organs, respiratory (including speech organs), cardiovascular, reproductive, digestive, genitourinary, hemic and lymphatic, skin, and endocrine." (The Americans with Disabilities Act 2010)

"A physical impairment might be defined as a disabling condition or other health impairment that requires adaptation …. The physical disability the person experiences may be either congenital, or a result of injury, muscular dystrophy, cerebral palsy, amputation, multiple sclerosis, pulmonary disease, heart disease or other reasons. Some persons may experience non-visible disabilities that may include respiratory disorders, epilepsy, or other conditions." (Disabled-world.com 2012)

Note: Although *hearing impairment* and *visual impairment* can be considered physical disabilities, they've got their own sections in this book. Right here, right now, we're talking about the other body stuff—the muscles, the bones, the organs. When these entities don't work like normal (whatever that is?!) we, in our label-happy way, like to refer to this as "physical disability."

DID YOU KNOW?

19.5 MILLION PEOPLE in the U.S. have some sort of ambulatory disability.
(Erickson, Lee, & von Schrader 2012)

What causes physical impairment?

Prenatal Causes

Some physical disabilities are acquired before birth. Certain diseases or infections that mom contracts during pregnancy can result in an infant's physical impairment. A genetic mutation may occur or there may be genetic incompatibility between mom and dad. Limbs and organs may not fully develop or may develop with defects. Alcohol and drug use during pregnancy can lead to physical impairment.

Perinatal Causes

Other physical disabilities can be traced to events that happen during birth. Lack of oxygen to the baby can cause brain damage and cerebral palsy. Injury during birth (misuse of forceps, for instance) can lead to physical impairment. Babies born prematurely can have physical disabilities.

Postnatal Causes

Some physical impairments are caused by events after birth. Accidents and illnesses can affect our brains and bodies, leaving us with mild, moderate, or severe physical disabilities.

Way, Way Postnatal Causes!

Yes, that is a medical term. Not really…but we wrote it to remind you that physical disabilities can be acquired at any age and from a wide variety of causes. Even normal aging leads to increased physical limitation and impairment. For most of us, it's simply a matter of time before we all join the club!

Language 101 for Physical Disability

SAY:

- ▶ a person with a physical disability
- ▶ a person with arthritis (or multiple sclerosis, or cerebral palsy … you get the idea)
- ▶ a person who has arthritis ("who has" is okay, too)
- ▶ a person who uses a wheelchair (or a walker or a scooter)

DON'T SAY:

- ▶ a physically disabled person (this isn't person-first language)
- ▶ a person "who suffers from" quadriplegia (or spina bifida, or … whatever. "Suffers from" is a stereotypic phrase coming from the medical model of disability.)
- ▶ a person who is wheelchair-bound or wheelchair confined (This language is limiting and negative. We don't say "person who is glasses-bound"!

Figure 2 Lynda Miller, EMU Presenter
Image courtesy of author

MYTH #1

People with physical disabilities also have cognitive impairment.

NOT TRUE. Some folks do, many do not. NEVER ASSUME!

Some Common Types of Physical Disabilities

Arthritis

Arthritis is inflammation of one or more of your joints. The main symptoms of arthritis are joint pain and stiffness, which typically worsen with age. There are two main types of arthritis, osteoarthritis and rheumatoid arthritis. Osteoarthritis is caused by normal wear and tear of the joints; rheumatoid arthritis is an auto-immune disorder. Juvenile rheumatoid arthritis is the most common type of arthritis in children younger than sixteen years of age. The condition can be severe and life-long, or intermittent and short-lived.

Cerebral Palsy (CP)

Cerebral palsy is a non-progressive disorder of movement, muscle tone, or posture caused by injury or abnormal development in the immature brain. Signs and symptoms appear during infancy and toddlerhood. CP is characterized by exaggerated reflexes or rigidity of the limbs and torso, and can be accompanied by abnormal posture, involuntary movements, and unsteadiness and gait abnormality when walking. There is great variation in motor ability with CP, from mild, barely noticeable impairment to severe spasmodic or rigid movement such that the individual requires a cane, walker, or wheelchair to ambulate. Speech and cognitive functioning may or may not be a co-factor.

Congenital Heart Defect

Congenital heart defects are problems in the structure of a newborn's heart. These defects can be mild, and resolve on their own, or they can be serious, requiring medical intervention. Serious heart defects become evident soon after birth. Less serious defects may not be noticed until later childhood. Mobility may be affected; some children have shortness of breath or tire quickly during physical exercise. Because some children with congenital heart defects have a long recovery time from surgeries or procedures, they may be developmentally behind other children their age.

Muscular Dystrophy

Muscular Dystrophy is a genetic disease that progressively weakens an individual's skeletal and muscular systems. There are several different kinds of Muscular Dystrophy, some of which appear in childhood, others in adulthood. Each type affects different muscle groups and has a different prognosis. Some people with Muscular Dystrophy have trouble swallowing or breathing. There is no cure for Muscular Dystrophy, but many individuals are helped by surgery and physical therapy. Certain medications may slow the progression of the disease.

Multiple Sclerosis

Multiple sclerosis (MS) is a disease where a person's immune system attacks the wrong target, namely the covering, or myelin sheath, of the brain and spinal cord nerves. Bouts of MS cause inflammation and injury to the myelin sheath, and may cause blockage in nerve transmissions. As a result, a person may have trouble controlling vision and body movements. MS usually strikes between ages 20 and 40, and affects women twice as often as men. Treatment includes medication and physical therapy; persons with MS may require canes, walkers, and other mobility devices.

Parkinson's Disease

Parkinson's Disease is a gradually developing disorder of the nervous system that often begins with a slight tremor, but ultimately affects all body movement. Parkinson's Disease may cause stiffness or slowness in both gross and fine motor movement, and may impair speech. Symptoms worsen over time. There is no cure, but medications can improve symptoms.

Spina Bifida

Spina Bifida is a condition caused by the failure of the fetus' spine to fully close in utero. Because the spine's nerves are exposed, they may be injured and the damage may be permanent. Depending on the severity of the damage, the infant's motor abilities may be significantly impaired. It is also fairly common that children with spina bifida develop learning disabilities. Treatment options include surgery, and many children will need to use braces, crutches, or wheelchairs.

Spinal Cord Injury

Damage to any part of the spinal cord may cause permanent impairment in strength, sensation, and control of body functions below the site of the injury. Partial to full paralysis may occur. Surgery and physical therapy are the primary treatments for spinal cord injury. Persons with this type of injury often use wheelchairs and other assistive technologies. Advances in robotics may enable greater mobility in the future.

Stroke

When the blood supply to part of your brain is interrupted, your brain does not receive important oxygen and nutrients. This is called a stroke, and brain cells can actually die. Early intervention by trained medical personnel may reduce damage and potential complications. Sometime, however, the damage is done, and a person's gross and fine motor abilities may be impaired. Rehabilitation including physical therapy is necessitated; some patients recover, at least partially (Mayo Clinic 2012).

Legal Protections for Persons with Physical Disabilities

The Americans with Disabilities Act (ADA) prohibits the discrimination of persons with disabilities in employment, transportation, public accommodation, communications, and governmental activities. It is an especially important law for persons with physical disabilities as it calls for greater accessibility of buildings, facilities, and transportation systems. You've seen the ramps and push-button doors—those are in place because of the ADA. The ADA also requires employers to make reasonable modifications to their workplaces so that persons with disabilities can do their jobs. This is very important. There are a lot of misconceptions about the employment of people with disabilities. For instance, many employers assume it will be expensive to make "reasonable accommodations" to their workplace so that a person with a disability can work there. Not true! The U.S. Department of Labor's Office of Disability Employment Policy reports that for the minority of workers with disabilities who do need some sort of special equipment or accommodation, 56 percent of these cost less than $600, with many costing nothing at all. Other employers worry that people with disabilities will miss work often. Again, these assumptions are not valid. Studies show that absentee rates for persons with disabilities are no greater than for persons without disabilities.

Because we've deliberately or inadvertently segregated people with disabilities from active society for so long, we are unfamiliar with appropriate supports and practices that will facilitate greater accessibility and participation for people with disabilities and ALL THE REST OF US. It's time we got to know each other again. My father speaks of his childhood friend, a boy everyone knew was "slow" to learn and do things. "We all knew that Bill needed a hand now and then, but really he was just part of our gang. No big deal." How can we, in 2013, create a world in which disability, and accessibility, is "no big deal"?

Universal Design and Assistive Technology

All of us benefit from the universal design movement in education, architecture, and manufacturing whereby teachers, architects, and product designers try to maximize accessibility from the start, but these efforts are even more important to persons with physical disabilities. Imagine having to choose what restaurant to dine at by considering first the number of steps required to get in the building. When people who design lessons, buildings, and products put their "accessibility" caps on from Day 1, a lot more folks, young and old, will participate and succeed at learning, going, using, and doing.

Assistive technology (AT) is also vital to full participation. Mobility aids like canes, walkers, wheelchairs, and braces can assist individuals in moving through their homes, communities, and workplaces. Alternative computer access and input devices like voice recognition and switches make it possible for people with even the most significant disabilities to communicate, ambulate, learn, explore, and fulfill their own unique potential. Assistive technology is defined as any item, piece of equipment, or product system, whether acquired commercially, modified, or customized, that is used to increase, maintain, or improve functional capabilities of individuals with disabilities. Assistive technology can be no/low or high tech, and can be homemade or purchased. We are limited only by our imagination and ingenuity when determining what AT might make a positive difference for a person with disabilities. The task is to identify what the barrier is between a person (or student) and what he or she needs to do. Then, we put the appropriate assistive technology in place to break down or bypass that barrier and facilitate the doing! That AT might be as simple as a rubber pencil grip that enables a person with fine motor impairment to write, or as complex as a computer-based talking communication device for a non- or partially verbal individual.

Resources on Physical Disabilities

Books

As I Am, A True Story of Adaptation to Physical Disability
Dr. Karen Hutchins Pirnot and Garret Frey; Peppertree Press

Just One of the Kids: Raising a Resilient Family When One of Your Children Has a Physical Disability
Kay Harris Kriegsman and Sara Palmer; Johns Hopkins University Press

Moving Violations: War Zones, Wheelchairs, and Declarations of Independence
John Hockenberry; Hyperion Books

My Body Politic: A Memoir
Simi Linton; University of Michigan Press

Journals

Disability and Health Journal
Journal of Developmental and Physical Disabilities
Physical Disabilities: Education and Related Services

Organizations

Adaptive Sports Foundation
http://www.adaptivesportsfoundation.org/

Center for Applied Special Technologies
http://www.cast.org/

Christopher & Dana Reeve Foundation
http://www.christopherreeve.org/

Disabled-World
http://www.disabled-world.com/

Easter Seals
www.easterseals.com

Mobility International USA
http://miusa.org/

National Center on Health, Physical Activity, and Disability
http://www.ncpad.org/

The Arc
http://www.thearc.org/

United Cerebral Palsy
http://www.ucp.org/

United Spinal Association
http://www.unitedspinal.org/

Chapter 7

ADHD: Attention Deficit/ Hyperactivity Disorder

David C. Winters

Why the H?

Two Types of Behavior

- ► Inattention
- ► Hyperactivity or Impulsivity

Tell Me More

People with ADHD have patterns of behavior that involve inattention and/or hyperactivity or impulsivity (DSM-V, 2013).

Inattention includes behaviors such as

- ► Losing focus and making careless mistakes
- ► Appearing to not be actively listening
- ► Poor organization and follow-through (might start but then not complete)
- ► Avoiding tasks that require sustained mental effort
- ► Losing needed items and forgetting routine activities
- ► Being easily distracted

Hyperactivity or impulsivity includes behaviors such as

- ► Fidgeting or squirming
- ► Difficulty staying in seat when expected or needing to move around
- ► Difficulty playing or working quietly
- ► Talking too much, including blurting out
- ► Difficulty waiting for his/her turn
- ► Interrupting or intruding on others

A person may be identified as having ADHD with behaviors that are mainly inattentive, mainly hyperactive/ impulsive, or a combination of both. In addition, these behaviors may change as the person grows older.

While a person may be first identified as having ADHD during adulthood, most people receive the ADHD identification during childhood. Even those people who are identified at an older age will find that their symptoms began before age 12.

Figure 1 Difficulty with Selective Attention
Image © Andrea Danti, 2014. Used under license from Shutterstock, Inc.

Types of Attention

▶ **Selective Attention**

Selective attention is the ability to attend to a stimulus while ignoring competing stimuli. For example, when listening to a lecture, Stan must attend to the teacher's voice rather than other sounds and sights in and outside the room. If he is struggling with selecting the teacher's voice as the target for attention, he might begin listening to the birds outside the window, the fan in the air-conditioner, or the sound of a neighboring student's pen while taking notes.

▶ **Sustained Attention**

Once a person has selected the appropriate stimulus for attention, sustained attention is the ability to maintain that focus in the presence of other competing and often changing stimuli. For example, after Stan has begun to pay attention to his teacher's voice, he needs to continue to tune out the bird, fan, and pen sounds while the teacher is talking. He may also need to tune out other thoughts in his mind, such as his important ball game after class.

▶ **Divided Attention**

While a person needs to select and sustain attention to the important stimulus, very often the person needs to also focus on other important tasks, often called "multi-tasking." Divided attention allows the person to focus on more than one important stimulus simultaneously. For example, while paying attention to his teacher's voice, Stan will need to also focus on his paper while taking notes.

Not Just ADD/ADHD

- ▶ 50–60% have a co-existing disability
  - ▶ LD—20%
  - ▶ CI—20%
  - ▶ EI—60%

  ▶ POHI—66%
  ▶ ASD—25%

Etiology

Over the last several decades, researchers have proposed numerous causes of ADHD. Through this research, focus has centered on differences in brain structure and function. For example, the brains of many persons with ADHD have low levels of two important neurotransmitters, dopamine and norepinephrine, that play an important role in transmitting signals from one neuron to another (DuPaul, Barkley, & Connor 1998). Researchers have also found brain differences in the frontal lobe of the brain that handle motor control, executive function, and behavior inhibition (Biederman 2005).

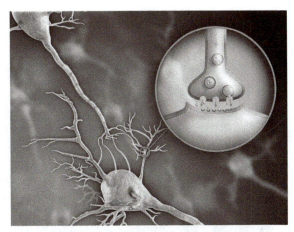

Figure 2 Neurons and Synapses
Image © Suzanne Tucker, 2014. Used under license from Shutterstock, Inc.

Genetics is a second major area of focus. Studies of identical and fraternal sets of twins have shown that genetics plays a significant role in the etiology of ADHD (Spencer et al. 2002). Parents and siblings of children with ADHD have a two to eight times greater risk to have ADHD themselves (Biederman 2005).

While certain environmental factors may influence ADHD, research has not been able to verify them as a cause. Therefore, poor parenting, food additives and diet, high lead levels, and exposure to alcohol and cigarette smoke do not cause ADHD (Biederman 2005).

To Med or Not to Med—That Is THE Question

Because research has highlighted neurobiological factors in ADHD, a popular, yet controversial, approach to help individuals with ADHD is to provide medication that counters the biophysical deficiencies. While many medications have been tried with people with ADHD, stimulants, such as Ritalin, and other medications that target dopamine such as antidepressants have been found effective (Spencer et al. 2002; Richard & Russell 2001).

However, many professionals, parents, and persons with ADHD themselves resist using medication, citing concerns ranging from unpleasant side effects to stunting physical growth to unknown long-term effects to increasing the risk for substance abuse.

Like all medications, those used to help people with ADHD have potential side effects. In their review of studies of long-term stimulant use in persons with ADHD, Lerner and Wigal (2008) found that most side effects lasted for short time periods when a person first began using the medication. Although medication use did not appear to produce significant negative cardiovascular, growth, tics, or long-term side effects, the authors did recommend careful monitoring by physicians.

Another concern with stimulant use involves the potential for later substance abuse. Wilens, Farone, Biederman, and Gunawardene (2003) reviewed studies that focused on long-term stimulant use and found that stimulant use actually reduced the risk for later substance abuse.

Richard and Russell (2001) recommend that parents and doctors consider five factors when deciding whether to treat a person's ADHD with medication:

1. Child's age: medications appear to be more effective with children age five or more
2. Non-medical interventions: Try non-medical interventions before trying medication
3. Side-effect risk: Because all medications have potential side effects, consider the benefits of the medication vs. the risk of side effects
4. Teacher opinion: Because classroom behavior may differ, sometimes significantly, from home behavior, consult the teacher's opinion for the need for medication
5. Parent concerns: Parents need to be educated about ADHD and the kinds of available treatments

Our Brain's Conductor

Executive Function

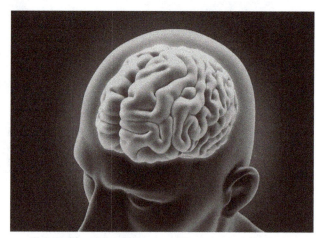

Figure 3   The brain controls executive function
Image © Nerthuz, 2014. Used under license from Shutterstock, Inc.

Brown (2006) likened executive function to an orchestra conductor. He noted that even if each instrumentalist is highly skilled in an instrument, the orchestra likely will not produce good music without a conductor to keep the instrumentalists together, set the tempo and volume, and cue entrances. Likewise, certain neural networks, called executive functions, manage cognitive functions through coordination and integration.

Working memory is one important executive function for persons with ADHD (Willcutt et al. 2006). Working memory allows a person to keep facts in mind while manipulating information, such as keeping a sentence in mind that you want to write while you spend a few moments focusing on the spelling of one of the words.

Another important executive function is response inhibition and selection (Willcutt et al. 2006), which helps a person ignore inappropriate responses in order to focus on the appropriate ones. For example, a person with poor response inhibition may blurt out the first answer that comes to mind when asked a question rather than taking a few moments to consider possible answers before choosing the most appropriate one.

A third important executive function is internalization of speech (Barkley 1997), which involves using self-talk to direct behavior as well as problem-solving. For example, when asked a question, a person may use self-talk to delay a response as well as to consider response options.

A fourth executive function is the self-regulation of affect, motivation, and arousal (Barkley 1997), which deals with emotional response to stimuli. These emotional responses include handling frustration, willingness to complete tasks, getting started, maintaining attention, and others.

How Can We Help the Person with ADHD?

At Home

- ► Provide choices
- ► Provide opportunities to help
- ► Give positive directions rather than stating what not to do
- ► Reinforce appropriate behavior
- ► Incorporate activities allowing movement and positive family relationships
- ► Maintain a consistent location, time, structure, and monitoring for completing homework
- ► Break down homework into small chunks with short breaks
- ► Use checklists
- ► Encourage personal responsibility for behavior
- ► Analyze events just before and just after a behavior issue happens to determine potential triggers or responses that result in or reward the undesired behavior
- ► Give clear, simple, positive behavior expectations
- ► Use calendars and visual planners, including computer, smartphone, and tablet apps
- ► Target problem areas such as morning time, bedtime, meal time, transitions, and vacations
- ► Provide external structure whenever possible
- ► Use the OHIO principle for paperwork—Only Handle It Once

At School

- ► Teach using UDL (Universal Design for Learning) principles
- ► Incorporate PBS (Positive Behavior Supports)
- ► Use visuals as well as color while teaching
- ► Incorporate demonstrations and hands-on activities
- ► Seat students near and facing the focus of instruction (teacher, screen, etc.)
- ► Limit extraneous visual and auditory stimuli in the room
- ► Use a brisk presentation pace
- ► Use paired and group activities
- ► Ask open-ended questions that encourage reasoning and critical thinking
- ► Allow opportunities for movement
- ► Encourage AT (Assistive Technology) use
- ► Provide written directions and assignment information
- ► Break down long-term and complex projects and assignments into smaller segments with distributed due dates
- ► Have students repeat or rephrase directions and key points of a conversation or discussion
- ► Structure and supervise transitions

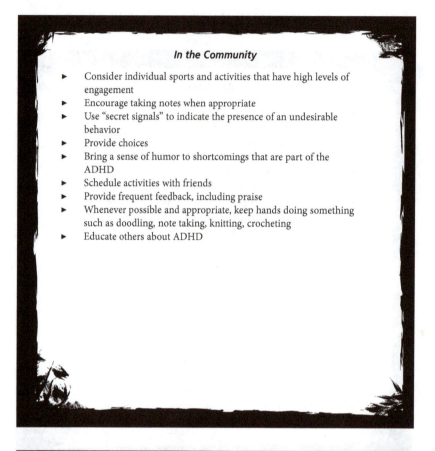

In the Community

► Consider individual sports and activities that have high levels of engagement
► Encourage taking notes when appropriate
► Use "secret signals" to indicate the presence of an undesirable behavior
► Provide choices
► Bring a sense of humor to shortcomings that are part of the ADHD
► Schedule activities with friends
► Provide frequent feedback, including praise
► Whenever possible and appropriate, keep hands doing something such as doodling, note taking, knitting, crocheting
► Educate others about ADHD

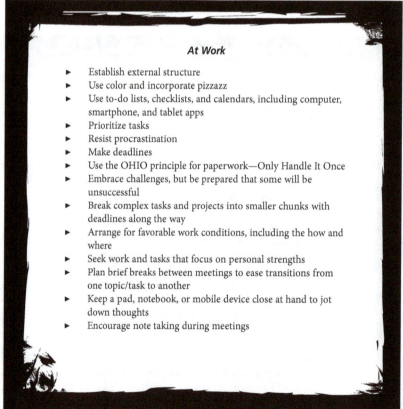

At Work

► Establish external structure
► Use color and incorporate pizzazz
► Use to-do lists, checklists, and calendars, including computer, smartphone, and tablet apps
► Prioritize tasks
► Resist procrastination
► Make deadlines
► Use the OHIO principle for paperwork—Only Handle It Once
► Embrace challenges, but be prepared that some will be unsuccessful
► Break complex tasks and projects into smaller chunks with deadlines along the way
► Arrange for favorable work conditions, including the how and where
► Seek work and tasks that focus on personal strengths
► Plan brief breaks between meetings to ease transitions from one topic/task to another
► Keep a pad, notebook, or mobile device close at hand to jot down thoughts
► Encourage note taking during meetings

Several of these suggestions have been adapted from Richard & Russell 2001; Hallowell & Ratey 1994.

Questions for Discussion

► Discuss how each type of attention could aid or hinder a person's performance at school or work.

► Discuss the potential benefits and drawbacks in using medication to help a person with ADHD. Discuss medication's effectiveness, benefits, and drawbacks that you have observed in a family member, classmate, or co-worker.

► Pick a common educational or work task and discuss how each aspect of executive function contributes to successful completion of the task.

Chapter 8

Talented and Gifted

Loreena Parks

… creative, imaginative, persuasive, sensitive, emotional, diverse, opinionated, fantasize, intellectual, playful, complex, impulsive, thinkers, original, artistic, flexible, introspective, bored, unconventional, independent, self-confident, motivated, spontaneous, adventurous, perceptive, intuitive …

Image © Anson0618, 2014. Used under license from Shutterstock, Inc.

Definition Discussion

There is no global or universal definition of what a student who is gifted and talented is. Many titles and acronyms are used such as: Talented and Gifted (TAG), Gifted and Talented Education (GATE), and Talented and Gifted (T/G). What teachers need are: special practices, educational settings, services, procedures, and theories that can help them when working with students who have been identified as TAG.

1. U.S. Department of Education (The Marland Definition)

The term "gifted and talented children" means children and, whenever applicable, youth, who are identified at the preschool, elementary, or secondary level as possessing demonstrated or potential abilities that give evidence of high performance capability in areas such as intellectual, creative, specific academic, or leadership ability, or in the performing or visual arts and who by reason thereof require services or activities not ordinarily provided by the school ... gifted and talented will encompass a minimum of 3 to 5 percent of the school population. (Marland 1972)

2. Jacob K. Javits Gifted & Talented Students Education Act of 1988 (PL 100-297)

Children and youth with outstanding talent perform or (who) show the potential for performing at remarkably high levels of accomplishment when compared with others, other age, experience, or environment. These children and youth exhibit high performance capability and intellectual, creative, and/or artistic areas, possess an unusual leadership capacity, or excel in specific academic fields. They require services or activities not ordinarily provided by the schools. Outstanding talents are present in children and youth from all cultural groups, across all economic strata, and in all areas of human behavior. (Jacob K. Javits Gifted and Talented Students Education Act 1994, 26)

3. Federal Government, NCLB (PL 107-110, Part A, Section 9101)

Students, children, or youth who give evidence of high achievement capability in areas such as intellectual, creative, artistic, or leadership capability, or in specific academic fields, and who need services or activities not ordinarily provided by the school in order to fully develop those capabilities. (No Child Left Behind (NCLB), Elementary and Secondary Education Act, PL 107-110, 2001)

The above three definitions are not entirely inclusive of all the characteristics exhibited by students who are considered talented and gifted. These students could typically exhibit one or more of Gardner's Multiple Intelligences.

1. Linguistic
2. Logical—mathematical
3. Spatial
4. Body—kinesthetic
5. Musical
6. Interpersonal
7. Intrapersonal
8. Naturalist

He has proposed, in his philosophy on Multiple Intelligences, that a student can demonstrate giftedness in any one or more of the above listed intelligences. (Kornhaber 2004)

Image © FERNANDO BLANCO CALZADA, 2014. Used under license from Shutterstock, Inc.

Ideally, educators should strive to maximize a student's ability in any or all areas in which the students display an unusual potential. Using Gardner's list is useful in helping to identify such areas of strength. Depending on how rigorously one looks at a student's potential, the TAG population might actually exceed the typical 3–5 percent of students identified as being talented and gifted.

Historical Background

Image © Robert Kneschke, 2014. Used under license from Shutterstock, Inc.

History of the talented and gifted has vacillated back and forth between the need for education for the elite vs. having education to foster democracy. The egalitarian attitude of special education supports that specialized education for gifted individuals is undemocratic, elitist, unnecessary, and wasteful.

Much information can be found addressing education of talented and gifted students as far back as 3000 BC. Interesting highlights include:

- ▶ **3000 BC**—Egyptians sent their best students (along with royalty) to court schools (Hunsaker 1995)
- ▶ **500 BC**—Confucius proposed special education for gifted children
- ▶ **AD 618**—Talented and gifted children were brought to the Chinese imperial court for special education
- ▶ **1600s—1800s**

  1. Japan—Children born of samurai nobility were provided differentiated curriculum containing Confucian classics, martial arts, history, moral values, calligraphy, and composition. Poor children were taught the value of loyalty, obedience, humility, and diligence. (Davis & Rimm 2004)

  2. West African Cultures—Children's status, recognized characteristics, or cleverness aided in the decision as to whether to provide them specialized education.

  3. 1800s—Charles Darwin and Sir Francis Galton both researched the potential connection between intelligence and heredity.

  4. Thomas Jefferson brought the egalitarian position to the forefront.

- ▶ **1900–1979**

  1. Alfred Binet developed the first intelligence test not only to identify gifted students but to also assess the interest of all students.

  2. Leta Hollingworth (textbook) and Lewis Terman (research) were noted for their work on gifted individuals.

  3. Russia's 1957 launching of the satellite Sputnik was an incentive to start programs in the United States for the talented and gifted with strengths in math and science. The United States felt it was in the national interest to surpass Russia in the space arena.

4. The civil rights movement was adamant that specialized education for students thought to be talented and gifted was another way of showering more onto an already privileged group of students (typically non-minority).

5. June Make attracted national attention to the needs of a subgroup of gifted students—those students with learning disabilities.

▶ **1980s—Present**

1. 1988—Jacob K. Javits Gifted & Talented Students Education Act

2. Funding for the education of talented and gifted students increased or decreased along with trends of whether to provide or not to provide special TAG services.

3. Some states do and some states do not have mandates in place to provide programs for gifted students.

Prevalence/Causes

IDEA '04 does not require that states report statistics to the federal government as to the numbers of talented and gifted students who are being identified or serviced.

Talented and gifted students come from all racial and social-economic groups. Generally, 3 to 5 percent of any given group of students is considered talented and gifted. These students can have a singular talent (i.e., math or language) or they can be gifted in multiple areas.

Image © michaeljung, 2014. Used under license from Shutterstock, Inc.

Diverse students including African American, Native American, Hispanic students, students with disabilities and ADHD are known to be underrepresented in TAG classes. This can be due to their diversity, being poor, inappropriate identification, and not having access to a TAG program.

Causes for lower percentage of the poor being enrolled or successful in these programs include: low expectations, educators' attitude toward these diverse students, and culturally biased criteria for admission to these programs.

Female students are also underrepresented in TAG programs. Societal expectations and peer pressure are two reasons for this phenomenon.

Characteristics

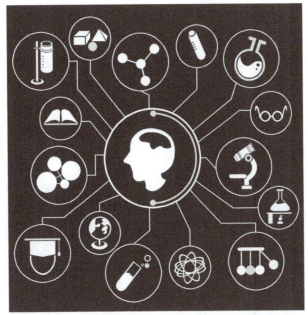

Image © phipatbig, 2014. Used under license from Shutterstock, Inc.

Table 1 shows some of the ***Characteristics of Talented and Gifted Students*** but this is not a complete or exhaustive list. Talented and gifted students may or may not display some or most of these characteristics. There are also students who fall within the current NCLB definition but for a variety of reasons fail to exhibit any of these characteristics in the classroom setting.

TABLE 1 Some Characteristics of Talented and Gifted Students	
▶ Often perfectionist	▶ Conceptualizes and synthesizes
▶ Often idealistic	▶ Experiences great stress from failure
▶ Heightened sensitivity	▶ Observant
▶ Asynchronous	▶ Great memorization ability
▶ Sequential or spatial learner	▶ Has wide interests
▶ Much curriculum known before class begins	▶ Produce "Own copy" vs. "Copying"
▶ Problem solver	▶ Athletic abilities can be challenging
▶ Success is defined by receiving an "A"	▶ Good manipulative skills
▶ Has an unusual talent in one or two areas	▶ Has ability to stay focused on a topic
▶ Independent thinker and autonomous	▶ Strength of character
▶ Original thinking	▶ Unusually self-expressive
▶ Sense of humor	▶ Takes responsibility
▶ Improvises	▶ Dislikes drill and routine
▶ Does not mind being different	▶ Takes risks
▶ Reasons abstractly	▶ High energy level
▶ Criticizes self	▶ Invents
▶ Intense	▶ Improvises
▶ Nonconforming	▶ Has a large vocabulary
▶ Uses different modes of expression	▶ Concerned about ethical issues
▶ Learns rapidly	▶ Leadership abilities
▶ Self-starter	▶ Adapts well

Image courtesy of author

Education of the Talented and Gifted Student

Typically school districts address the needs of TAG students through the use of enrichment, acceleration, and differentiation. Any or all of these three can happen in special programs or right in the general education program.

Each district has their own philosophy on what they offer for students who are considered talented and gifted. A teacher follows the district's orientation on this. However, a teacher in the general education classroom has the challenge of dealing with all students and must decide on how they will handle these needs as well as working with students who are talented and gifted.

Technology is an important aspect of everyone's life and can be used to augment any program at any level provided and accepted by the school district.

Image © Monkey Business Images, 2014. Used under license from Shutterstock, Inc.

Enrichment

Anything that enhances the current curriculum and aids in making a topic come to life for students. Some of the things that have been used traditionally include field trips, real life situations as in setting up a school store, simulations, use of technology, independent studies, and mentorships.

Acceleration

The teaching of subject matter using faster-paced methodologies to help alleviate repetition or redundancy and to aid in boredom or behavior issues. Many school districts have incorporated advanced placement (AP) classes, which cover subject matter in a shorter time period; ability grouping is often used to populate their AP classes. Often students can attend a local community college or university in order to obtain credits before they actually are in attendance at institutions of higher education.

Differentiation

Teachers who feel that their job is to help all students be as successful as they can will incorporate differentiation into their classroom. Differentiation can include enrichment and acceleration as the teacher facilitates a curriculum topic so that the needs of all students in the classroom are met. Table 2 is an example of a spelling lesson for a student who is talented and gifted. The lesson could be expanded to include the needs of other students in the classroom as well.

TABLE 2 Sample Adaptations for a Spelling Class	
Class Spelling Assignment	Sample of Differentiation Activities for a TAG Student
► Be able to spell, define, and use a list of spelling words	► Spelling list could be in two languages (example: Spanish and English) ► Learn origins of words on the spelling list ► Explore derivatives of words on the spelling list ► Choose from several different spelling lists ► Draw pictures that depict knowledge of the spelling list words

Image courtesy of author

Advice to Future Teachers from 5th Grade Talented and Gifted Students

Image © Monkey Business Images, 2014. Used under license from Shutterstock, Inc.

► "Teachers, please do not always have the talented and gifted student have to head up a group project. Sometimes we just want to work on our own ideas and projects."—*Author unknown*

► "Do not put us in a special class that only wants us to do more work … sometimes we would like to do less work but be able to create more on our own."—*Author unknown*

► "Please do not treat us as different from everyone else in our school."—*Author unknown*

► "Let us just be!"—*Author unknown*

► "Whenever we can take a field trip it seems to be a lot more fun than staying in the classroom most of the time."—*Author unknown*

Questions for Discussion

▶ Have you ever thought that you might be talented and gifted? If so, what **characteristics** do you feel you have that would put you in that category?

▶ What are your thoughts on the **educational placement** of students who are talented and gifted? Should they be placed in special classrooms, alternative settings, etc., or fully included in the general education population?

▶ What would you include on a formal **Fact Sheet** to help teachers identify which students in your classroom might be talented and gifted?

▶ If you were teaching a high school novel (such as *The Great Gatsby, Romeo and Juliet*, etc.) what **accommodations** might you include in your lesson that would help to motivate and challenge all students, as well as those who are talented and gifted?

▶ Share your reflections if you have seen any of the movies listed in **Table 6.** Are there any other movies that should be added to this table?

Useful Resources

TABLE 3   Organizations to Connect With
GT World http://www.gtworld.org
National Association for Gifted Children (NAGC), Washington, DC http://www.nagc.org
The Association for the Gifted (TAG), Council for Exceptional Children, Arlington, Virginia http://cectag.com/
World Council for Gifted and Talented Children http://www.worldgifted.org
Supporting the Emotional Needs of the Gifted, Inc. http://www.SENGifted.org
National Office for American Mensa, Gifted Children Program, Arlington, Texas http://www.us.mensa.org
National Research Center on the Gifted and Talented, Storrs, Connecticut http://www.gifted.uconn.edu

Image courtesy of author

TABLE 4   Some Outstanding TAG Websites
Hoagies' Gifted Education Page http://www.hoagiesgifted.org
Odyssey of the Mind http://www.odysseyofthemind.org

Image courtesy of author

TABLE 5   Special Programs and Research Centers Available
College of William and Mary Center for Gifted Education http://www.cfge.wm.edu
Duke University Talent Identification Program (TIP) http://www.tip.duke.edu
Jacob K. Javits Gifted and Talented Students Education Program http://www.ed.gov/programs/javits/index.html
National Consortium for Specialized Secondary Schools of Mathematics, Science, and Technology http://www.ncsssmst.org
Northwestern University Center for Talent Development http://www.ctd.northwestern.edu

Image courtesy of author

TABLE 6   Movies That Might Be of Interest
Good Will Hunting (1998). Miramax
Searching for Bobby Fischer (1993). Paramount
Class Act (1992). Warner Brothers
Little Man Tate (1991). Orion
The Goonies (1985). Warner Brothers/Amblin Entertainment
Weird Science (1985). Universal Pictures
Amadeus (1984). Republic Pictures

Image courtesy of author

Chapter 9

Intellectual Impairment

Jackie McGinnis

Several years ago it was my privilege to observe an outstanding student teacher as she led a class of thirteen 3rd–5th graders through the process of writing a name poem. These thirteen students were receiving their language arts instruction while in a self-contained classroom for students with mild/moderate intellectual impairment. After the large group instruction, students individually started work on their poems. I moved closer to a girl who was beginning to list her interests and activities in order to start her poem. We worked together, for some time, when we started to look at the words that she would use to describe herself. I said, "Well, what do you think, what is one word that you would use to describe who you are?" This smiling, glasses-wearing young girl didn't miss a beat when she replied, "Fabulous"! I mirrored her wide grin when she said this and said "I agree, let's write that word!"

Image © Denis Kuvaev, 2014. Used under license from Shutterstock, Inc.

Later I reflected on this wonderful exchange. I wondered if this ten-year-old would continue to have this positive self-image as she continued her education. Would the fact that she had Down syndrome, the most common genetic cause of intellectual impairment, mean that she would struggle to be accepted by her peers? Would it mean that she would not have a career, or healthy loving relationships and/or be able to live, work, and play however she chose? When others thought of her intellectual impairment would they see someone who is less than perfect, someone to pity, someone to tease and bully? Would the supports necessary be in place at the right time and every time needed so she could continue to feel fabulous and be included in activities and settings of her choosing?

The purpose of this chapter is to provide accurate information regarding intellectual impairment and issues related to definition, possible causes, and individual characteristics. In the areas of education, employment, and adult life, the challenges faced by persons with intellectual impairments and their loved ones will be discussed. This chapter is written using person first language and the philosophy that given the needed supports, persons with intellectual impairment are capable of learning, loving, and living to their own individual, self-determined, fabulous potential!

Definition

The American Association on Intellectual and Developmental Disabilities [AAIDD] (2013) defines an intellectual disability as characterized by significant limitations in both intellectual functioning and adaptive behavior. The disability also manifests itself before the age of eighteen.

Intellectual functioning which refers to reasoning and problem solving can, in one way, be measured by an IQ test (AAIDD 2013). Traditionally labels of intellectual impairment begin at a score of 70 (mild) to moderate (50), severe (20) and profound. Adaptive behaviors are defined in three distinct skills sets. The conceptual skills set or the ability to read and complete computations, social skills set such as following rules or developing relationships, and finally a practical skills set, including using transportation, and self care (AAIDD 2013).

Table 10.1 Adaptive Behavior		
Conceptual skills	Social skills	Practical skills
language and literacy; money, time, and number concepts; and self-direction	interpersonal skills, social responsibility, self-esteem, gullibility, naïveté (i.e., wariness), social problem solving, and the ability to follow rules/obey laws and to avoid being victimized	activities of daily living (personal care), occupational skills, healthcare, travel/transportation, schedules/routines, safety, use of money, use of the telephone
American Association on Intellectual and Developmental Disabilities. (2013). Intellectual Disability. *Definition of Intellectual Disability.* Retrieved from: http://aaidd.org/intellectual-disability/definition/faqs-on-intellectual-disability		

This definition can be used to provide labels that an individual must have in order to access health, financial, and educational services. These same labels can be stigmatizing and lead to discrimination. R Word is an international organization dedicated to ending the use of the r word (retard(ed)), in any dehumanizing or humiliating fashion (R-word.org 2013). Schools can also implement disability awareness activities, or team building classes so that students without disabilities can support and advocate for students with disabilities. It is also important to build a school climate that celebrates and supports different abilities, realizing that every student can come to school without fear of bullying or discrimination.

Causes

In about one-third of cases of intellectual impairment, the cause will not be known (The ARC 2013). Research by Beirne-Smith, Patton, and Kim (2006) categorize causes of intellectual impairment into two categories, psychosocial and biological. Psychosocial issues are related to poverty and cultural deprivation. Children living in poverty are at a greater risk for poor health and nutrition, are exposed to environmental toxins, and often do not receive the medical care that is required. They may not have the same types of early cultural or educational experiences as other children. These issues can put them at a greater risk for intellectual impairment (The ARC 2013).

Biological causes include genetic conditions and specific problems that may occur during pregnancy, at the time of birth, and after birth. Human genes carry physical, mental, and personality traits (Beirne-Smith et al. 2006). There are many different genetic diseases that can be linked to intellectual impairment. The most common are the chromosomal disorder, Down syndrome, and the leading inherited cause of intellectual impairment, Fragile X, a gene disorder found on the X chromosome (The ARC 2013). There is also a single gene disorder called PKU (phenylketonuria), which left untreated can also lead to intellectual disability.

During pregnancy, maternal malnutrition, disease, and drug/alcohol use can increase the risk of a child being born with intellectual impairments. Fetal Alcohol Spectrum Disorder is a disorder that is 100% preventable. There are important things that a woman can do during pregnancy to be healthy, including cessation of drugs/alcohol and smoking. Additionally, appropriate affordable health care services, affordable food, and living in an environment free of neglect and abuse will only increase every woman's chance of having a healthy baby.

In reviewing possible causes of intellectual impairment during birth, it is important to remember that these conditions may put an infant at higher risk of developing an intellectual impairment. These conditions include prematurity, oxygen deprivation, or specific birth injury. Finally, after a child is born, childhood disease, accident, and shaken baby syndrome can lead to injury of the brain and central nervous system, with a resulting intellectual impairment.

Characteristics

Cognitive/Motivational

There are certain cognitive and motivational characteristics that are typically present in persons with an intellectual impairment. However, it is important to remember that not all persons will demonstrate the same skills and/or challenges in these domains. Certainly there will be noted differences depending on the degree of intellectual impairment (usually defined as a continuum from mild to moderate to severe). With that in mind, a general definition of each domain is provided, knowing that individuals will come with their own unique performance characteristics.

In the cognitive domain, challenges are evident in the areas of language, attention, memory, and generalization of learned skills to new settings and /or materials (Wehman, McLaughlin, Wehman 2005). Receptive and expressive language skills can be delayed to varying degrees and while all persons with an intellectual impairment can learn new skills, the style and pace of learning will be unique. The learning process that requires pulling information into the sensory register, making sense of the information, relating it to known facts, and storing the knowledge for later retrieval will be slower and less efficient than the process for typical learners. Additionally, once information is learned in one environment with one set of materials, transfer of this knowledge to a different scenario will not be automatic.

In the social/emotional domain there are motivational characteristics that will impact learning. Along with learned helplessness and the belief that they cannot be successful even when it is possible the term outerdirectedness (Crane 2002) describes a learner who waits before responding, looking outside themselves to other people for the answers. These learners fear taking a risk, based on their firm belief that they couldn't possibly know the correct answer or contribute.

The good news is that there are techniques that caregivers, teachers, and others can systematically employ to help individuals with these challenges (Wehman et al. 2005). Specific prompting techniques, general case instruction, and detailed task analysis are research based practices that can enhance learning for persons with intellectual impairment (Collins 2007).

Medical/Mental Health Characteristics

In order to provide appropriate supports to individuals with intellectual impairments, knowing other conditions that may accompany an intellectual impairment is important. These characteristics are briefly presented and more in-depth information should be sought as needed. Medical characteristics may include cerebral palsy, seizure disorder, hearing loss, vision loss, and specific health issues (e.g., respiratory, nutritional, self-care). Characteristics of depression, anxiety, hyperactivity, obsessive compulsive disorder may or may not be present as part of the individual's mental health.

Intellectual Impairment and Schooling, Living, Playing, and Working

How does having an intellectual impairment impact one's ability to get an education, have a successful career, live in your own dwelling, and develop meaningful relationships? While certainly a person with intellectual impairment may need supports to participate in some or all of these areas of life, it is certainly possible that persons with intellectual impairment can lead successful and fulfilled lives. In order to support goal attainment in these areas, planning that emphasizes helping a person lead a self determined life is best practice.

Self Determination as it relates to persons with disabilities was first used in thinking about transition planning for students who were preparing to exit the high school environment (Wehman & Palmer 2003). This type of planning approach that focuses on the desires and aspirations of the person at the center of the plan promotes the individual's ability to focus and control their own life (Wehman & Palmer 2003). One of the key features of a person centered plan is determining the type and intensity of supports that may be needed to actualize an individual's dreams and goals (AAIDD 2013).

Education

In the area of education, the label intellectual disability can negatively impact both where an individual learns and what curriculum they access. This may be less true for persons with milder intellectual impairment, but as Dr. Martha Snell discusses, the more traditional labeling, where students were classified as moderately, severely, or profoundly impaired is quite problematic. Snell (2010) states,

> "But this traditional approach has had some pretty bad effects on inclusion. Far more than any other disability group, students with intellectual disability have been separated from their peers who have no disabilities. For example, 51 percent of students with intellectual disabilities still spend the large majority—more than 60 percent—of their day away from peers who don't have disabilities. In contrast, other disability groups spend about 18 percent of their day away from their non-disabled peers. So we have a lot of segregation or separation of students because they have a label of intellectual disability." (fourth section question on levels of support.)

There is a growing body of research demonstrating that students with severe or significant intellectual disabilities can learn and benefit from instruction in the general education curriculum (Clayton et al. 2006; Copeland & Keefe 2009; Stainback, Stainback, & Stefanich 1996). In order to improve opportunities for students with intellectual impairment, teachers must be better prepared and supported to welcome students with even the challenging learning needs into their classrooms.

Adult Life

Transition planning and self-determination are necessary components in planning for a student's future after they have finished their formal education (Rowjewski et al. 2012). It is important to demonstrate to future employers, landlords, and adult system service providers that persons with intellectual impairments are capable of working and living independently.

Traumatic Brain Injury

In the regulation for the Individuals with Disability Education Act (IDEA), Traumatic Brain Injury is defined as an acquired injury to the brain caused by an external physical force that results in total or partial functional disability or psychosocial impairment, or both (IDEA 2004). Traumatic Brain Injury is not a trauma that is part of a birth injury, or congenital or degenerative condition. The Brain Injury Association of America (2013) is an organization dedicated to provide access to individuals in the areas of trauma care, rehabilitation, lifelong disease management, and individualized services and supports in order to live healthy, independent, and satisfying lives (1).

Specific services and supports will vary from person to person. Specialists in occupation, physical, and speech language therapy will work closely with the individual and their family to support educational and day-to-day living requirements.

Chapter 10

My Life Is Awesome!

Megan Hoorn, Deon Chaneyfield, and James Kleimola

Figure 1   Deon Chaneyfield
Image courtesy of author

My life is awesome! I live in Ypsilanti Michigan with my mom. My niece lives with us sometimes too. I go to school and I help people in the classroom sometimes or I go help out. I am 25.

I work in Ann Arbor city club. I clean there. I also work at another job, cleaning there also. I hang out with friends. We walk to stores or watch a movie, talk, play with my little niece, hang out with my brothers. I love sports! I like to watch 'em. I'm just making new friends and getting to know them.

My favorite thing to do is to ride around with my family. I have to make choices like do I want to leave Ypsi. I want to live in Chicago. Hopefully I would like to get an apartment and live with a friend. I would like to find another good job. My dream job is to work custodian probably at like a restaurant or something.

I don't have no kind of drama in my life, I just stay to myself. I look how other people live in this world. I see what they want to do. My mom raised me well to be a young man. I'm pretty proud of that.

Figure 2 James Kleimola
Image courtesy of author

I have CP (cerebral palsy). There's no reason to feel sorry for me, I can do a lot of things. It makes fine motor skills difficult. But I can overcome those challenges, we all have challenges. It doesn't bring me down, it lifts me up.

In a typical day I do my chores, I do laundry, dishes, cleaning. I help my mom around the house. Its great you know, I feel blessed.

Right now I live with my mom but in 2 weeks I will be moving into Cornell courts with my roommate Biyi from Nigeria. I wanted to live on my own, and I wanted to be independent. You can't rely on your mom all the time.

The hardest part about living in my own apartment is that you have to keep it maintained. The best part about living in my own apartment is that I get to spend time with friends. I get to watch my sports and invite people over. My favorite thing to do is to hang out with friends and watch sports. I get to invite family over as well. I like it you know? I want my own personal space, my own place. I want to live on my own somewhere safe, where there is no crime.

I help the football team with equipment and picking up stuff, and cheering them on. I eat dinner with the team, and after that I go to hang out with them afterward until their meeting starts.

This year I will be working for the EMU Echo delivering newspapers. I want to work with football, for the NFL working with equipment.

I also do Best Buddies, I am the buddy director and my job is to plan for activities and make sure everything is done right. I am a Christian and I live by Christian values. I go to Cross and Resurrection Church on EMU's campus. I play guitar during distribution.

I'm also involved with Peak biking program. It's basically all cyclists can ride with people with disabilities. They teach you how to stop and brake. I am part of the complete streets biker legislation. If a motorist hits a cyclist they should have consequences.

Chapter 11

Hearing Impairment

Linda Polter

Three Components Needed to Describe Hearing Loss

Type—Where is the problem?

Conductive

- ▶ Blockage in or damage to the *conductors*—those structures that conduct the sound waves to the cochlea
- ▶ The conductors are those structures in the outer ear and the middle ear
- ▶ The problems are usually temporary and most can be medically or surgically treated
- ▶ Results in a mild to moderate hearing loss
- ▶ Use of hearing aids may be part of the treatment, as well as medical management
- ▶ Damage in the inner ear—with the cochlear or the auditory nerve
- ▶ Cannot be medically or surgically "cured"
- ▶ Results in a severe or profound hearing loss
- ▶ Use of hearing aids and/or a cochlear implant may be part of the treatment

Mixed Loss

- ▶ A combination of conductive and sensorineural hearing loss
- ▶ Results in something that caused a conductive loss in an individual who has a sensorineural loss
- ▶ The conductive loss may be medically or surgically treated

Central Auditory Loss

- ▶ Caused by problems to central auditory system in the brain
- ▶ Hearing acuity is intact and these individuals will pass traditional hearing assessments

Degree—How much hearing does a person have?

- ▶ Hearing acuity is measured by an *audiometer*, testing specific frequencies and intensities
- ▶ *Audiologists* use a system as shown here to describe the degree of hearing loss
- ▶ *Unilateral*—a loss in one ear

Age at Onset—When did the hearing loss occur?

▶ *Congenital*—existing at birth
▶ *Pre-lingual*—a hearing loss that is sustained prior to the acquisition of language
▶ *Post-lingual*—a hearing loss that is sustained after the acquisition of language

Hearing Aids

▶ Electroacoustical devices which are typically wore in or behind the ear
▶ These amplify sound

Cochlear Implants

▶ An electronic device whose implanted internal component converts sound to electrical impulses, which are then sent to the auditory nerve and then to the brain
▶ These may provide sound detection and improved speech reception and production

Hearing Screening and Evaluation

Ways a young child may be screened and evaluated for a hearing loss

Automated Brain Stem Response (ABR)

▶ Sounds are presented through earphones
▶ Baby is sleeping or resting quietly
▶ Brain stem responses to sound are measured through small electrodes taped to the baby's head
▶ Responses are processed through a computer

Otoacoustic Emissions (OAE)

▶ A small probe tip is inserted into the sleeping baby's ear canal
▶ Measures the function of the cochlea

Behavioral Testing

▶ Procedures that can be conducted when the child is old enough to turn his/her head in response to a pure tone sound
▶ Measures the quietest sounds a child can detect

Acoustical Impedance

▶ This test can be administered to individuals of any age
▶ Can identify problems in the middle ear (e.g., presence of fluid, status of the tympanic membrane)

Effects of Hearing Loss

▶ It may cause a delay in the development of auditory processing skills that are prerequisite to efficient language learning.
▶ It may cause a delay in the development of receptive and expressive language, as well as speech skills.
▶ It may cause a delay in the development of academic achievement.
▶ It may cause communication difficulties.
▶ It may impact long-term educational opportunities and vocational choices.

Individuals Who are Deaf or Hard of Hearing Communicate in Various Ways

- **Auditory-Oral Methods:**
  Individuals utilize their residual hearing (or a cochlear implant) to listen and use spoken language

- **Manual Methods:**
  Individuals use American Sign Language (ASL) which is considered the language of the Deaf Community

Speech, language, and communication are important to human beings living together in a society. When interacting with individuals who are deaf or hard of hearing, don't let communication challenges get in the way of meaningful relationships.

Questions for Discussion

- Is deafness a disability or a culture?

- Can an individual who is deaf be part of both the Deaf community and a hearing community?

Chapter 12

Life with a Hearing Loss

Lisa Jordan

Image courtesy of author

I have a moderate-severe hearing loss in my left ear and a profound loss in my right ear. From the time I lost my hearing, I have worn hearing aids in my left ear since my right ear does not have enough residual hearing to benefit from an aid. I have developed a stronger left eye and perfected my head tilt so that I can look at a person's mouth to lip-read and optimize microphone direction. Hearing aids allow me to hear sound and speech, and lip-reading allows me to discriminate what is being said. In a one-on-one conversation with no background noise and optimal lip-reading conditions, I can determine at least 85% of what is said. To fill in the gaps I draw on the conversation topic and knowledge of the pattern of speech of the speaker.

I am open to new technological advances in hearing aids and currently wear a CROS system, which means the hearing aid I wear in my non-hearing right ear wirelessly transmits the sound to the hearing aid in my left ear. As my hearing levels have remained mostly constant over the years, and due to the lopsided nature of my hearing loss, I am not yet a candidate for cochlear implants.

My hearing loss results from a bout of meningitis in the fall of 1985 (before the meningitis vaccine was available). Before my illness at eighteen months I had a decent, growing vocabulary and walked; meningitis erased all those developments. I re-learned to walk and talk. Within weeks my parents scheduled appointments with audiologists to have me fitted for a hearing aid and with speech pathologists. From the beginning my mom used an FM system (a speaker wears a microphone which transmits the sound directly to a receiving device such as a hearing aid or standalone hearing device), worked on speech, and taught me how to use my hearing aids. My mom sought to know all that she could about services, my options, and what she needed to do to make sure I thrived. She was my strongest advocate.

My parents made the decision to raise me only oral (a rehabilitation approach which utilizes residual hearing through amplification, lip-reading, and speech), based on the professional school of thought at the time and because of exposure to sound and speech before the loss. My strongest early memories are of playing with an Apple computer at the speech pathologist's office, practicing speech, and being aware of hearing aids. I wore a hearing aid connected by wire to a battery pack that was carried via body harness in the front. At times I became annoyed wearing my hearing aids. As a toddler on one occasion I threw the hearing aid onto the lawn and my family combed the grass looking for the aid. Gradually I became accustomed to the ritual of wearing hearing aids—storing them in a safe, dry spot, carrying hearing aid batteries, charging the battery pack, and avoiding water.

From kindergarten to twelfth grade, I had an annual Individualized Education Program (IEP), teachers for the deaf and hard of hearing (TDHoH), used an FM system, always sat in front—a little to the right—and went to speech therapy. Teachers' voices became familiar and dependable through the FM system and I rarely missed anything. Speech therapy in elementary school was held in a janitor closet-sized space and involved rote repetition. In middle school and high school, for speech therapy, I recorded myself reading out loud, and on the playback would have to pick out trouble areas and critique my speech. The speech teachers were strict to follow the IEP, and were unmemorable.

The TDHoH worked with my teachers to coordinate services and advocated for me when the teachers did not provide those services. They taught me self-advocacy, how to navigate the school settings, and discussed daily issues. I was a willing participant in all of these activities, up until the last couple years of high school, when I started to rebel by canceling speech appointments and meetings with my TDHoH. I became increasingly self-conscious and did not want to be removed from class for speech therapy or meetings with my TDHoH. My TDHoH teacher wanted me to assert myself with my regular teachers and take charge of making sure my needs were met. I wanted to coast, sit in the back of the classroom, was certain I could navigate the college world, and felt the teacher couldn't help me with social issues. I strived to be an outstanding student to show that I was capable of being normal. In response to the challenges I succeeded academically, but withdrew socially.

In high school I was lost in the social environment: conversation topics were constantly switching, classmates couldn't be bothered to repeat sentences, most environments were loud, and they spoke fast. It was a losing battle to tell every person "please slow down," "please repeat what you said," "use a different phrase," etc. I felt like I always needed help and assistance. I flustered easily and my face would turn bright red in response to anything people said. I assumed that people made fun of me, and that I would always miss out on what was happening. I wanted to be someone other than a person with a hearing loss.

I was confused about my identity—was I Deaf? Was I hearing? People would often say "you do so well" which was meant to be a compliment, but to me it was somewhat insulting, highlighted differences and overlooked my constant efforts. I just couldn't fit in and became increasingly aware of how different I was. I felt torn between two worlds. To be in the hearing world, I grappled with the burden that I would always have to work to hear and ask others for assistance. Deafness is an invisible handicap. People do not easily discern a hearing loss without experience, and even then, people are not always willing to be of assistance. It's hard for people to grasp the magnitude of the loss and my efforts, as the hearing loss is not visible and my adaptations to the hearing world are unnoticeable.

For college I toyed with the idea of going to Gallaudet and Rochester Institute of Technology for the Deaf. I visited Gallaudet and met the chancellor. I learned that most of the classes I wanted to take would be at neighboring colleges and that mostly I would gain a culture at Gallaudet. A culture, I had read, that would not be accepting of hard-of-hearing people raised orally with limited ASL. With the whole world seemingly open to me, it seemed narrow to enter a small niche culture. It seemed like the opposite side of the coin to struggle in a Deaf environment for acceptance and full communication. Both places were far from home and family, and although I have struggled in family social environments, it was unappealing to be without their support. I chose not to attend either university and attended a small liberal arts college and continued in the mainstream.

I took ASL courses to fulfill my language requirement in college. My ASL professor was the only deaf person in the rural area, and mostly used sign with interpreters and teaching. College was not as easy as expected. I had become comfortable with my accommodating teachers, and with classmates in high school who were familiar with the FM system. In college I pushed for my professors to accommodate me, reminded them when they didn't, and asked for note takers. In large auditoriums it seemed to make little difference whether or not I sat in front, and the FM systems often did not help enough. Walking up to the front of the classroom in my freshman year to deliver the FM system was a task I dreaded; it felt like an announcement and wasn't the way I wanted to introduce myself to my classmates.

Post-college I studied for a year in sub-Saharan Africa. I became involved in the deaf and hard-of-hearing community there and learned the sign language of the country. My classmates were on the same level; they struggled to be included and learn the spoken national and local languages. Frankly, it was easier for me to be deaf there. I was already a noticeable foreigner and went days without wearing my hearing aids. The community there was tenuous, large, and striving for language uniformity. I made friends with the local leaders of the deaf community and learned of their efforts to reach the rural deaf and inform them of HIV/AIDs and sign language. I marveled at their accomplishments and desire to help others less fortunate. There were misconceptions both ways—people did not think an American could have a hearing loss and do well with a hearing aid, and I could not even conceive of a large, take-charge deaf community in that part of the world.

I'm still learning how to navigate the hearing world—in the workplace, in personal relationships, and with support services. As an adult I accepted my hearing abilities and mostly settled the identity issues. Perhaps the phrase I hated so much ("you do so well") is also a source of strength, as I can succeed well enough in the hearing world. I have found supportive people who help in a kind manner without being asked, or learn how to help. I learned to ignore the people who just won't accommodate me—even when asked and reminded. I learned how to preface conversations with the important tidbits about my hearing loss when needed in crucial situations. I learned that no one hears well in a bar or loud environment, and that I have an advantage by lip-reading. I choose not to tell everyone I meet about my hearing loss, as some social interactions are so fleeting. I'm still sensitive about my speech and try to self-monitor correct speech, but sometimes I end up being more self-conscious, shy, and tongue-tied.

With my partner I feel jealous that he is so easily included in social interactions and, by no fault of his own, I am left behind. Sometimes I feel like it's an unfair burden on him, as he is the person I ask to repeat tidbits and he also acts as my advocate. On the other hand, knowing what he does about my hearing, he could do more to communicate with me in a manner that's more beneficial. Some days I am lazy or tired, and speak to him from another room expecting him to find me so I can see his face. He's comfortable communicating with me if I choose not to wear my hearing aids. We are learning together, finding a way to communicate that improves and strengthens our relationship.

I have concerns for the future for when I have kids. I have concerns about safety—how will I know they are crying and need me? How will they be able to share their pains with me? Will they make fun of my hearing loss? Will they have a speech impediment due to my deaf accent? The gibberish of first speech is understandable to others but not me. Kids who are able to converse are often confused when I can't understand them. I trust that I will understand my own children through familiarity. Perhaps I have made a mistake in not becoming fluent in ASL, as that could serve me well in the future with kids, and if I lose more hearing. In the meantime, I will do what I can with what I have.

Chapter 13

Visual Impairment: Low Vision and Blindness

Alicia Li

With our intact senses we carry out daily activities without thinking about what might happen and what we would do if any of our senses were lost. Many activities and functions undoubtedly will be affected and hindered if vision, which is responsible for more than 50 percent of the information that enters the brain, is lost (Li 2004). However, a significant number of individuals without normal functional vision excel in their jobs or achieve unimaginable tasks regardless of the adversity (e.g., lawyers, teachers, computer programmers, athletes, counselors, etc.). There are at least 300 occupational fields in which they are succeeding and finding satisfaction (American Foundation for the Blind 2012). Compare to a century ago the amazing achievement of persons today with visual impairments did not happen overnight. The education, training, and resources available to this segment of the population as well as the attitude changes and support of the society has played a critical role in the success of individuals who are visually impaired in leading successful, productive, and fulfilling lives. Today, individuals with visual impairments are considered more similar than different from nondisabled people. For example, they don't have a sixth sense. As a result of lacking functional vision, they may develop and depend on other senses, such as hearing and touch, beyond that of sighted people. They do dream as all of us do, except their dreams are filled with sensations, odors, tastes, tactile images instead of visual images. They speak the same language, therefore we should not refrain from using terms as "see," "look," and colors-related words. They may use different sensory modalities for learning and living. Their needs as human beings are no different than those of sighted people, such as being respected, loved, supported, taking responsibilities, and fulfilling dreams and goals.

I. Definitions

> "Visual impairment including blindness means an impairment in vision that even with correction, adversely affects a child's educational performance. The term includes both partial sight and blindness."
> [IDEA, §300.8 (c)(13)]

In addition to the IDEA definition above, Michigan, as many other states, determines the eligibility for special services of visual impairment (VI) based on a multidisciplinary evaluation team including an ophthalmologist or optometrist that a child exhibits one or more of the following:

"(i) A central visual acuity for near or far point vision of 20/70 or less in the better eye after routine refractive correction.

(ii)   A peripheral field of vision restricted to not more than 20 degrees.

(iii) A diagnosed progressively deteriorating eye condition." [Michigan Administrative Rules for Special Education (MARSE, 2012, R 340.1708, p. 15].

Visual acuity, the sharpness of vision, refers to the eye's ability to distinguish the details. In 20/70, the top number (the numerator) indicates the vision testing distance (i.e., how far the child stood from the eye chart, such as the Snellen "E" chart, when he was tested). The bottom number (the denominator) tells us what was the smallest line the child was able to read or identify. 20/70 also means that a person with 20/20 vision can read the "E" at 70 feet, while those with visual acuities of 20/70 need to be at 20 feet away to read the same target (Dennison 2003). Visual field refers to the area that can be seen when looking straight ahead. The normal visual field that most of us can see is an area of about 160–180 degrees.

Another term, low vision, has been commonly used as partial sight to refer to individuals who have a best-corrected visual acuity between 20/70 and 20/200 in the better eye. In fact, the term *low vision* has, for the most part, become the more predominant term than *partial sight* (Corn & Lusk 2010). Students with a visual acuity of 20/200 or less, or a peripheral field of 20 degrees or less in the better eye after correction are classified as legally blind (Hatlen 2000). This is a term used by the federal government to allow them to receive special tax benefits and materials from the federal government. For example, according to the Code of Regulations, individuals who are legally blind are entitled to receive higher disability and retirement benefits from the Supplemental Security Income (SSI) program. They are also entitled to exemptions and deductions on federal and state taxes such as property or real estate taxes (McDowell, n.d.). The exemptions and deductions vary from state to state. Students who are legally blind are entitled to receive free educational materials from American Printing House for the Blind through the Federal Quota Program (to be detailed later under VI. Education). In spite of different labels, most individuals with VI have residual vision, and only about 10 percent of them are totally blind (Griffin et al. 2002).

II. How the Visual System Works

In order to see, light must exist. The light rays reflected off of objects enter the eye through the cornea, pupil, and lens before they strike the retina (see following illustration). The *cornea* is transparent and a curved surface with the strongest bending power of the eye. Astigmatism, myopia (nearsightedness), and hyperopia (farsightedness) will occur when the smoothness and shape of the cornea is affected. After passing through cornea, the light rays go into an area filled with *aqueous humor* (gel-like fluid). An imbalance between the production and drainage of it results in high eye pressure and subsequently glaucoma. The light rays then go through the *pupil*, which is the opening in the center of the iris, the colored part of the eye. The size of the pupil varies as the lighting of the setting changes. The visual pathway is transparent and at times the *lens* becomes cloudy as people advance in age. This is commonly known as cataracts. Another critical function of the lens is to bring an object at near and far into focus by adjusting its thickness. This accommodative ability becomes weaker and weaker (a condition called "presbyopia") as people age over 40 by losing the elasticity of the lens. The light rays travel through it and hit the *retina,* where they are changed into electrical/neural signals and are then sent to the *occipital lobes* of the brain through the *optic nerve* for interpretation. The retina is made up of the innermost layer of the eye with nerves and special cells including the two types of photoreceptors, the rods and cones. The rods enable us to see gross forms and movement whereas the cones give us ability to see colors and fine details.

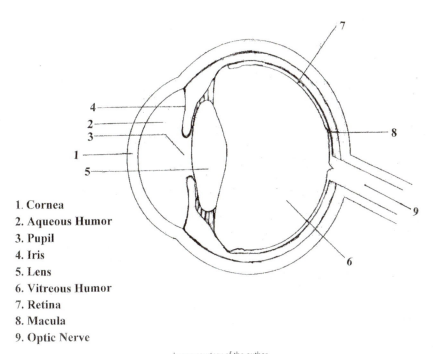

1. Cornea
2. Aqueous Humor
3. Pupil
4. Iris
5. Lens
6. Vitreous Humor
7. Retina
8. Macula
9. Optic Nerve

Image courtesy of the author

III. Types of Visual Loss and Causes

When things go wrong with parts of the visual system, various eye disorders lead to any or a combination of types of visual loss described below (Dennison 2003):

A. **Acuity Loss**

A person with acuity loss does not see his or her world as clearly as s/he should. This is the result of a wide range of causes that affect any part of the visual pathway delineated above (i.e., cornea, lens, retina, optic nerve, etc.). Severe refractive errors including myopia, hyperopia, and astigmatism, where the images are not formed on the retina, cause acuity loss. Other examples of causes are cataracts (cloudiness of the lens), retinal detachment, retinopathy of prematurity (the abnormal retinal development in premature infants), damage to the retina caused by albinism (lack of pigment in the skin and lightly colored iris), aniridia (partial or completely absent iris and underdeveloped retina), coloboma (incomplete closure of the pupil and may involve other parts of the eye including retina), glaucoma (high eye pressure), and optic nerve hypoplasia (underdeveloped optic nerve).

B. **Field Loss**

The areas that a person with field loss can see are limited. Field loss may occur with and without reduced visual acuity. There are varying types and degrees of field loss. Examples of different types of field loss are as follows: islands of vision (as if looking through Swiss cheese), central field loss (the detail and color vision may be affected), scotoma (blind spots in a person's visual field), and hemianopsia (a loss of half the visual field).

The person who has blind spots in his/her visual field may hold his/her head in a different position trying to get around the blind spots when looking. Like acuity loss, field loss can be caused by any disorders which interfere with the travel along the visual pathway such as cataracts, retinal detachment, or a brain tumor on the optic nerve.

C. **Oculomotor Problems**

This is a type of visual loss pertaining to the movement of the eyes. Six pairs of muscles and the nerves governing them are primarily responsible for the eyes' movement in all directions. Any disruptions to the coordination of the six muscles, such as any or a combination of the muscles are too tight, loose, short, or long (muscle imbalance), can cause different types of oculomotor problems. Amblyopia (lazy eyes) and strabismus (crossed eyes) are two typical oculomotor disorders. Patching, glasses, medication, even surgery may be used to correct the problem.

D. **Processing Problems**

As stated earlier, light rays enter the visual pathway and reach the vision center or occipital lobes located in the back of the brain for interpretation. Although the last type of processing visual loss may occur with an abnormal eye, the main disorder lies in the processing of the visual information transmitted to the occipital lobes and leads to a disorder called cortical visual impairment (CVI) or cortical blindness. There is no cure (such as medication, glasses, or surgery) for CVI, but a vision stimulation program may improve the child's use of his/her vision.

IV. Demographics

In its *2007 Annual Report*, American Printing House for the Blind reported that 57,696 students were listed in the annual registry for school-aged children, which is used for the purpose of distributing educational materials through the quota system (American Printing House for the Blind 2007). In this report, 10 percent are considered to be braille readers, 27 percent to be visual readers, and 7 percent to be auditory readers. The remaining students are either pre-readers including infants, preschoolers, or older students with reading potential (23 percent) or nonreaders who show no reading potential (34 percent). The actual number of children with VI is greater than those reported in the American Printing House for the Blind registry because the registry focuses primarily on the students' reading data, and a significant number of them may not be identified due to their other disabilities which mask the impact of their visual impairments (Corn & Lusk 2010). They are also likely to be labeled under those categories instead of visual impairments. The leading causes of VI in infants and children are retinopathy of prematurity, CVI, and eye abnormalities such as retina related disorders (APH 2011).

School-aged children with VI actually constitute a small proportion of the entire VI population. More than two-thirds of people with visual impairments are older than 65 years of age (APH 2011). In 2004, National Eye Institute supported a research project providing an in-depth description on the prevalence of a number of eye conditions (i.e., age-related macular degeneration, cataracts, diabetic retinopathy, and glaucoma) among Whites, Blacks, and Hispanics (National Eye Institute 2004). The findings revealed that age-related macular degeneration is the leading cause of blindness among Caucasians in the United States (Corn & Lusk 2010). Macula, 4 millimeters in diameter, is a small portion of the retina containing most cones for sharp central vision. Age-related macular degeneration (AMD) is the leading cause of central vision loss in adults over 50 years of age in the United States and its prevalence increases after age 65 (Friedman et al. 2004; Schwartz 2010). AMD causes gradual and permanent central vision loss, but the peripheral vision is usually retained. In other words, individuals with AMD may lose the ability to read and see details but continue to move and travel around freely without difficulties. A combination of genetic and environmental factors such as cigarette smoking and exposure to ultraviolet light have been found as possible contributing factors of AMD (Haddad et al. 2006; Murphy 1986). American Printing House for the Blind (2011) reported that the leading causes of visual impairment in elderly persons are AMD, glaucoma, diabetic retinopathy, cataracts, and optic nerve atrophy.

For African Americans, cataracts and glaucoma are the leading causes of blindness, and glaucoma occurs at three times the rate in African Americans than it does in Caucasians (Corn & Lusk 2010; National Eye Institute 2004). The prevalence for glaucoma also rises rapidly in Hispanics above the age of 65 (National

Eye Institute 2004) (Visit http://www.eyecareamerica.com/eyecare/conditions/glaucoma/simulator.cfm for a glaucoma simulator). Prevent Blindness America (2008) found that there were also geographical differences in the prevalence of visual impairments in the 40-and-older age group. For example, Alaska had the lowest rate while Hawaii and Rhode Island had the highest (Prevent Blindness America 2008). In its 2012 "Vision Problems in the U.S." report, Prevent Blindness America identified a significant increase in visual impairments and blindness among older Americans over the past decade, including an 89 percent spike in diabetic eye disease. Research also suggests that:

> "ethnic groups have lower awareness of the need for preventive care, and often less access to receiving comprehensive eye care. …cultural and language barriers can further stand in the way of ethnic populations receiving adequate eye care and treatment." (Prevent Blindness America 2012)

V. Characteristics

A. Intelligence

VI alone will not impact a person's cognitive skills. However due to medical advancement, more and more babies, who would not have survived decades ago, live with complications including vision problems such as CVI, the leading cause of VI for infants, toddlers, and preschoolers.

B. Learning

Students with low vision frequently are placed in general education classrooms accessing general education curriculum alongside their nondisabled peers. They read standard (regular) or large print with or without accommodations. Students who continue reading regular print may become tired or fatigue easily. Taking constant breaks helps resolve this problem. Accommodations include adjusting size, lighting, contrast, glare, and/or colors to meet the student's needs.

Students with severe VI and cannot read print even with accommodations will need to learn through tactile and/or auditory channels. Braille, the primary tactile medium for the blind, is a coded system of reading and writing that was first invented by Louis Braille in 1824. The use of braille does not come naturally. Instead, it needs extensive training on tactual discrimination so the braille learners are able to distinguish the fine differences among the dot combinations. Besides, extensive training and practice are definitely needed for the braille learners to master the braille they need in different types of reading, such as math, science, and music, which are different from literary braille.

Image © Lisa S., 2014. Used under license from Shutterstock, Inc.

C. **Social skills**

Beginning in infancy, people learn social skills through watching. Making eye contact, smiling, showing facial expressions and body language of different emotions (happy, angry, sad, etc.), initiating, maintaining, and terminating conversations are attributed largely to visual clues. Without usable sight, nonverbal cues, such as rolling eyes, a shrug of the shoulders, and the social meanings they represent are unlikely to be acquired. Incidental learning that sighted people take for granted is lacking in students with VI. As a result, step-by-step direct instructions in social skills are critical for them to learn skills that are basic and which sighted students possess without learning such as making eye contact when being spoken to.

VI. Education

A. Due to the lack of usable vision, students who are blind apparently require a wide variety of compensatory skills trainings and adaptations in communication (reading and writing), travel, daily living, and academic learning:

1. **Braille:** This is a tactile system of reading and writing. It employs six raised dots arranged in two parallel rows each having three dots. They are numbered, downward, 1 through 3 in the left column and 4 through 6 in the right column. Braille is written in two forms, uncontracted (Grade 1 braille) and contracted (Grade 2 braille). Uncontracted braille spells words out letter by letter. In contracted braille, there are 189 different contractions and 76 short-form words. Contracted braille is used to save space. Nevertheless, braille books are bulky and require additional space for storage.

BRAILLE ALPHABET

Image © Laralova, 2014. Used under license from Shutterstock, Inc.

2. **Orientation & mobility** (O & M): Orientation is the ability to use the senses to understand one's position and relationship to objects in the environment. It is a process of knowing where one is at any given time in an ever-changing environment. Mobility means the ability of moving around safely and efficiently. O & M skills are essential for people with severe visual impairments for traveling from one place to another. Currently, there are three common O & M forms for the blind, sighted guide techniques, cane travels, and dog guides. They are not used exclusively from one another, e.g., cane travels with occasional sighted guide. In today's technology era, more advance-

ment has been done to electronic travel aids (ETA), another O & M form to help people without sighted travel. However due to the cost of ETA, it is not being considered as one of the convenient and inexpensive modes of travel.

Image © Lisa S., 2014. Used under license from Shutterstock, Inc.

3. **Instructional materials:** The adapted materials that students with VI need for assessment and learning at school require special design and are at higher-than-usual costs. The Congress recognized this and passed "An Act to Promote the Education of the Blind" in 1879 to establish the American Printing House for the Blind (APH) and the federal quota system. APH was founded with federal money to produce textbooks in braille and large print, and to develop or adapt instructional materials for students who are blind (Hatlen 2000). APH explains the federal quota system as follows:

> "A Congressional appropriation, designated to provide educational materials for students who meet the definition of blindness, is made each October in the federal budget. This allotment is divided by the total number of eligible students and clients in educational or instructional programs at less than college levels on the first Monday of the preceding January. This division results in a per capita amount that is then multiplied by the number of registered students in each Federal Quota account. This amount is credited to each respective account, thus establishing each account's "quota" for the federal fiscal year." (APH 2012)

APH provides assessment materials such as the Brigance Diagnostic Comprehensive Inventory of Basic Skills, Revised, 1999; Woodcock-Johnson III, etc. Instructional materials for a variety of subjects are one of APH's primary focuses: English and language arts, literacy education, mathematics, science and health, social studies (history, geography, and economics), fine arts, business and vocational education, and physical education. Other areas of instructional materials that APH makes available are for visual efficiency, O & M (concept development), assistive technology and electronics, daily living and social interaction, and recreation and leisure. Most of these materials can be ordered for use at home or school through the federal quota system.

4. **Accommodations for students with severe VI in inclusive environments**:
   ▶ Open or close doors or drawers fully, any half-open/close doors or drawers can be dangerous.
   ▶ Any objects hanging from the ceiling and getting in the student's face should be avoided.
   ▶ It's important to keep the layout of the room constant, and notify the student if changes need to be made.
   ▶ Provide verbal instructions/descriptions of the activities in the setting all the time.
   ▶ Place the student away from cluttered areas, such as doors, pencil sharpeners, etc.
   ▶ Provide a hard copy of outlines, key concepts, or summaries in braille.
   ▶ When a sighted guide is leading a student, the guide should be half a step ahead of the student who is holding onto the guide's arm above the elbow. At no time does the guide lead the student by pushing him/her ahead. If the guide must leave in the middle of a conversation or activity, the student should be told.
   ▶ Use the clock position when telling the student the location of an object, e.g., the glass of water is at the 11 o'clock position.
   ▶ Encourage and help the student use his/her assistive technology devices, including magnifying visual aids/glasses, synthetic speech (e.g., JAWS), braille translators (e.g., Duxbury Braille Translator), braille embosser (e.g., Tiger Braille Embosser), and braille note-taker (e.g., Braille Note).

VII. Adaptations for Individuals with Low Vision

In the population of VI, there are more individuals with residual vision than being totally blind. For example, approximately 80 percent of students with VI have sufficient residual vision to read print (Wilkinson & Trantham 2004). This section is devoted to enhance the use of vision in persons with residual visions and to increase the visibility of objects viewed through manipulating environmental factors (such as illumination, glare, contrast, and colors). Examples of these environmental manipulations are delineated below (Kapperman & Koenig 1996; Watkins 1989; Quillman & Goodrich 2004):

A. **Illumination**

Fluorescent lighting contains large amounts of blue light whereas incandescent lighting contains large amounts of yellow and red light. Fluorescent lighting gives better area illumination than does incandescent lighting, but scatters, flickers, and buzzes. Incandescent lighting provides better contrast due to its quality and directionality and is better for most near tasks such as reading. For individuals with low vision, it is advised to use a combination of fluorescent lighting for overhead illumination and incandescent lighting for spot illumination. Another way to meet the person's lighting needs is to use a combination of overhead lighting and an adjustable neck or swing-arm lamp that can be moved closer for near tasks. Using lighting with a dimmer switch (rheostat) is also a helpful alternative.

B. **Glare**

Many ocular conditions such as cataracts and albinism are sensitive to glare. Curtains, drapes, and venetian/vertical blinds can be used to control the glare from outdoor light. Covering a polished floor with an area rug is a good way to eliminate glare.

C. **Colors**

Using colors is a simple and effective way to organize different items, e.g., sorting papers for different subjects by using different color folders. Another common use of color is to place colored acetate sheets over purple and blue printed materials to enhance contrast.

D. **Contrast**

The following is a list of methods to increase contrast in a household:

► Placing warm colors (red, orange, and yellow) next to cool colors (green, blue, and violet).

► Using light and dark including the use of basic colors, e.g., light brown next to dark brown.

► Wrapping drawer, cupboard, and other handles with contrasting bright fluorescent tape against their respective backgrounds.

► Lining the inside edge of cabinet/cupboard doors with highly contrasting tape so that any open doors are easier to see.

► Using a contrast between the table and eating utensils (e.g., using contrasting placemats; white plates on a plain dark tablecloth).

► Using light objects against dark backgrounds and dark objects against light backgrounds. For example, when measuring liquids, light/dark liquids contrast well with a dark/light piece of paper glued to the wall.

► Using a contrasting colored non-skid mat in the tub to help prevent slipping and to make it easier to see the tub.

► Using a contrasting bathmat draped over the edge of the tub.

► Placing color contrasting tape around light switches.

Increasing visibility:

► Affixing brightly colored fluorescent tape or attaching cut-out figures to glass doors.

► Draping a towel over the back of a piece of furniture.

► Using magnifying mirrors to help when shaving or applying makeup.

► For steps and stairs inside and outside of the house, mark the edge and riser of the steps with a contrasting adhesive, paint, or safety tape.

VIII. Career Development and Individuals with Visual Impairments

Persons with visual impairments have long had a high unemployment record. In the late 1970s almost 70 percent of adults with VI were not participating in the labor market (Kirchner & Peterson 1988). In the 1992 National Longitudinal Transition Study of Special Education Students (Wagner et al. 1992), the authors reported over 60 percent of students with VI were unemployed three years following graduation. No better records have been located to indicate the unemployment for this section of the population today. Fortunately, numerous efforts have been made to reduce the depressing statistics.

The primary piece of federal legislation that provides services to persons who are blind or visually impaired throughout the United States is the 1992 Amendments (PL 102-569) to the Rehabilitation Act of 1973 (Moore, Huebner, & Maxson 1997). Title I of the Rehabilitation Act of 1973, as amended, provides the primary framework for the provision of vocational rehabilitation services to people who are blind or visually impaired.

"…the state agency for individuals who are blind or other agency which provides assistance or services to adults who are blind, is authorized to provide vocational rehabilitation services to such individuals, such agency may be designated as the sole state agency to administer the part of the plan under which vocational rehabilitation services are provided for individuals who are blind … (29 USC & 720 et seq.)."

Several important services for persons who are blind or visually impaired, such as assessment, vocational training, rehabilitation teaching services, orientation and mobility services, sensory devices and other technological devices (e.g., low vision aids), and rehabilitation technology services, are provided under the amended Rehabilitation Act of 1973.

In hiring people with VI, many employers are concerned with safety issues, performance on the job, and the cost for accommodation. A study on occupational injuries and illnesses by the National Industries for the Blind, entitled "Incidence of Occupational injuries and illnesses among Workers Who Are Blind," reported that workers who are blind do not have a higher incidence rate of illness and injury than the national average based on data collected from 1995 through 1997 (AFB 2007). High retention and performance/productivity were reported by numerous agencies. Contrary to common thought, typical accommodation costs are very low. In most cases of low vision, only improved lighting and magnification are required (AFB 2007). For more expensive accommodation, the state agency serving people who are visually impaired frequently supports, in part or in whole, the employers who hire workers who are visually impaired.

In today's technological era, information and resources are readily accessible. A website designed by American Foundation for the Blind, "AFB Career Connect," is by far the most comprehensive Internet resource for people who are visually impaired attempting to enter the job market as well as for employers who are interested in hiring people who are visually impaired. AFB Career Connect offers information for job seekers, employers, professionals, mentors, and family and friends. It is not just the content presented, but the site offers a place for mentoring and asking job-related questions.

IX. Partnerships with Families and Communities

In preparing individuals with VI to become independent and productive members of society, families start at the beginning and throughout the continuum. Bonding establishment, daily living skills, social skills, communication skills, and cognitive skills are all rooted and developed in the family arena in which the child spends most of his/her day. To a different extent each family experiences shock, denial, or the entire grief process as soon as the "eye conditions" are diagnosed at any time of the life cycle (i.e., congenital or adventitiously blind; child or adult blindness). Regardless, they should be the ones providing support and assistance to the person with VI. Family members may not have full VI knowledge and/or skills, so collaborating with service providers is an excellent means to fill in the gap. Family support is always one of the first steps to empower the person with VI. Overprotection or thinking the person needs help all the time creates a candidate for helplessness. It's critical for families to equip themselves with a myriad of resources to be knowledgeable of the things their family member with VI needs, e.g., AFB FamilyConnect, NICHCY (National Dissemination Center for Children with Disabilities), and associations for parents of children with VI in every state.

In addition to family support, community awareness and accessibility is equally important. Although the ADA law has expanded opportunities for individuals with disabilities, there continues to be a huge place for community improvement for persons with VI. The stereotype bias prevents people from getting near persons with VI because they do not know what to do or say. In fact, a simple step of going over and asking: "Do you need help?" is sufficient, no mystery or special ways. Simply ask and they will let you know how to help.

X. Summary

Although students with VI are one of the smallest disability categories, the incidence of VI increases with age (D. Smith 2007). As a matter of fact, increases are expected in the numbers of both children and adults with VI (Corn & Lusk 2010). As more infants survive at lower gestation and weights, more children will experience vision problems and multiple disabilities (National Advisory Eye Council 1999). In addition, as medical advances continue to extend life expectancy, adults are at risk of developing age-related visual impairments, such as AMD (Janiszewski et al. 2006). Rates of severe vision loss are predicted to be doubled in the next three decades along with the size of the country's aging population (Prevent Blindness America 2008). With decades of efforts, students with VI have a better chance of being included in general education classes, but the integration into the adult world continues to be restricted. Due to the stereotypes of blind people being fragile and incapable of many things, their employment and participation in the mainstream of society remain restricted. Improvement in this area is absolutely and desperately needed from everyone in our society. A tiny step of acceptance and support of people with VI can make an unimaginable impact on their lives.

Questions for Discussion

▶ How can a safe and adequate physical and social environment be prepared for individuals with blindness or low vision at home, school, and/or work?

▶ What are some possible accommodations a teacher can provide for students with blindness or low vision in general education classrooms?

▶ Besides cultural differences, what diversity issues need to be addressed for individuals with blindness or low vision at school and/or at work? Include age of onset (congenital VS adventitious VI), socioeconomic status/access to medical intervention, eye disorders (resulting in reduced visual acuity and/or visual field restriction), and learning media (braille VS large print) in your discussion.

▶ How can technology assist individuals with blindness or low vision at school or in the workplace?

▶ What can be done to increase or enhance the inclusion of individuals with blindness or low vision in school and/or the workplace?

Chapter 14

Learning Disabilities

Karen Schulte

Introduction

Learning disabilities—they comprise the largest group of students receiving special education services and are perhaps the most misunderstood of all the disability areas. Understanding a person with a learning disability is often like solving a mystery: gathering clues from assessment data and observation about how the person's mind processes information, forming a hypothesis about what would help the person be a more effective learner, trying out these ideas, and then "back to the drawing board" if the hypothesis turned out not to be correct. One might also think of understanding a person with a learning disability as similar to putting together a complex puzzle, each person with his or her own unique learning style or pattern.

The term learning disability was first introduced in 1963 by Sam Kirk, replacing terms such as brain injured, perceptual handicaps, and neurologically impaired (Lerner & Johns 2012), to represent a large and heterogeneous group of students who process or understand information differently than their peers. In 1975, learning disabilities were included in the first major federal legislation mandating special education, Public Law 94-142 Education of All Handicapped Children Act, now called Individuals with Disabilities Education Act (IDEA). Although there were many problems with the definition of learning disabilities included in PL94-142, the definition went basically unchanged from 1975 until the 2004 reauthorization of IDEA. At that time there were major revisions in the way learning disabilities are defined and identified, and, as a result of this, the field of learning disabilities finds itself in a time of adjustment and redefinition.

Approximately four to six percent of public school students are identified as having learning disabilities (Learning Disabilities Association of America 2012). These 2.4 million students represent the largest group of students, 41%, receiving special education services in our public schools (U.S. Department of Education 2010). Despite their numbers, the long-term achievement of students with learning disabilities has not shown significant improvement, and outcomes remain relatively poor:

▶ Almost half of all high school students with learning disabilities are performing at least three grade levels below their actual grade level in both reading and math (Wagner et al. 2003).

▶ Close to 20% of students with learning disabilities drop out of high school, compared with 8% of the general population of high school students (U.S. Department of Education National Center for Education Statistics 2010).

▶ Adults with learning disabilities are employed at a disproportionally lower rate than those without disabilities, and a significantly higher number of adults with learning disabilities are not working due to lack of education (Kaye 2010).

The field of learning disabilities is currently engaged in refining the definition of learning disabilities, extending and deepening the understanding of learning disabilities and improving the design of services and strategies to better meet the needs of this large and varied group of students. This chapter will cover the current definition of learning disabilities; a framework for thinking about the processing skills involved in learning disabilities; characteristics of students with learning disabilities; types of learning disabilities; and the identification of students with learning disabilities.

Adults With Learning Disabilities Describe What It Is Like...

"School was hard for me because I was always catching up. My work took me longer to do, but that was ok because I was getting it done."

"In first grade, I couldn't read the books because they were too difficult for me. I had a difficult time sounding out the words and figuring out what the words were. Because of the problems I had with vowels, by the time I figured out a word I forgot what I had read."

"Due to my struggles I have developed an anxiety problem. This anxiety happens when a teacher asks me a question I do not know or when we are doing read aloud and there is a possibility I may be called on. I was always nervous about what other students thought when I would leave the room for resource room, where I would get help on assignments, take tests or catch up on late work."

Image courtesy of author

Definition

There are many definitions of learning disabilities, leading to some confusion in the field! IDEA 2004 defines a specific learning disability, in part, as:

> ...a disorder in one or more of the basic psychological processes involved in understanding or in using language, spoken or written, which disorder may manifest itself in imperfect ability to listen, think, speak, read, write, spell, or do mathematical calculations. The term includes such conditions as perceptual disabilities, brain injury, minimal brain dysfunction, dyslexia, and developmental aphasia (300.8).

This part of the federal definition is often referred to as the *theoretical definition* and has remained unchanged since 1975. It defines a learning disability as a difficulty in a variety of areas, including reading, writing, spelling, and mathematics, caused by a disorder or difference in the way a person processes information, and implies an underlying neurological cause.

The National Center for Learning Disabilities describes a learning disability as "a neurological disorder that affects the brain's ability to receive, process, store, and respond to information (National Center for Learning Disabilities 2012). The National Joint Committee on Learning Disabilities has developed quite a lengthy definition of learning disabilities, which includes, among other things, difficulties acquiring or using reading, writing, or mathematical skills and the presumption of a neurological or central nervous system dysfunction (Interagency Committee on Learning Disabilities 1988).

What Does All This Mean?

A learning disability:

▶ Is caused by a neurological or central nervous system dysfunction,
▶ Is present from birth,
▶ Impacts the way a person's brain receives, processes, stores, or acts upon information,
▶ Impacts a person's ability to learn in the same way other people do, and
▶ Causes difficulty with various learning tasks such as reading, writing, and mathematics.

Image courtesy of author

Exclusionary Clause

Because of the complex nature of the neurological involvement in learning disabilities and our limited diagnostic tools, it is often difficult to document the presumed neurological cause. The theoretical definition included in IDEA 2004 addresses this through what is known as the exclusionary clause:

> …Such term does not include a learning problem that is primarily the result of visual, hearing, or motor disabilities; of mental retardation; of emotional disturbance; or of environmental, cultural, or economic disadvantage (300.8).

Although the factors mentioned in the exclusionary clause may be present in a student with a learning disability, assessment teams must rule out these factors as the *causes* of a student's processing differences or learning difficulties, thus confirming *by exclusion* a neurological cause.

MYTH

Persons with learning disabilities are dumb.

FACT

Persons with learning disabilities have average or above average intelligence.

Image courtesy of author

Processing Skills

Because a learning disability is caused by a *dysfunction or difference* in the way a person processes (receives, understands, stores, and acts upon) information, it is important to understand what we mean by "processing skills." There are many frameworks, each of them using different terms, to describe processing skills. One way to think about them is using an "input-processing-output" model (see following illustration).

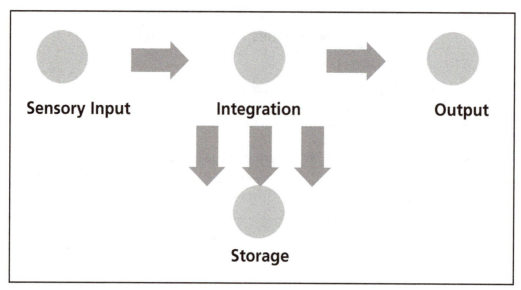

Input—Processing—Output Model
Image courtesy of author

Sensory Input

▶ Visual processing: Visual processing is how the brain interprets incoming visual information, including *perception* (recognizing visual input), *discrimination* (seeing differences between visual information) and *connecting* visual input with previously learned information.

▶ Auditory processing: Auditory processing is the way in which the brain interprets incoming auditory information, including *perception* (recognizing auditory input), *discrimination* (hearing differences between auditory input), and *connecting* auditory input with previously learned information.

Integration

▶ Attention: Attention refers to the ability to *determine what is important to pay attention to, pay attention to input for the appropriate length of time, ignore distractions, and stay on task.*

▶ Processing speed: This is how *quickly* the brain can interpret incoming information and connect it with previously learned information.

▶ Organization: This is the ability to *"chunk," paraphrase, summarize, categorize, and otherwise organize information.*

▶ Sequencing: This is the ability to put ideas into a *logical order.*

▶ Abstraction: This is the ability to think about and *understand concepts*, including problem solving and cause and effect.

Storage

▶ Memory: Memory includes short-term memory (*remembering things for only a few seconds—like remembering a phone number just long enough to dial it*), active working memory (*holding many different things in your mind at one time—like when you are reading a paragraph and have to remember multiple ideas or when you are listening to directions and have to remember many different steps*), and long-term memory (*storing ideas, concepts, facts, processes, and procedures for future use and being able to retrieve them when needed*).

▶ Visual Memory and Auditory Memory: These terms refer to the ability to *remember things you hear or things you see.*

Output

- ► Speaking and writing (sometimes referred to as graphomotor skills), fine motor skills, and gross motor skills
- ► Visual Motor Integration: This involves integrating what is seen with motor movements (like *copying down something from the board*).

MYTH

Persons with learning disabilities see letters backwards
and reverse letters while writing.

FACT

A small percentage of persons with learning disabilities have visual perception
processing disorders which cause them to see or write letters backwards,
but this is not true of the majority of persons with learning disabilities.

Image courtesy of author

A learning disability occurs when the differences in the way a person's brain processes information are significant enough to impact his or her ability to learn. Recent research indicates that the majority of students with learning disabilities have difficulty with *automatization*—the ability to process information rapidly, automatically, and efficiently (Waber 2010). It seems that many students with learning disabilities are inefficient or slow information processors, especially when dealing with complex information.

Adults With Learning Disabilities Describe What It Is Like...

"Living life as a dyslexic person has made me realize I have to work harder than the average person. I know I have to learn things differently than the others, but I am happy to know that I can learn as much as them. I also realize that I can never give up if I am going to be successful. Through my hard work and determination I learned I can do anything I want to as long as I set my mind to it. I don't mind catching up—it is a way of life to me."

Image courtesy of author

Characteristics of Persons with Learning Disabilities

Persons with learning disabilities comprise a very heterogeneous group of learners, with no two persons exhibiting the exact same *learning profile*, or combination of characteristics. It is a mistake to stereotype persons with learning disabilities as being all the same. However, the following list identifies some of the more common characteristics and demonstrates how a learning disability may change throughout a person's life.

Preschool

- ► Speaks later than most children
- ► Pronunciation problems
- ► Slow vocabulary growth, often unable to find the right word

▶ Difficulty rhyming words
▶ Trouble learning numbers, alphabet, days of the week, colors, shapes
▶ Extremely restless and easily distracted
▶ Trouble interacting with peers
▶ Difficulty following directions or routines
▶ Fine motor skills slow to develop

Grades K–4

▶ Slow to learn the connection between letters and sounds
▶ Confuses basic words (*run, eat, want*)
▶ Makes consistent reading and spelling errors including letter reversals (*b/d*), inversions (*m/w*), transpositions (*felt/left*), and substitutions (*house/home*)
▶ Transposes number sequences and confuses arithmetic signs (+, −, ×, /, =)
▶ Slow to remember facts
▶ Slow to learn new skills, relies heavily on memorization
▶ Impulsive, difficulty planning
▶ Unstable pencil grip
▶ Trouble learning about time
▶ Poor coordination, unaware of physical surroundings, prone to accidents

Grades 5–8

▶ Reverses letter sequences (*soiled/solid, left/felt*)
▶ Slow to learn prefixes, suffixes, root words, and other spelling strategies
▶ Avoids reading aloud
▶ Trouble with word problems
▶ Difficulty with handwriting
▶ Awkward, fist-like, or tight pencil grip
▶ Avoids writing assignments
▶ Slow or poor recall of facts
▶ Difficulty making friends
▶ Trouble understanding body language and facial expressions

High School Students and Adults

▶ Continues to spell incorrectly, frequently spells the same word differently in a single piece of writing
▶ Avoids reading and writing tasks
▶ Trouble summarizing
▶ Trouble with open-ended questions on tests
▶ Weak memory skills
▶ Difficulty adjusting to new settings
▶ Works slowly
▶ Poor grasp of abstract concepts
▶ Either pays too little attention to details or focuses on them too much
▶ Misreads information (Ldonline 2012)

MYTH

People with learning disabilities will "grow out of them".

FACT

Learning disabilities are lifelong, although people learn to compensate
for them and can achieve great things!

Image courtesy of author

Types of Learning Disabilities

Even though persons with learning disabilities have a wide variety of characteristics, there are many frameworks that attempt to categorize learning disabilities into certain types of learning problems. One of the most common frameworks includes the following types of disabilities:

Dyslexia: Dyslexia is a specific type of reading disability in which the person has difficulty remembering sound-symbol relationships (*remembering the sounds of letters and letter combinations*). Reading disabilities make up about 80 percent of all learning disabilities (Shaywitz 2004) and, although dyslexia is the most common type of reading disability, there are other types of reading disabilities as well.

Dyscalculia: This is a disability impacting mathematic abilities. About 26 percent of students with learning disabilities have difficulty with math (Lerner & Johns 2012).

Dysgraphia: This is a very specific term describing a disability involving the fine motor movements involved in handwriting.

Language-Based Learning Disabilities: These disabilities involve difficulty understanding or using language effectively (*including listening, speaking, reading, and writing*).

Nonverbal Learning Disabilities: This refers to a type of learning disability involving a neurologically based inability to understand or respond appropriately to social cues and information.

Executive Functioning Learning Disabilities: These include learning disabilities involving difficulty with planning and organizing time and space. This type of learning disability can impact many aspects of a person's life.

MYTH

Attention Deficit Hyperactivity Disorder (ADHD) is a learning disability.

FACT

Although many persons with learning disabilities have difficulty with the
processing skill of attention, ADHD is NOT a type of learning disability.
ADHD is a separately defined disability, although many people
have both a learning disability and ADHD.

Image courtesy of author

Identification of Students with Learning Disabilities

In addition to the *theoretical definition* included in IDEA 2004, another section of the definition of learning disabilities included in IDEA is often referred to as the *operational definition*. This underwent major revisions in IDEA 2004 and provides specific guidance for schools on how to identify students with learning disabilities.

Underachievement

A basic premise in the identification of students with learning disabilities is the idea that the differences in the way a person processes information impacts his or her ability to learn. Thus, underachievement is a primary characteristic of persons with learning disabilities. As stated in IDEA 2004:

> ...the child does not achieve adequately for the child's age or to meet State-approved grade level standards in one or more of the following areas, when provided with learning experiences and instruction appropriate for the child's age or State-approved grade level standards:

▶ Oral expression
▶ Listening comprehension
▶ Written expression
▶ Basic reading skill
▶ Reading fluency skills
▶ Reading comprehension
▶ Mathematics calculation
▶ Mathematics problem solving (300.309).

A key component of an assessment to determine the presence of a learning disability is the documentation of underachievement in one or more of these areas. It is important to note that students with learning disabilities have average to above average general intelligence; the underachievement is not caused by below average intelligence. *This is often misunderstood by teachers, parents, and the general public. Many students with learning disabilities, in fact, have above average intelligence and demonstrate areas of giftedness.*

Adults With Learning Disabilities Describe What It Is Like...

"I have noticed that it takes me a lot longer to do the work than most other people. I have to plan things out and write everything in advance before I can even begin the assignment. I have to do a lot of mental prepping before doing my work or before going to my jobs or class because I am a very impulsive person and struggle with structure and organization. It's something that I kind of battle with on a daily basis."

Image courtesy of author

Response to Intervention and Pattern of Strengths and Weaknesses

Schools may use a variety of different methods to identify students with learning disabilities. Two of the more common methods are Response to Intervention (RtI) and Pattern of Strengths and Weaknesses (PSW). RtI is a process of identification involving tiers of "scientific, research-based" instruction. The number of tiers required is not specified in any regulations or laws, however most schools use a process involving three tiers.

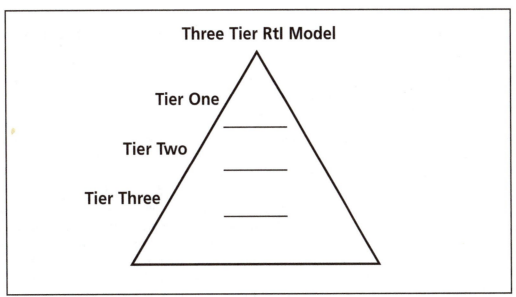

Image courtesy of author

Tier One: Scientific, research-based instruction for all (general education)
Tier Two: More intensive interventions for students who need it (general education)
Tier Three: Assessment for identification of a learning disability

How Does RtI Identify Students with Learning Disabilities?

RtI identifies students with learning disabilities by *exclusion*—the idea is that if a student does not achieve while receiving tier one or tier two instruction, and if all of the other possible causes of learning problems identified in the exclusionary clause have been ruled out, then the student must have a learning disability—it is assumed that a learning disability is the only other possible cause of the learning problem.

Image courtesy of author

PWS is another common method of identifying students with learning disabilities. By carefully assessing a student suspected of having a learning disability, specific processing strengths and deficits are identified and linked to specific academic achievement strengths deficits. For instance, it may be determined that a person has a very specific deficit in active working memory which is significantly impacting his or her reading comprehension. A pattern of learning strengths and needs emerges and yields significant information for designing appropriate interventions.

Most schools use a combination of RtI and PSW. RtI is used as a process to monitor the achievement of all students. For students who are not successful after receiving tier two interventions, an assessment using a PSW model is used to identify whether a learning disability is present.

Adults With Learning Disabilities Describe What It Is Like...

"Everyone should be more educated about the disability because I have not been the only person who is affected by it, my family has put up with a lot as well and it would have been much more helpful for everyone to understand why someone was acting the way that they were."

"Growing up with dyslexia has not only been hard for me but it has been twice as hard for my parents. My parents have been great advocates to help me get the services I deserve whether it be tutoring or pulling me out of public school for a more individualized education. Homework with reading and writing involved has always been and will always be a struggle for me. Throughout school years homework would always cause arguments at home. My parents would try to help, however they would teach me in a different way—and that caused stress and confusion for me. This homework struggle will never end; even in college my parents are helping me. I have now come to the realization that I will always need someone to look over my work because there are mistakes that I will never notice."

Image courtesy of author

A Summary of The Definition and Identification of Persons With Learning Disabilities

Neurological Impairment

Processing Disorder

► Input
► Integration
► Storage
► Output

Underachievement

► Oral Expression
► Listening Comprehension
► Written Expression
► Basic Reading Skills
► Reading Fluency Skills
► Reading Comprehension
► Mathematics Calculation
► Mathematics Problem-Solving

Image courtesy of author

Additional Resources

Books

Cimera, R. (2007). *Learning disabilities: What are they?* Lanham, MD: Rowman & Littlefield Education.

Harwell, J. & Jackson, R. (2008). *The complete learning disabilities handbook.* San Francisco, CA: Jossey-Bass.

Lerner, J. & Johns, B. (2012). *Learning disabilities and related mild disabilities: Characteristics, teaching strategies, and new directions,* 12th Edition, Belmont, CA: Wadsworth Cengage Learning.

Levine, M. (2002). *A mind at a time.* New York: Simon & Schuster.

Websites / Associations

All Kinds of Minds
www.allkindsofminds.org

Learning Disabilities Association of America
www.ldanatl.org

LD OnLine
www.ldonline.org

National Center for Learning Disabilities
www.ncld.org

Other

Video: Misunderstood Minds, WGBH Boston Video.

Chapter 15

Speech and Language Disorders across the Lifespan

Rhonda Vander Laan Kraai
Lizbeth Curme Stevens

Introduction

All people communicate, and most do so effortlessly through speech. Such communication is the essence of our humanity, as we talk to others to exchange information, to obtain basic needs and wants and, of perhaps greatest importance, to connect on a personal level. Too often this is taken for granted, unless we are rendered unable to do so. For many individuals communicating comprises a daily challenge. The struggle to communicate impacts not only those persons themselves with speech and language impairments but their families, friends, and communication partners as well. This chapter describes diverse types of communication disorders whose onset may occur at any time during the lifespan. It also provides examples of many techniques and devices used to ameliorate or even circumvent communication disorders. Finally, suggestions for how to support individuals who struggle to communicate are made.

Communication and Communication Disorders

Communication. Speech and language development begins in infancy. Communication skills include but are not limited to speech and language and continue to be refined throughout life. Figure 1 exemplifies early communication in children.

Figure 1 Children engaging in communication
Image courtesy of author

In the words of Dr. Cathy Nutbrown, professor and early childhood educator at the University of Sheffield, UK, we need to respect children's rights and provide nurturing environments for growth:

> Pausing to listen to an airplane in the sky, stooping to watch a ladybug on a plant, sitting on a rock to watch the waves crash over the quayside—children have their own agendas and timescales. As they find out more about their world and their place in it: they work hard not to let adults hurry them and we need to heed their message. (Nutbrown 1996, 53)

In sum, communicating with others is a part of our daily existence. Within homes, schools, workplaces, and public spaces we say "Good morning," ask for latte at the coffee shop, answer the telephone at work, and purchase movie tickets at the theater. We listen to lectures, teachers giving directions, our supervisor giving a new strategic plan, and children's laughter.

When any one of these actions becomes more challenging and difficult, it makes the ease of communication disappear. The natural act of interacting becomes more difficult and can cause social, academic, and vocational problems. The results at any time in life can be devastating.

Communication disorders. A communication disorder is defined as:

> An impairment in the ability to receive, send, process, and comprehend concepts or verbal, nonverbal and graphic symbol systems. A communication disorder may be evident in the processes of hearing, language, and/or speech. A communication disorder may range in severity from mild to profound. It may be developmental or acquired. Individuals may demonstrate one or any combination of three aspects of communication disorders (ASHA 1993).

Various types of communication problems and their prevalence are listed in Table 1. We discuss these more specifically in a following section.

TABLE 1   Incidence and Prevalence of Selected Communication Disorders
Disorder Incidence/prevalence
Aphasia: 80,000 people are diagnosed with aphasia annually ▶ 1,000,000 people in the U.S. have aphasia ▶ 85% of aphasia cases are the result of strokes ▶ 25–40% of stroke survivors have aphasia
Autism: Approximately 1 out of 88 children have autism
Hearing loss: Two to three babies in 1,000 born each year have a hearing loss Fifteen percent of adults report a degree of hearing loss
Language impairment: About 8% of kindergarten students have a specific language impairment Between 6 and 8 million people in the U.S. have some kind of language impairment
Speech disorder: Approximately 5% of students in first grade have a speech disorder
Stuttering: Approximately 1% of the general population (i.e., about 3 million people) stutters
Voice: Approximately 7.5 million people in the U.S. have trouble using their voices
Sources: American-Speech-Language-Hearing Association (2013); National Aphasia Association (2013); National Institute on Deafness and other Communication Disorders (2013)

History, Social, and Cultural Issues

History. Communication disorders date back to ancient times, BC. There are accounts of people stuttering throughout history. Some early treatments included: (a) putting stones in the speaker's mouth while speaking; (b) surgery on the tongue; and (c) placing a fork in the mouth to support the tongue (Goldberg 1989). People with communication difficulties were often viewed derisively as entertainment for the pleasure of others.

FIGURE 2 Brandon's Story

When I was a kid I had a speech problem say about started when I was about 7. My grandfather studdered and my uncle studders. I had speech thereapy done during school time and i guess now that I am older it is getting worse.

It effected me in ways because I do not like talking to certain people because I get embarrassed or clowned. I don't like talking to a whole bunch of people because half the time they clown. It makes me sad but there is nothing I can do about it because my granddad studders and my uncle studders. People start to tease me about the way I talk. I remember when they use to call me retarted and other names—even now but I don't worry about that anymore. I guess now that I look at it a different way because half of the people I hang out with and most of the people on the radio had the same speech problems and that makes me feel better because they talk about their speech problems and therapy and they are ok.

(Brandon Davis 2013)

This history began to change in the United States around the turn of the century when the first school-based speech program opened in Chicago in 1910 (Battaglia 2010). Shortly thereafter (in 1913) New York City started a program to treat children who "stammered." The first university speech clinic opened at the University of Wisconsin in 1914 to help train future speech-language pathologists. In 1925, a professional organization dedicated to advancing the study of speech problems and their treatment was formed and called the American Academy of Speech Correction (Duchan 2002). Its present name is the American Speech-Language-Hearing Association (ASHA) (www.asha.org)

Social and Cultural Issues. Communication exchanges are directly governed by conventions linked to a person's affiliation with a cultural group that include aspects of values, perceptions, attitudes, and history. Within the social construct, the group affiliation determines whether a person within that group has a communication disorder. The cultural group acts as the judge when deciding when, how, with whom, and what topics will be discussed with others in that group. What is appropriate in one cultural communication exchange may not be appropriate in another (Battle 2012). Various regional and ethnic dialects are additional examples of speech differences that are not considered disorders but reflect the standards of an individual's respective community.

Speech-Language Disorders

Types of Disorders

SPEECH

▶ Articulation
▶ Voice
▶ Stuttering

LANGUAGE

▶ Phonology
▶ Morphology

- ► Semantics
- ► Syntax
- ► Pragmatics

Speech is one of the ways that we communicate with others. Through speech we communicate orally from one partner to another. For some people, speech may be late in developing and behind the typical schedule. For others speech acquisition may not occur due to various physical and/or cognitive disabilities. Alternatively, speech may develop and then be lost through a traumatic brain injury, resulting in other methods of communication being utilized based on individual needs.

Speech Disorders

Speech disorders consist of articulation, voice, or fluency disorders. **Articulation** disorders are the most common group of speech disorders. Types of articulation disorders may include: substitution of one sound for another such as "fee for three." There may be several sound substitutions in a child's speech that may make their speech "unintelligible" or difficult to understand. A child may omit sounds from words such as "hou for house." If there are patterns such as many final consonant deletions, their speech will be very difficult to understand. In that case, it may be called a **phonological** disorder. Another type of articulation disorder is when there are distortions of the speech sounds in words such as lisping, or dysarthric type speech which results in difficulties in the timing of breathing, more labored speech, and precise articulation movements of the lips, tongue, and mouth. Lastly, you may notice additions of sounds in words such as "capitol for capitol."

    Voice disorders can be detected throughout the lifespan. Disorders of the voice can affect characteristics of the voice such as volume, quality, and pitch. A voice disorder can appear because of vocal abuse, or the result of any type of injury to the brain or larynx or the result of a cleft palate. Volume may be a characteristic that you notice immediately, it is when a voice is too quiet to hear or too loud and inappropriate for the setting. Quality of voice may include such characteristics as hoarse, breathy, strained, or nasal. There are many different causes for these types of disorders, so a medical professional should always be consulted when a concern arises.

    Within **fluency** disorders, stuttering is the most common type. When a person stutters, it is noticed that their speech is not smooth or rhythmic but is interrupted by repetitions, blocks, or prolongations of sounds. You may hear an example of stuttering such as "my, my, my arm hurts." If it is a fluency disorder, it will occur occasionally with accompanying physical movements such as the head moving or the mouth blocking the words from being articulated. Most stuttering begins in childhood; however, it can occur after a brain injury.

Language Disorders

Language is a complicated process that is comprised of rule systems, such as form (phonology, morphology, and syntax), content (semantics) and use (pragmatics) (Bloom and Lahey 1978). Further, "It encompasses complex rules that govern sounds, words, sentences, meaning and use. These rules underlie an individual's ability to understand language (language comprehension) and the ability to formulate language (language expression)" (Bernstein & Tiegerman-Farber 2009, 5). Language disorders can occur in the areas of phonology, morphology, syntax, semantics, and/or pragmatics (See Table 3 on page 105 for a time line of typical development for these school-age language components).

Phonology is a rule system that helps direct the combination of sounds and the ability to blend and segment sounds to form words as well as sequencing those sounds to produce words. A phoneme is the smallest sound element that changes the meaning of a word (i.e., /p/ is the phoneme that beings the word /pat/). Phonemes also have individual properties that distinguish them from other phonemes such as acoustical characteristics, place of articulation as well as how they are made (see Table 3).

Morphology governs how words are formed by putting morphemes together to form meaningful words. A single morpheme can change the whole meaning of a word. For example, *cat* and *walk* are free morphemes. When a bound morpheme is attached such as *-s* or *-ed, cat* becomes *cats* and *walk* becomes *walked* (see Table 3).

Syntax is a rule system that determines the structure of sentences. It specifies the order of and organization that words must take in order to produce sentences (Bernstein & Tiegerman-Farber 2009). Children start with short "sentences" and move on to longer, more complex sentences structures.

Semantics

This aspect of language involves meaning about objects, events, and people and the relationship among them. It includes both the ability of the speaker to convey appropriate meaning as well as the listener understanding the meaning being communicated (Bernstein & Tiegerman-Farber 2009). There is an obvious difference between the vocabulary levels used by children and adults. Children may use the word *cool* to indicate that a drink is cold; however, an adult may use the word *cool* to imply that they like an object, statement, or event. Children begin understanding and using vocabulary in a very concrete way and then advance to more abstract use of their language.

Pragmatics

The use of this aspect of language is important in order to convey wants and needs in the social context of life. Encompassed in this component of language is the need to communicate, keeping in mind how the listener perceives that message as well as learning how to manage the conventional rules of conversation both verbally and nonverbally.

Speech and language difficulties can occur in adulthood as well. **Aphasia** may occur when an individual suffers an injury to the brain. Understanding and expressing language may become difficult for the individual and require the services of a speech-language pathologist to assist in the development of a form of communication.

Assistive Technology and Augmentative/Alternative Communication

Students with communication disorders comprise a diverse group with varying needs for assistive technology (AT). They benefit from support designed to enhance their comprehension and/or expression of spoken as well as written language. Teachers work collaboratively with speech-language pathologists to achieve desired outcomes for students.

AT may be classified into two types:

1. technology directly interfacing with the communication breakdown (which alters the signals either sent or received)

2. technology used to instruct or remediate the student's problem (through training or therapy incorporating it)

Type 1: Message altering technology

Input. Technology to support the understanding of speech and language includes many forms routinely provided for students with hearing impairments such as hearing aids (see Chapter 11). Some of this equipment, such as classroom sound field FM systems originally designed only to support this group, has proven beneficial for other students as well (e.g., students with autism spectrum disorders (ASD), central auditory processing disorders (CAPD), as well as English language learners (ELL)). Such technology has even been implemented in general education (e.g., FM systems used in both kindergarten classrooms and at the secondary level in classes where world languages are taught) reinforcing the idea of Universal Design and its benefit for all.

Output. For a very small number of students with complex communication needs using conventional speech and/or writing to communicate is not possible. Such children/adolescents may require augmentative and/or alternative communication (AAC). AAC is "the practice of using compensatory treatments to supplement or replace natural speech and writing…" (Ogletree and Oren 2006). AAC may be affected through aided or unaided symbols (Beukelman and Mirenda 2013). Aided symbols require technology and include line drawings, picture communication symbols, and objects whereas unaided symbols like signs and finger spelling are produced on the body. Technology for AAC includes but is not limited to "high tech" speech generating devices (SGDs) as well as low-tech supports (e.g., communication boards and books). Recently with the advent of tablet computers a new generation of technology has emerged. Examples of some special "apps" for speech output include *Proloquo2Go, TouchChat, Speak it!* An example for written communication is *Dragon Dictation*. However, not all off-the-shelf technology works well for everyone. Dedicated SGDs which have been developed specifically for individuals with physical and/or cognitive challenges remain a trusted albeit more costly alternative. Leading manufacturers include Prentke-Romich, Dynavox, and Tobii. It is beyond the scope of this chapter to provide a comprehensive listing of all AAC options. The interested reader should consult the resources provided and be aware that technology changes rapidly. Selection and implementation of an appropriate AAC system is a collaborative team effort and typically an ongoing process for children and adolescents.

Type 2: Instructional Technology

There are now likely thousands of instructional programs in various formats (e.g., computer software, apps) for students who struggle to speak or write effectively. Many of these can be implemented within the classroom by the teacher and/or the speech-language pathologist and are appropriate for all students (e.g., *Kidspiration, Inspiration, Expanding Expression Tool*). Other products are specifically designed to address the child with a disability and range widely from supports for social communication to speech production (e.g., *Articulate it, Speech sounds on cue*). For additional information consult the resources which follow. Check websites for software or app reviews or listings by knowledgeable professionals (e.g., Judith Kuster, Sean Sweeney, Jane Farrall). The link to a useful guide for evaluating apps is provided in the resources (see VanHouten).

In conclusion, technology to support individuals with communication disorders of various types and degree is readily available. Its selection and implementation should be based upon a collaborative effort of all stakeholders considering the specific needs of the individual and evidence supporting its efficacy. Using Feature Match guidelines, which compare characteristics across systems, is especially helpful in selecting AAC systems (In resources, see Gosnell; Marfilius & Fonner; Parker & Zangari).

Resources/Links

AAC Information

http://www.aac-rerc.com
Rehabilitation Engineering and Research Center in Communication Enhancement, collaborative funded by NIDRR (National Institute on Disability and Rehabilitation Research) and U.S. Dept. of Education-Office of Special Education and Rehabilitative Services (OSERS). Includes webcasts on various topics and numerous resources and publications.

http://aac.unl.edu
University of Nebraska-Lincoln has information including AAC device tutorials, definitions of AAC glossary under Academic page, frequently used vocabulary lists for different age groups and many other resources.

http://www.asha.org/NJC/
Information on provision of services (including AT) to persons with severe disabilities.

http://unl.edu/yaack/
Augmentative Alternative Communication (AAC) Connecting Young Kids.
Part of the University of Nebraska-Lincoln site with information concerning children and AAC devices such as when and where to secure help regarding AAC; information on how to choose the best AAC system, etc.

Still not working!!!

http://www.wati.org
Wisconsin's assistive technology institute. Many free materials to support AT with various types of students. Includes downloadable handbook on AT including a chapter on AAC supports.

AAC Dedicated Products

http://www.tobii.com
Tobii Assistive Technology, Inc. (Tobii ATI), leading developer of innovative eye tracking hardware.

http:// www.atia.org
Assistive Technology Industry Association (ATIA), an organization of manufacturers and sellers of technology-based assistive devices and services, including speech generating devices; search this site by state, country, category of interest (e.g., AAC, autism, etc.).

http://www.dynavoxtech.com
Large line of SGDs available through Dynavox.

http://www.mayer-johnson.com
Boardmaker program, widely used symbols for communication boards and books is available here.

http://www.prentrom.com
Prentke Romich Company (PRC), another leading manufacturer offers numerous SGDs.

Apps Information

http://www.a4cwsn.com
Apps 4 children with Special Needs. Includes app reviews, demonstrations, and lists.

http://www.momswithapps.com
Provides reviews and free or reduced prices on apps.

http://www.janefarrall.com
Jane Farrall Consulting. Information on literacy, AAC and AT. Both Android and iPad apps listed.

http://www.therapyapp411.com
Information and reviews of apps used by SLPs, OTs, PTs, and others from blogs/postings by various contributors.

http://www.speechtechie.com
Sean Sweeney's review of apps and websites and their use in therapy.

http://www.otap-oregon.org/Documents/iapp%20evaluation%20Rubric.pdf
Downloadable tool to evaluate learning-educational apps by Jeannette Van Houten, M.Ed, ATP (2011).

AT Instructional Resources and Feature Matching Tools

http://www.commuicationdisorders.com
Comprehensive website on communication disorders created by Judith Kuster, Emeritus Professor, Mankato State University; past author of column on internet for ASHA.

http://www.childrenshospital.org/clinicalservices/site2016/mainpageS2016P19.html
Feature Matching Communication Applications
Jessica Gosnell, Children's Hospital Boston

http://praacticalaac.org/praactical/introducing-relaaacs-rubric-for-evaluating-the-language-of-apps-for-aac/
RUBRIC for Evaluating the Language of Apps for AAC: RELAACs
Robin Parker and Carole Zangari (2012)

http://www.spectronicsinoz.com/conference/2012/pdfs/handouts/kelly-fonner/Feature_Match_Checklists_JAN2012.pdf
Scott Marfilius & Kelly Fonner (2012)

Interventions for Students with Speech and Language Disorders

Several options for delivering needed services are now available to the person with speech-language challenges. In the school setting, a **speech-language pathologist** will screen, evaluate, and create an Individual Education Plan (IEP) for a student who is eligible for speech-language services. Depending on the individual needs of the student, those services may be provided as a pull-out option where the student is seen by the speech-language pathologist in the classroom or a therapy room with other students. Classroom-based services may be an option where the speech-language pathologist works with the classroom teacher providing direct instruction or in collaboration with the classroom instruction. Services may change based upon the needs and progress of the student. No one option is right for all students. In addition, community-based, clinic, or hospital speech-language therapy services are typically available for those outside of the school community who need intervention in order to improve their communication skills. These services are also provided by a certified speech-language pathologist.

Adapting Settings for Those with Speech and Language Disorders

Information processing is a frequent concern, therefore, slow down while giving directions, and repeat as appropriate.

Offer both visual and auditory information whenever possible.

Give numerous opportunities for responding. Often extra time is needed to formulate questions and responses in a classroom or conversational exchange.

Model social skills and allow time to practice greeting, initiating a conversation, maintaining and ending a conversation.

TABLE 3 Milestones of Language Development in School Aged Children Across Domains/Modalities				
ORAL (Speech/Listening)				WRITTEN (reading/writing/ spelling)
AGE FORM		CONTENT	USE	
Phonology	Morphology & Syntax	Semantics	Pragmatics	
5–6 years Mastery of morphophonemic rules re plural s (e.g., /s/ vs /z/ vs /Iz/; can blend & segment sounds and manipulate phonemes in words	Passives understood; morphology beginning to be used to infer meaning of new words; use of sentences which are both more complex syntactically and correctly formulated	Beginning use of multiword (vs. single word) definitions; expressive vocabulary of 2,600 words & 20,000–24,000 understood	Mostly direct requests used; repetition used for conversational repair; production of minimally four types of narratives	'Learning to read' by decoding (identifies sounds for printed letters & synthesizes across letters); learns some sight words & conventional spelling for some words; writing more simple than speech
7–8 years Production of all sounds & blends (American English)	Derivational suffixes used (e.g., *-er, -ist, -y, -ly*); some passives, elaborated noun phrases, adverbs, conjunctions, and some mental and linguistic verbs used; Understand conjunctions (e.g., *because, so, if, but, before, after, then*)	Pronouns used anaphorically (i.e., refer to a previously named noun); word definitions include synonym, categories; words understood to have multiple meanings	Indirect requests & hints understood; most deictic terms understood & used; narrative plots produced w/ beginning, end, problem, & resolution	Dictionary used to define new words; Decoding skills effective for reading unfamiliar words; Learns spelling patterns (e.g., *-ight* pattern words); writing level akin to speech complexity; mixes oral and literate styles in writing
9–10 years	Mental and linguistic verbs (e.g., *believe, promise)* used; Pronouns referring to elements outside immediate sentence used; Reflexive pronouns used (e.g., *herself, himself*); Reversible passives produced (e.g., *the ball was thrown by the boy*)	Vocabulary in school texts increasingly abstract & specific than that of conversation; students expected to get information from text ~knows 40,000 words by 10 yrs.	Topics sustained through many conversational turns; perceived source of conversational breakdowns addressed; all elements of narrative story grammar produced	'Reading to learn' w/ focus on reading for information; becoming fluent w/ automatic & efficient decoding; writing takes on more literate style w/ subordinate clauses

11–12 years	Expression of precise intent through stress & emphasis	*If* and *though* understood; Reversible passives produced (e.g., *the girl was kissed by the boy*); Derivational suffixes mastered by 12 yrs. (i.e., ful, less, ly, ness, al, ance, -men, -ity, ify, -ous, -ive)	Able to create abstract definitions; ~50,000 words understood	Abstract topics of conversation sustained	Reading on a general "adult" level; reading to expand vocabulary
13–15 years		*Unless* understood; All types of clausal embedding understood.	Some proverbs understood	Jokes w/ lexical & syntactic ambiguities understood	Multiple points of view considered when reading; level writing level complexity begins to exceed that of speech
16–18 years	Vowel-shifting rules used (i.e., vowel pronunciation varies across word derivations as in: *s**a**ne* vs. *s**a**nity)*	More words used per communication unit in written vs. spoken language; Increased use of verb tenses w/ perfect aspect (e.g. *I have eaten all the cookies*)	Command of ~60,000 word meanings ~80,000 by 18 yrs.	Sarcasm, double meanings, and metaphors used; multiple perspectives are recognized	

Source: Stevens (2011)

Chapter 16

Emotional Disabilities/ Emotional and Behavioral Disorders (ED/EBD)

Gil Stiefel

Emotional Disturbance or Emotional Disability (ED) (referred to Emotional Impairment (EI) in Michigan or Emotional and Behavioral Disorders (EBD) in several other states) represents one of the most diverse, disabling, and controversial categories of special education. Emotional Disturbance is a complex construct with causes appearing to span the range of biology, family, and societal problems. The most commonly accepted definition of ED is based on five criteria first proposed by Bower in 1960 (Bower 1981; 1982) Although the eligibility criteria for this disability have been described as vague (Hallahan and Kauffman 1977) and subjective (Forness 1996), they have remained unchanged and are incorporated in IDEIA. More specific guidance in the interpretation of these criteria is often provided by other authority, such as state education departments, or regional or local educational agencies.

Issues in the Definition of Emotional Disturbance

IDEIA Definition of Emotional Disturbance or Disability

§ 300.8 A condition exhibiting one or more of the following characteristics over a long period of time and to a marked degree that adversely affects a child's educational performance:

► An inability to learn that cannot be explained by intellectual, sensory, or health factors.
► An inability to build or maintain satisfactory interpersonal relationships with peers and teachers.
► Inappropriate types of behavior or feelings under normal circumstances.
► A general pervasive mood of unhappiness or depression.
► A tendency to develop physical symptoms or fears associated with personal or school problems.

Emotional disability includes schizophrenia. The term does not apply to children who are socially maladjusted, unless it is determined that they have an emotional disturbance.

Image courtesy of author

What is a "long period of time"?

IDEIA does not specify a duration of time although the intention is to avoid labeling a student who is temporarily reacting to a situational trauma. Several months (often, at least six) is referred to in the literature as an appropriate standard.

What is a "marked degree"?

The problems are significant and apparent to school staff members who observe the student in a variety of settings and situations as well as more severe or frequent than the normally expected range of behavior for individuals of the same age, gender, and cultural group. It is implied that the student has been unresponsive or insufficiently responsive to previous intervention efforts.

What is an "adverse affect" on a child's educational performance?

Some teams of professionals, following their school district policies for evaluating ED, have taken a narrow view, confining this definition simply to academic progress, because the federal definition does not specifically include social learning or behavior as educational performance. This definition might be understood as excluding any student whose academic achievement appears in the average or above range despite the severity of emotional disturbance. In the preponderence of cases, however, greater weight has been placed on the "functional performance" emphasis of IDEIA. These cases have included social competence in the definition of "educational performance." Thus, while a student may demonstrate satisfactory performance on classroom tests, the disruptive effects of their behavior on the learning environment for themselves and others would also be taken into account in determining eligibility for services.

The Six Criteria

Intellectual, sensory, or health factors—are essentially exclusionary criteria, meaning that a child would not be considered emotionally disabled if their behavior or affect is better explained by another disability. For example, a student with an intellectual disability might not comprehend socially inappropriate aspects of their behavior.

Satisfactory peer and teacher relationships—no operational definition of this concept is provided in IDEIA and is left to the discretion of the school or school district evaluation team composed of educators and school mental health personnel (school social worker, psychologist) with input from parents/guardians.

Inappropriate behavior—no operational definition of this concept is provided in IDEIA and is left to the discretion of the Multidisciplinary Evaluation Team (MET) composed of educators and school mental health personnel with input from parents/guardians.

Pervasive mood of unhappiness or depression—More than a temporary, expected responses to stress—definitions of various forms of depression are provided in the Diagnostic and Statistical Manual (DSM) (APA 2000) (discussed below) although it is not stipulated whether a student would need to be considered "clinically depressed" by the DSM criteria in order to qualify for services.

Physical symptoms or fears—these are typically associated with student refusal to attend school or extreme tardiness but must be differentiated from a refusal to attend school because of a specific threat or educational neglect on the part of the parent/guardian.

Exclusion of socially maladjusted—criteria for this differential diagnosis (especially in the case of socially maladjusted AND emotionally disturbed) do not appear in IDEIA or in the DSM although DSM diagnostic criteria for Oppositional Disorder, Conduct Disorder, or Antisocial Personality may be considered (APA 2000). This issue will be discussed later in this chapter.

Most Diverse

Emotional Disturbance encompasses a very wide range of feelings and behaviors. The Diagnostic and Statistical Manual is used by most mental health professionals for the diagnosis of Emotional Disturbance. The DSM follows a "medical model" in that patterns of behavioral symptoms are used to diagnose the underlying emotional "illness." The diagnostic descriptions and categories in the Manual are reviewed every several years as our understanding of the various disorders evolves. A useful way of organizing these categories is to think about for whom does the behavior or feeling cause a problem.

Internalized behavioral problems

produces discomfort for student—may be associated with behavioral inhibition—signs tend to be more subtle

- ► Sadness
- ► Anxiety
- ► Fearfulness
- ► Withdrawal
- ► Eating Disorders

Externalized behavioral problems

produces discomfort for everybody else—may be associated with behavioral exhibition

- ► Inattention
- ► Hyperactivity
- ► Aggression
- ► Opposition/Resistance

Image courtesy of author

While students with internalized behavior problems are more likely to elicit a sympathetic response if they come to the attention of adults in the school setting, students with externalized problems are more likely to evoke annoyance or anger. Within western cultures individuals are viewed as "responsible" for their own behavior despite the extensive work of Skinner and others from the field of behavioral psychology who have demonstrated the role played by the environment and external conditions of reinforcement in the control of behavior. Meanwhile, disciplinary measures may be employed to eliminate inappropriate behaviors without evidence that they are effective, especially with students demonstrating such externalized conditions as Oppositional Defiant Disorder, Attention Deficit Hyperactivity Disorder, or Conduct Disorder.

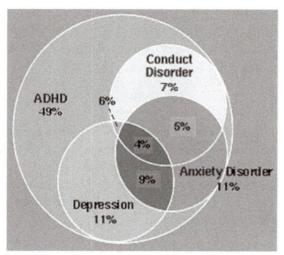

Figure 3 Emotional Disabilities often overlap.
This is referred to as comorbidity.
Source: www.forums.com/forums/shortread.php?t=90604

Most Disabling

Despite the difficulties with definition and identification, the needs of these students must be addressed. Emotional Disturbance is perhaps the most disabling of disabilities in terms of long-term outcomes. As examples, students identified with Emotional Disturbance have the worst graduation rate of all students with disabilities, at least twice the dropout rate of students with other disabilities (Blackorby & Wagner 1996). According to the National Longitudinal Transition Study of special education students, the arrest rates of youth with disabilities who dropped out were significantly higher than those who had graduated (Wagner, Newman, et al. 1991). Three to five years after dropping out, the cumulative arrest rate for youth with serious emotional disturbance was 73 percent. Further, students who had been identified with Emotional Disturbance were twice as likely as students with other disabilities (e.g., developmental or learning) to be living in a correctional facility, halfway house, drug treatment center, or on the street after leaving school (Wagner 1995; Wagner, Blackorby, et al. 1993).

Most Controversial

Controversies regarding ED arise from a number of issues. These include subjectivity and individual differences in teacher expectations and tolerances of student behavior, cultural differences of students and the exclusionary social maladjustment clause in the definition.

Teacher expectations and tolerances may be impacted by their behavior management skills, the resources available in the school, and the expectations of school administrators. For some classroom teachers, high levels of noise and movement in the classroom are an acceptable norm while for others this situation would be intolerable. The level of classroom management skills a teacher possesses would impact when behaviors would be managed within the classroom versus referral for external assistance. Schools and adjacent communities also vary in terms of the non-special education resources available for student support. School adminstrators' evaluations of teachers' classroom management skills may intentionally or non-intentionally serve to suppress teacher referrals to special education. Some school administrators prefer that students with "acting out" behaviors not be referred since this may limit disciplinary options. All of these contribute to disparities in who gets referred and for what reason.

In theory, students should not be considered as ED if the behaviors at issue reflect cultural differences. Specifically, the definition of emotional or behavioral disorder (E/BD) proposed by the National Mental Health and Special Education Coalition (Forness & Knitzer 1992) reads as follows:

> The term emotional or behavioral disorder means a disability characterized by behavioral or emotional responses in school programs so different from appropriate age, cultural, or ethnic norm that the responses adversely affect educational performance, including academic, social, vocational, and personal skills.

In actuality, however, research suggests that referrals of students for assessment of ED by general education classroom teachers are often based on limited understanding of behavior in relationship to cultural influences (Gay 2000; Riccio et al. 2003). This is seen in statistics that consistently indicate very significant disproportionality with twice as many African American male students referred as well as subsequently identified as ED despite the fact that the proportions of students identified with such other disabilities as autism, speech and language, or hearing impairments are the same across the groups (disproportionality is also seen in the identification of Intellectual Disabilities and Learning Disabilities). A similar disproportionality is also seen for Hispanic males (National Center for Education Statistics 2010).

Source: Suzanne Tucker/Shutterstock. com

The Social Maladjustment clause has been described as making the definition of ED self-contradictory (Gresham 2005). While the presenting behavior of students described as socially maladjusted may be the same as a student considered ED, the inferred motives for this behavior differ. The primary argument used to support the exclusion of socially maladjusted students from placement in emotionally impaired programs is that students with social maladjustment are not truly disabled. These children are believed to engage in deliberate acts of self-interest to gain attention or to intimidate others, while experiencing no distress or self-devaluation about their own internalized distress about their behavior (Clarizio 1992; Kelly 1993; Slenkovitch 1986). On the other hand, the consideration of Social Maladjustment calls for not just whether or not specific aberrant behaviors have occurred, but the evaluators' perception of the *intention* of this behavior or whether the student is experiencing *internalized* distress as the result of this behavior. According to the Bazelon Center on Mental Health Law, "the majority of students who have been identified as emotionally disturbed by their school have a conduct disorder and thus exhibit some of the behaviors for which others are suspended or expelled. Sorting students into two groups—suspending one group and giving the other access to special education ... cannot be justified from the research." This distinction is important because if the student's behavior is seen as the result of Social Maladjustment, they are *not* afforded the protections provided by the Free and Appropriate Public Education (FAPE) provisions of IDEIA for students with disabilities.

Causes

Contemporary views of Emotional Disturbance refer to biopsychosocial causes in which various systems at the biological, psychological, familal, and larger social levels interact to produce varying outcomes. While some of the factors increase the risk or likelihood of emotional disturbance, others may act to mitigate these risks.

At the biological systems level, genetics are viewed as risk factors in such disorders as Schizophrenia and Bi-Polar Disorder. However, despite what is viewed as a substanital inheritability component associated with these disabilities, the genetic contribution should not be confused for inevitability. For example, children of a Schizophrenic parent have a 13 percent chance of developing Schizophrenia vs. a 1 percent chance in the general population (Burton 2012), thus more than eight out of nine children with a Schizophrenic parent DO NOT develop Schizophrenia. High levels of chronic stress, poor dietary habits, environmental toxins, biological toxins, as well as genetics can cause neurological stress that may produce an imbalance in neurotransmitter levels leading to other changes reflected in mood, behavior, and social attitude. Such imbalances may affect sleep, cardiac function, metabolism, weight, organs, and glands. Of particular relevance to educators is that these imbalances also affect learning, focus, and cognitive functions. Symptoms associated with neurotransmitter imbalance produce a variety of ailments that include, but are not limited to: fatigue, chronic muscle and joint pain, inappropriate hunger, food cravings, irritability, hostility, inability to focus, inability to concentrate, depression, agitation, excessive body fat, obsessive and compulsive behaviors, sleep disturbances, physical stress, emotional stress, recurrent diarrhea, constipation, headaches, and migraines (IMCHB 2001).

At the family systems level, abuse and neglect are frequently mentioned as contributing factors to many different forms of Emotional Disturbance (Child Welfare Information Gateway 2013). Other risk factors include death of a parent or other family member, substance abuse by a parent or other family member, observed violence in the family, or less dramatic, simply inadquate management of a temperamentally difficult child.

At a broader societal system level, poverty is a primary contributor to risk factors related to Emotional Disturbance in as much as conditions of poverty result in an inability to satisfy basic needs, a lack of control over resources, a lack of education, and poor health. In addition, those in poverty are the most likely to be the victims of violence and crime and those attendant risk factors (Meichenbaum 2008). One of the criticsims leveled against the classifying of a child as "Emotionally Disabled" is that it may create the perception that the disability is "intrinsic" to the child, thus further "victimizing" the child while not addressing these external causes.

At the same time it is recognized that many individuals facing some or even many of the risk factors described above show little or no sign of Emotional Disturbance. Contemporary views of ED refer to a "Diathesis-Stress" model to account for these individual differences. A *diathesis* refers to the disposition or characteristics of an individual, their level of vulnerability/invulnerability, which may be based upon their biology or environmental history. Just as individuals differ in other physical characterstics at birth, some individuals may be more constitutionally vulnerable than others (e.g., more prone to illness or variations in temperament). *Stress*, or a stressor refers to an ongoing event or circumstance that challenges the coping abilities of an individual. This model attempts to explain the circumstances in which an individual with a high level of vulnerability may develop emotional problems even in the face of what might be viewed by others as low levels of stress. Alternatively, an individual with a low level of vulnerability might experience significant stressors with few adverse consequences. Meichenbaum (2008) describes this "class of phenomena characterized by good outcomes in spite of serious threats to adaptation or development" as *Resilience*. *Protective Factors* are conditions or attributes that foster the development of resilience.

In the school setting one of these protective factors is referred to as "School Connectedness." School connectedness is the *belief by students that adults in the school care about them as students and their learning*. School connectedness is related to academic, behavioral, and social success in school. It should be noted that some studies have found that protective factors may differ across gender, race, and cultures. For instance, girls tend to become resilient by building strong, caring relationships, while boys are more likely to build resilience by learning how to use active problem-solving (Bernard 1995).

Assessment

Assessment of ED involves a number of components designed to obtain a comprehensive profile of the student and their behavior and performance in the educational setting and in other settings, such as adaptive behavior within the broader community. This assessment should include relevant medical and psychoeducational information, a description of the intervention strategies used to improve the behaviors and the length of time the strategies were utilized prior to special education referral unless the referral is parent initiated. Behavior and emotion are assessed through several methods described as indirect and direct. Indirect methods include interviews and behavior ratings scales completed by the student themselves and adults who have regular and direct contact with the student. Direct methods include systematic observation of the behavior of concern while recording such aspects of the behavior as the context, frequency, and intensity. On some occasions, student self-monitoring might also be utilized. This information is then pooled by the Multidisciplinary Evaluation Team which attempts to develop hypotheses concerning the "function" of the behavior (referred to as a Functional Behavior Analysis (FBA)) and determines whether the behaviors have persisted over such an extended period of time and marked degree that the student requires special education services as a student with a disability.

Interventions

Intervention approaches vary considerably depending on the presenting behaviors or issues of students and therefore require a variety of skill sets on the part of the special education teacher. Key among these is that the Special Educator may serve as a "touchstone" teacher, who among school professionals, should have the most flexibility to meet regularly with the student to coordinate services, review work, set goals, give feedback, and target four key areas that often cause difficulty: work completion, handing work in, social interactions, and physical activity. This person may serve to provide input to and coordinate with families and medical or other behavioral professionals.

Another skill set used by the Special Educator in the school setting is to assist in the development of a Functional Behavior Analysis (FBA) for students experiencing behavioral/emotional difficulties. The intent of the Functional Behavior Analysis (FBA) is to identify the cause or function of such behaviors and provide a change of context or "replacement" behavior that reduces or eliminates the inappropriate behavior. This approach is referred to as Positive Behavior and Intervention Supports (PBIS). The Special Educator serves a key role in monitoring the effectiveness of the proposed Behavior Intervention Plan (BIP).

If needed, the Special Educator develops modifications and accommodations to respond to students' fluctuations in mood, ability to concentrate, and the side effects of medications. This might include breaking academic work into manageable tasks, teaching basic homework, study, and goal-setting skills, constantly monitoring work, and helping depressed students to self-monitor their frustration level, their need for physical activity or a break, or physical symptoms (such as a dry mouth from medications) and to take the initiative to solve the problem. In conjunction with classroom teachers and other staff, Special Educators may facilitate cooperative classroom projects and club activities that encourage depressed students to interact more with their peers. The overall goal of this variety of interventions is to communicate to students that adults in the school setting do care about them and their learning.

Chapter 17

Autism Spectrum Disorders

Sally Burton-Hoyle

Introduction

There has been a striking increase in the identification of children with autism worldwide. News and TV programs featuring persons with autism have made society aware of the disorder in general. However, in order to understand and accept all individuals as community members it is critical that we learn about the range of abilities and impairments across the *spectrum* of autism.

Currently, the diagnosis of autism is based on a group of disorders, with a range of abilities/disabilities specific to each person. The impact on communication, socialization, and the ability to self-regulate behavior may look different across the population of persons with autism, thus it is called Autism Spectrum Disorders (ASD). There is a saying that "If you have met a person with autism then you have met *A* person with autism." Even though a general diagnosis is often made, each person on the spectrum experiences the world differently and with varying strengths and types of needs. This chapter will cover the history and evolution of the many definitions and diagnoses of Autism Spectrum Disorders as well as the issues related to a comprehensive understanding of characteristics associated with ASD.

Dr. Leo Kanner, an American psychiatrist, was the first to both formally identify and classify children who exhibited the similar patterns of behavioral excesses and deficits that he called autism. In his 1943 paper, "Autistic Disturbances of Affective Contact," he observed, studied, and reported on ten children with behavioral symptoms that he termed "autistic." The children Kanner wrote about had a variety of symptoms which resulted in impaired communication and socialization. The individuals were non-verbal, withdrawn, unable to relate to others, and displayed odd movements such as spinning and twirling.

Image courtesy of author

During this same time period, in Austria, Hans Asperger was studying individuals who were verbal but unable to communicate, socialize, and empathize with others. Asperger observed numerous similarities to Kanner's subjects. Asperger's findings were originally written in German. With the exception of limited verbal communications, none of his work was translated to English until the 1980s. Thus, the comparisons between autism and Asperger's were not made until the 1990s when Asperger's findings were first included in the Diagnostic Statistical Manual (DSM).

Today, the DSM is used by psychiatrists and psychologists to describe and categorize psychiatric illnesses. It is updated both periodically and upon discovery of new disorders by the American Psychiatric Association (APA). The terms autism and Asperger's are now included under the term "Autism Spectrum Disorders," representing the range of abilities and level of impairment across the spectrum. It is important to note that The American Psychiatric Association (APA) has implemented new diagnostic criteria for the fifth edition of the Diagnostic and Statistical Manual of Mental Disorders (DSM-5) for autism. DSM-5 was released in late May 2013 (http://www.dsm5.org/Pages/Default.aspx).

Types of Autism

Autistic Disorder *(also called "classic" autism)*

This is what most people think of when hearing the word "autism." People with autistic disorder usually have significant language delays, social and communication challenges, and unusual behaviors and interests. Many people with autistic disorder also have intellectual disability (cdc.gov/ncbddd/autism/facts.html).

Asperger's Syndrome

People with Asperger's syndrome usually have some milder symptoms of autistic disorder. They might encounter social challenges and demonstrate unusual behaviors and interests. However, they typically do not have problems with language or intellectual disability (cdc.gov/ncbddd/autism/facts.html).

Pervasive Developmental Disorder—Not Otherwise Specified
(PDD-NOS; also called "atypical autism")

People who meet some, but not necessarily all, of the criteria for autistic disorder or Asperger's syndrome may be diagnosed with PDD-NOS. People with PDD-NOS usually have fewer and milder symptoms than those with autistic disorder. The symptoms might cause only social and communication challenges (cdc.gov/ncbddd/autism/facts.html).

New DSM 5 Information

As of May 2013 PDD-NOS and Asperger's will no longer be diagnosed by professionals making a medical diagnosis of ASD and all identified individuals will be referred to as having ASD. These persons with ASD will be referred to as having one of three severity levels. Severity is measured by medical professionals; those Individuals whose severity falls outside the bandwidth of these three levels but who exhibit significant social communication challenges may be diagnosed as having Social Communication Disorders (SCD).

The Center for Disease Control (CDC), the federal agency that monitors disease nationally, is the primary source for statistics about autism. During the late 1980s, in response to increased public alarm, the CDC began to collect data on the number of persons living within designated states/regions who had been diagnosed with autism. Early reports showed that autism was rare, occurring in only 4–5 out of 10,000 persons in 1940, although no official data was taken at that time. In 1990 the CDC discovered that the prevalence of autism diagnoses had increased to 10 out of 10,000 persons.

Over the years the surveillance and screening of autism disorders has grown more sophisticated. Authorized as part of the Children's Health Act of 2000 (42 U.S.C. § 280i (a)(1) (2000)), the CDC developed and currently maintains the ADDM (Autism Developmental Disabilities Monitoring) network. ADDM is comprised of a group of programs funded by CDC in order to determine the number of people with autism spectrum disorders (ASDs) in the U.S. The ADDM sites collect data using the same surveillance methods, which are modeled after CDC's whole programs, to study the prevalence of this disorder.

Prevalence is the number of cases of a condition that exist at a particular time in a defined population				
Identified Prevalence of Autism Spectrum Disorders ADDM Network 2000–2008 Combining Data from All Sites				
Surveillance Year	Birth Year	Number of ADDM Sites Reporting	Prevalance per 1,000 Children (Range)	This is about 1 in X children...
2000	1992	6	**6.7** (4.5–9.9)	1 in 150
2002	1994	14	**6.6** (3.3–10.6)	1 in 150
2004	1996	8	**8.0** (4.6–9.8)	1 in 125
2006	1998	11	**9.0** (4.2–12.1)	1 in 110
2008	2000	14	**11.3** (4.8–21.2)	1 in 88
Source: http://www.cdc.gov/features/countingautism/				

ASD Then and Now

In 1964 the prevalence of autism was 2 in 10,000 and was considered so rare that teachers, social workers, and other professionals and community helpers never received any formal education about the disorder. With the increased incidence of identified ASD cases it is now more important than ever for communities, schools, and other agencies to become knowledgeable about ASD.

Causes and Controversy in Autism

ASD is a lifelong developmental disability with very little known of its root cause. Studies have shown that it tends to run in families so genetics are thought to be part of the issue. Research regarding exactly which genes may be responsible for passing down autism in families and what role their environment may play in its increase is ongoing. Many ASDs tend to occur in people who have certain genetic or chromosomal conditions. About 10 percent of children with ASDs have also been identified as having Down syndrome, fragile X, and other genetic and chromosomal disorders. According to the CDC there are several other factors that may lead to an increased probability that a child will develop an ASD. Children who have a sibling or parent with an ASD are at a higher risk of being diagnosed. While childhood vaccinations are no longer linked to ASDs, when taken during pregnancy, prescription drugs containing valproic acid have been associated with a higher risk of ASD diagnoses. We now know that the once common belief that poor parenting practices cause ASDs is not true; and there is now some evidence that the critical period for developing ASDs occurs before birth. However, initial concerns about vaccines and infections have led researchers to consider risk factors before and after birth. Finally, a small percentage of children who are born prematurely or with low birth weight are at greater risk for having ASDs (http://cdc.gov/ncbddd/autism/facts.html)

Case Study

When Tim was born in 1964 his family was thrilled to finally welcome a son into the world. After four daughters their son would carry on the family name, which is important in any family. As an infant, Tim was different from his siblings; he seemed aloof and distant. The infant seemed to look beyond his parents and did not engage with them as their daughters had. It is typical for infants to follow the voices of their parents/caregivers or gaze toward those persons they are most familiar with. In Tim's case, he did none of those things and seemed uncomfortable being held and was uninterested in following the voices of his parents and family members. He did, however, play patty-cake with his big sister and was able to say "mama and dada" at the age of 15 months. At 20 months Tim began to withdraw from touch and affection, and all verbal communication ceased.

He was tested for hearing, vision, and speech problems at age 3 and his parents began asking doctors to test him for possible disorders. The doctors told the family: "he is a boy and boys are always late in speaking" or "well, he is your first son and you cannot compare him to his sisters." Finally, Tim was placed on a waiting list for a medical and psychological evaluation at a local university medical center. After several months, the diagnosis was complete. The family was called into the medical center and the experts told them the following: "Your son has autism and will not be more than a pet around the house." "Can he work at a job one day?" the father asked. One of the experts told the parents to focus on their four daughters and perhaps find a residential placement for the boy. The parents went home and told their youngest daughter, who was14 at the time, "Your life is never going to be the same again, your brother has autism"; the father went into the back yard and wept.

Image courtesy of author

Autism and the Family

At the current rate, 1 out of every 88 children is diagnosed with autism. Often forgotten amid these times of crisis is the fact that autistic children are part of a larger family unit. The developmental tasks and responsibilities of families with autistic children are monumental and include securing financial resources, maintaining appropriate socialization opportunities for each of its family members, and providing adequate education, recreation, and overall family satisfaction. The addition of a family member with autism can have a tremendous impact on the family unit and requires constant support across the lifespan of the autistic child. Doheny (2012) identified five major areas of impact on families that include: adjusting parental expectations, worrying about the siblings of autistic children, tending to the marriage, holding onto family traditions, and making a social life.

Reevaluating Hopes and Dreams

Throughout pregnancy, families dream about what their child will be like. Who will he/she look like? How big will they be? Will it be a boy or a girl? Plans for the future begin through college trusts, wills, a bigger house, but autism is not considered or planned for with most families. Upon the realization and subsequent diagnosis of autism, families must adapt cognitively for a different journey with their child and family. The variance of adaptation depends on the family and how they approach the challenges of life in general.

Caring for Other Siblings

Siblings of persons with autism have unique strengths and needs because of the experiences they share. Sibling support is encouraged through groups which help them understand autism and their role in their brother's or sister's life. It is critical that siblings without autism be honored for their roles. Families are encouraged to listen to the opinions of the siblings regarding their brother/sister. Family balance is a critical skill and parents are encouraged to set aside specific time to be with each of their children.

Marriage and the Family Unit

The addition of an autistic child to a family is a challenge to any marriage. A basic skill of balancing the autistic child's needs with the necessary, shared intimacy with a spouse is difficult but imperative to the strength of the relationship. The notion of "date night" is always encouraged but not possible in many situations. When there is a child with autism in the family attending to the needs of the child/children and the spouse is difficult and relationships can become strained. The entire family unit may be in jeopardy if both partners do not work cooperatively for overall family satisfaction. Concurrently, financial duress may occur if families endeavor to spend family resources that they cannot afford in an effort to "cure" their child. According to family support experts, the divorce rate is 50 percent across the general population. The same is true of families who have a child with autism. It is said that the diagnosis of autism is either the reason that couples work together and thrive in their relationship or the reason that they divorce. Family support is necessary from the beginning so that families do not feel isolated and unprepared to care for their autistic child.

Maintaining Basic Family Functions

Family traditions can be upheld even with the inclusion of a child with Autism. It is challenging to participate in traditional family get-togethers when there is a change in routine, food, people and locations. Visual aids such as picture schedules, calendars, and checklists which support their child's understanding and expectations of the day can be useful. Other support mechanisms like daily planners can help families determine where and how long they will be in a location that might be unfamiliar to a child with autism. Families who learn to informally educate other family members about their autistic child's needs set the occasion for a positive experience maintaining family traditions.

Socializing Outside the Home

Families of children with autism will suffer if they remain isolated from their community. When they are ready, families can begin to enjoy social outings with others who share the challenge of parenting children with autism, or with neighbors who understand and respect the boundaries that a family may need (webmd.com/brain/autism/features/autism-and-family-relationships).

Autism: The Big Picture

It is important to look at the big picture when understanding ASD. Because of the spectrum of abilities/disabilities it is important to remember the following. Just because a person can speak it does not mean he/she knows how to socialize or communicate. Every person with autism has difficulty understanding HOW, WHEN, and WHERE to interact with others, as a result, navigating their unique, individual environments is a challenge. Difficulties with socialization can be misleading and it is important to remember that intelligence has nothing to do with the diagnosis of autism. All persons with ASDs can lead fulfilling lives, as independently as possible, within their communities.

Defining Autism

Autism is covered by the "Individuals with Disabilities Education Improvement Act" (IDEA) of 2004 (formerly the "Education for all Handicapped Children Act" of 1975). Codified and defined in the Code of Federal Regulations (C.F.R.) under "Subtitle B—Regulations of the Offices of the Department of Education" (34 C.F.R. § 300.7 (c)(1) 1999), the federal legislative definition reads as follows:

> "Autism means a developmental disability significantly affecting verbal and nonverbal communication and social interaction, generally evident before age 3, that adversely affects a child's educational performance. Other characteristics often associated with autism are engagement in repetitive activities and stereotyped movements, resistance to environmental change or change in daily routines, and unusual

responses to sensory experiences. The term does not apply if a child's educational performance is adversely affected primarily because the child has an emotional disturbance as defined in paragraph (b) (4) [sic: this should say (c)(4)] of this section.

(ii) A child who manifests the characteristics of "autism" after age 3 could be diagnosed as having "autism" if the criteria in paragraph (c) (1) (i) of this section are satisfied."

Autism was added as a separate category of educational services in 1990. In order for a student to receive assistance from their public school system they must first be deemed eligible for special education services. Each state must, at least, meet the federal requirement but check your state's definition.

Diagnosis and Identification of ASD

Families, schools, and community agencies work collaboratively to address the concern of possible autism diagnoses. Depending on the level and severity of each case, a child may be diagnosed anytime between one year of age and middle school. However, it is not uncommon for adults to be diagnosed with autism/Asperger's as well. Typically, before diagnosis, a family will approach their school district, family doctor, or a university medical center for assistance and guidance regarding an initial autism assessment. Depending on the age of the individual, possible assessments may include any or all of the following: observation, a family interview regarding early childhood development, speech and hearing, and occupational therapy evaluations.

Each system (educational or medical) has eligibility requirements for services. For instance, a medical diagnosis could meet the requirements for services or support from an insurance company or a mental health care provider but not for educational services. Just because an M.D. might diagnose a child with autism does not mean that the child will be eligible for special education services. Doctors, schools, and mental health systems are all different and rely on different requirements and assessments. As a result, doctors cannot dictate how schools operate and schools may not tell medical personnel how to diagnose patients.

The Variance of Autism

Determining eligibility for autism services has been a challenge to health care professionals. They must have experience in assessment and diagnosis across a variety of individuals who display the core deficits of autism. The following scenarios depict the range of ability and disability within the spectrum of autism. They each make the case that whatever your functioning level is, the diagnosis of autism creates a unique and individualized set of challenges and supports necessary for community participation. Just because someone is verbal and can speak does not mean that they can effectively communicate. What do you think both Jim and Austin need in order to participate in their homes, school, and community?

Jim

Jim was four years old and would cry when his pre-school teacher would ask him to follow a simple direction. If she provided physical direction to the task he would scream, kick, and refuse to move forward. The more verbal encouragement that the teacher and her staff would apply the more Jim would scream. He would sometimes flap and twirl or scream with his fingers in his ears. He had some language that he would use over and over again directly from a cartoon that he watched obsessively while at home. The family said that when he watched the cartoon it was the only time that they could get dinner ready or have a conversation with their other children. The rest of the family only watched TV in their own rooms away from Jim. If Jim saw or heard the other TV programs he would change them to the channel that he was watching. The family learned to mute the TV so that captions were all that was on. Jim ate only chicken fingers. The family would attempt to serve nutritious alternatives such as fruits and vegetables but Jim would scream and throw the foods. The family reluctantly complied with Jim's requests.

Austin

Austin had a sophisticated vocabulary and at the age of seven and could tell you, with great detail, about robotics and the various theories related to the best robotics. His IQ was registered at 135 but he could not complete classwork. Austin could read at the tenth grade level but could not comprehend the material. He could speak but could not communicate his wants and needs to his parents. Toilet training was never really accomplished and by the age of eighteen Austin was still unable to use proper hygiene when using the toilet. Taking daily showers, brushing his teeth, and combing his hair were tasks that his parents eventually gave up on. Austin entered college but was on his way to being expelled because he would dominate classroom conversations during discussion time. He believed that any question posed to the class was direct communication to him. He did not see anything wrong with what he was doing and blamed other students for being "idiots" (http://www.cornwall.gov.uk).

TABLE 1 Criteria for Functioning Level		
Mild Level of Impairment	Moderate Level of Impairment	Severe Level of Impairment
People with mild autistic spectrum disorders have normal intelligence, and in many cases, they score well above normal on IQ tests. Despite this, they may struggle with some tasks requiring them to make changes in their regular routines.	A person with moderate autism may have some degree of mental retardation, or he or she may have a normal IQ of about 100. This person may find self-care tasks challenging.	Some individuals with autism, especially those with low functioning levels, also have a degree of mental retardation. This usually includes an IQ of below 70 and problems with adaptive behaviors like self-care and communication.
Someone with mild autism may struggle with the finer points of social interaction, including eye contact, maintaining a back-and-forth conversation, interpreting body language and tone of voice, and interacting with others at an age-appropriate level. This person may have difficulties taking the perspective of others	A person with a moderate autism spectrum disorder will appear aloof. He or she may not try to interact with others, and it may be very challenging to initiate an interaction with this person. However, someone with moderate autism is generally aware that others are in the room.	It is very difficult to interact with someone with severe autism. The individual may not be aware of what others are saying or doing, and it may take significant effort to gain his or her attention.
(http://cdc.gov/ncbddd/autism/signs.html) (http://www.nimh.nih.gov/health/topics/autism-spectrum-disorders-pervasive) (http://www.nimh.nih.gov/health/topics/index.shtml)		

Characteristics over the Lifespan

Autism may be evident at an early age with some individuals and not obvious until middle school or later for others. The ability of families to grasp the differences that their child displays also varies. Some families recognize developmental differences right away and seek support. Parents may not recognize deficits because they also displayed similar issues with socialization and/or communication when they were younger; they simply do not see a problem. It is up to the community to be supportive of individuals who may appear different and also cognizant of free or low-cost resources for families. It is always a sensitive issue to offer information or guidance to families regarding the possibility of a disability. As responsible community members it is our duty to learn the warning signs and indicators associated with autism.

In Table 2, some of the characteristics apply to small children but many are life-long issues that persons across the spectrum may demonstrate.

TABLE 2   Characteristics of Autism
▶ Not respond to their name by 12 months of age
▶ Not point at objects to show interest (point at an airplane flying overhead) by ▶ 14 months
▶ Not play "pretend" games (pretend to "feed" a doll) by 18 months
▶ Avoid eye contact and want to be alone
▶ Have trouble understanding other people's feelings or talking about their own feelings
▶ Have delayed speech and language skills
▶ Repeat words or phrases over and over (echolalia)
▶ Give unrelated answers to questions
▶ Get upset by minor changes
▶ Have obsessive interests
▶ Flap their hands, rock their body, or spin in circles
▶ Have unusual reactions to the way things sound, smell, taste, look, or feel
(http://cdc.gov/ncbddd/autism/signs.html)

Myths

There are myths associated with autism. It is not uncommon for families of children with autism to deal with these myths on a daily basis. One family was advised when their child was loud in the grocery store that if they got rid of the yeast in their diet that the child could be cured of autism. Table 3 displays common myths and possible realities associated with each myth.

TABLE 3 Autism: Myth vs. Reality	
Myth	Reality
Persons with autism want no contact with others and are in their own world.	People with autism are just like us and appreciate contact with those that they like and who honor some of the barriers that are a part of their disorder. Some persons with autism are sensitive to smells such as perfume, smoke, and other things. If we crowd the person and bombard them with smells, they may react in challenging ways.
Persons with autism can be cured of their autism through diet.	Just like us, persons with autism grow and mature and are able to handle more of life's challenges. To date, however, there is no single treatment that leads to a cure.
Persons with autism should live in residential settings with people who are experts in autism.	Persons with autism should live with their families when they are school age. After that, with persons that they appreciate who can also respect their needs, afford to meet their needs, and provide them with opportunities to display their strengths.

If a person with autism does not speak by the age of 4 then they will never speak.	Language development occurs most often during early childhood but individuals may learn to initiate conversation and speak at various times in their life. Approximately 60% of persons with autism are verbal but all may communicate through their behavior.
People with autism will never develop friendships or marry.	Many persons with autism develop friendships with those who have similar interests and many do marry.
Vaccinations cause autism.	According to the latest research, vaccinations have not been linked to autism.

Approaches to Treatment

Depending on the abilities of the autistic person and their support staff, various approaches may be successful when facilitated with respect. It is important to begin with the use of evidenced based practices. Evidence based practices are those interventions that are based on studies that have been published in medical and/or psychology or academic peer-reviewed journals. In such journals, the editor receives research reports from authors and sends the reports to several experts for honest feedback. Each study is scrutinized based on research methodology, soundness of conclusions, and contribution to scientific knowledge. Peer reviewed reports are more trustworthy than "studies" found on popular media outlets.

No Child Left Behind (NCLB) (20 U.S.C. § 6301 et seq.), the federal legislation that covers elementary and secondary education, mandates that educational settings and professionals utilize evidence based practices. Evidence Based Practices for schools have been reviewed and published in educational journals that are peer reviewed and are based on research that has been done in schools and with school children.

The National Autism Center has found several established treatments to be evidence-based practices for schools (see Table 4).

TABLE 4   Autism Treatments in Schools
▶ Modifying the environment before target behavior occurs
▶ Reinforcement of desired behavior
▶ Intense service delivery with rich student to teacher ratio
▶ Joint-attention
▶ Modeling positive behavior
▶ Naturalistic teaching strategies (natural environment)
▶ Peer-training
▶ Pivotal-response training
▶ Schedules
▶ Self-management
▶ Story-based interventions (scripts)
(http://www.nationalautismcenter.org)

"How can these Interventions lead to a better life?" This is a question that each family and professional must ask prior to seeking treatment. The Autism National Committee has identified some warning signs and questions that must be asked of professionals in regard to recommended approaches to treatment (see Table 5).

TABLE 5 Warning Signs
▶ Be suspicious of any treatment which makes grandiose claims, using words like miraculous, amazing, recovery, or cure.
▶ Be suspicious of any professional who publicizes or promotes their method as if it was a marketable commodity.
▶ Remember that many treatments are composed of an eclectic mix of active and inactive ingredients.
▶ The more clarity we can achieve by knowing what really helps the less time, energy, and money we will waste on inactive, incidental, and occasionally harmful treatment components. It is helpful to note the common features in many effective interventions across many disciplines.
▶ Be aware of environmental accommodations which slow down interactions, using a consistent pattern paced to the person's unique rhythm.

TABLE 6 Questions
▶ Is the patient receiving adequate time and attention from favorable peers and adults?
▶ Is the health care professional following the patient's lead?
▶ Is the health care professional using the patient's strengths?
▶ Is the treatment taking place in the home and typical community settings?
(http://www.autcom.org)

Summary

Autism impacts the ability of individuals to communicate, socialize, empathize, and navigate their environments. ASD is aptly conceptualized as a spectrum because of the variance in ability and deficit with each individual diagnosed. Unless we begin to look globally at the core deficits in diagnosis and treatment, and attempt to meet the needs of each individual within their home, school, and community, there can be no meaningful inclusion of individuals with ASD in our society.

Chapter 18

"My Body Won't Do What My Brain Wants"

Sandi McClennen

How Sensorimotor Disability Masks Intelligence

We have made a huge mistake in special education. Most of us have equated how well people talk and what they can do with how intelligent they are. And we have been wrong. The first step in acknowledging this has been to shift from thinking in terms of special education to thinking in terms of inclusive education. Instead of thinking about a separate group of students with "special needs," we acknowledge that academic skills run along a continuum, that every student has some kind of challenge that should be addressed, and that the challenges students face do not fit neatly into one category.

We must take our thinking one step further, however. Over the past thirty years, people labeled with "intellectual disability" (also called "cognitive impairment" or "mental retardation") have seized opportunities to share and discuss their experiences. Inspired by these discussions, some researchers have begun to question what we mean by these terms. And what we have learned changes everything. Behaviors that educators took to be signs of *intellectual* disability—poor speech or lack of speech, difficulty pointing or manipulating objects in response to questions, failure to follow instructions, unusual or disruptive behaviors—have been shown to result from physical and neurological challenges involving motor skills and sensory processing. And when students are provided with therapies to help them improve their motor skills and sensory processing and have been given accommodations to help them work around these challenges, they are able to demonstrate much greater intellectual capability. When they are also given access to a communication system they can use, students labeled as "intellectually disabled" are able to demonstrate learning and frequently perform at age level or better. The two largest affected groups are people with cerebral palsy and people with autism, but people with other diagnoses have also been in this situation (Joubert syndrome, Rett syndrome, Down syndrome, tuberous sclerosis, etc.).

In this chapter, you will learn that what you think you know about people with "severe disabilities" (also called "significant disabilities"), especially those who do not have functional spoken language, is wrong. And you will learn primarily from their own words.

Anne McDonald

Anne McDonald was an Australian woman who had athetoid cerebral palsy and was diagnosed with "static encephalopathy," which means brain damage around the time of birth (the cause of the cerebral palsy) which is not becoming worse with time. When cerebral palsy occurs, it is known that the part of the brain involved in motor control is damaged. It does not mean that intelligence or cognitive ability is necessarily affected. Anne reported in 2007, ". . . I can't walk, talk, feed or care for myself. My motor skills are those of a 3-month-old. When I was 3, a doctor assessed me as severely retarded (that is, as having an IQ of less than 35) and I was admitted to a state institution called St. Nicholas Hospital in Melbourne, Australia. As the hospital didn't provide me with a wheelchair, I lay in bed or on the floor for most of the next 14 years. At the age of 12, I was relabeled as profoundly retarded (IQ less than 20) because I still hadn't learned to walk or talk. . . My life changed when I was offered a means of communication. At the age of 16, I was taught to spell by pointing to letters on an alphabet board."

At age eighteen, Anne successfully sued the state to free herself from guardianship and from the state institution in which she was imprisoned. Although she needed physical support to point, she demonstrated to both psychologists and the judge in court that she could respond correctly to questions unknown to the person providing physical support. Anne went on to earn a degree from Deakin University in fine arts and history and philosophy of science even though she was never able to walk or talk, nor eat or use the bathroom without assistance. She was able, however, to become an influential advocate for the rights of people with disabilities through her writing. (To learn more about McDonald, go to http://www.annemcdonaldcentre.org.au/rowing-upstream-0. Sadly, McDonald died of a heart attack unrelated to her cerebral palsy in 2010.)

Sensorimotor Challenges

Motor skill challenges can also be experienced by people with autism, though the mechanism is different and less well understood than in cerebral palsy. Further, the movement differences observed in autism are entwined with differences in the way people on the autism spectrum experience perception—vision, hearing, touch, smell, taste, and vestibular function (sense of self in relation to space and gravity). We use the term "sensorimotor system" to refer to the process by which we detect changes in the environment through our senses and respond to those changes using our motor system.

Advocates on the autism spectrum call people without disability labels "neurotypical." Although each of us is unique, neurotypicals understand each other by assuming that their sensory and motor systems work about the same. They expect each other to be able to communicate by talking, to respond immediately and specifically to requests if they choose to, and to assume that lack of response means someone has chosen not to respond. Neurotypicals expect each other to show emotion in their facial expressions and even have a term, "poker face," to describe someone working to not show such emotion. Neurotypicals operate under expectations of an acceptable range of behavior in public and more specific behaviors to fit particular circumstances: for example, what is allowable in school during class and what is allowed in the halls when class is not in session; how to behave in church; how to behave at a picnic versus how to behave at a meeting. Neurotypicals make judgments about unusual or unexpected behavior of others in each setting.

This system generally works for people who have "normal" or typical sensorimotor systems. But when a person's sensorimotor system is quite different, as in autism and in those with some other diagnoses, we must stop thinking we understand that person based on what we observe. And because these differences vary so much even when people have the same diagnosis, we cannot even generalize from one person to another.

I'm going to give you an oversimplified idea of what goes into a response and an example of a neurotypical situation that allows you to think about it. Then you will read how different people diagnosed with autism describe their experience through their sensorimotor systems.

1. You either hear, see, smell, taste, feel something that makes you want to respond, or you have an idea that makes you want to engage in an action. (Keep in mind that we use the word "feel" to mean many different things—we feel something touch our skin, we feel emotion, we feel where we are in relation to space and gravity (upright/standing, prone/lying down, dizzy, etc.), and we know where each part of our body is in relation to each other part. All of these ways that we feel are relevant to this discussion.)

2. Based on this, you use your store of sensory information to formulate a plan for movement.

3. "Motor planning" is the name commonly given to working out how, what, and where to move, and in what order, so that the desired movements occur.

4. Execution occurs when the message is sent from the brain to the designated muscle groups. While this is happening, the brain must monitor how well the action was performed and make any necessary adjustments to the message, then send that to the designated muscle groups.

5. Successful movement requires the individual to be organized in three areas: (a) arousal; (b) emotional and motor regulation; and (c) focus and attention. [Arousal refers to the nervous system being in a state of readiness to respond with intention.] (Chadwick 2012)

Thousands of times every day, neurotypicals do this without conscious thought. They are even able to drive a familiar route without much conscious thought. How often have you arrived at your destination, then wondered how you got there safely because your mind was on all kinds of things unrelated to driving? (Note that on an unfamiliar route, or when the weather greatly affects driving, your mind is on your driving.)

To get a sense of conscious thought about sensorimotor movements, try to learn a new dance step or to make a change in the way you perform a particular sport to try to improve (changing your tennis serve or the way you dribble a basketball). Think about what your brain and body are doing as you work on learning this change. You are using many or all of these motor movements—starting, stopping, executing, continuing, combining, switching—and you are also influenced by all of your sensory perceptions, your emotions and your memories related to the movement (Donnellan, Hill, & Leary 2010).

People with autism and other diagnoses report experiencing sensory perception and motor regulation in ways that sound quite different from what neurotypicals experience. Because I assume that neurotypicals in general experience sensory perception and motor regulation much like I do, I assume that neurotypical readers of this chapter will probably have about the same experience of wonder as I do as they read the accounts that follow.

Chandima Rajapatirana offers this account: "Helplessly I sit while Mom calls me to come. I know what I must do, but often I can't get up until she says, 'Stand up . . . [The] knack of knowing where my body is does not come easy for me. Interestingly I do not know if I am sitting or standing. I am not aware of my body unless it is touching something . . . Your hand on mine lets me know where my hand is. Jarring my legs by walking tells me I am alive." (Wallis 2006)

Nick Pentzell explains: "To focus, I learn to glance at things out of the corner of my eye and see things in a peripheral way. This allows me to regard life in small doses. It is too confusing most of the time to look at things face on. Really, I am overwhelmed by what I see." (Young 2011, 167)

April Herren describes her situation: "I have loud hands! I need help finding my place in a room. I can't tell where my body is in relation to things. I need to continually feel my surroundings to know how I fit in my kind little place. I might look pretty weird to the general public, but it is how I can keep myself connected in the world. I really might not want to have loud hands. It is a part of who I am. I could not stop if I tried. . . I can't sit still. I can't do normal everyday tasks. I need little kind helpers to help with these things. I might not be very successful without them … To the average person it might seem weird, but I can't function without it. . . Really my body listens to itself. Really don't have much control over my body much of the time. Really don't have much control over many things most of the time. I might feel out of control with my life in the hands of others most of the time." (Bascom 2012, 91–92)

Barb Rentenbach writes: "My facial expressions do not always match my emotions. I can walk and move fairly well, but my fine motor skills are limited and my initiation impulse is extremely weak, so assistance is needed in almost every sphere." (Young 2011, 163)

Sarah Stup explains: "My voice is not connected to me. My speaking is not working for me because it says nothing or weird non-speech sounds. Sometimes it speaks real words, but not always what I want to say. With autism, my body doesn't do what I tell it to do." (Young 2011, 163)

Tom Page finds that "I can't even get a drink of water without a signal or prompt of some sort." (Young 2011, 165)

Wally Wojtowicz, Jr. describes his situation: "The inability to respond on demand underscores many autistic people's inability to perform many tasks put before them by other people or by their own mind. Autistic people have functioning minds, but we all don't have functioning control of our bodies when we are asked to do a task. I have trouble trying to consciously direct my body to perform simple tasks such as sitting down gracefully or putting my treasured nails and stones in my pockets rather than throwing them. It is the reason I gobble my food and gulp down a drink." (Young 2011, 165)

Beginning in the 1990s, there has been a slow but steady increase in neurological research verifying what people with autism have been telling us about how they experience being alive—not only in the wide variation in the way sensory input is perceived but their difficulty in controlling their bodies. (See Donnellan and Leary 2012, for extensive lists of this research until publication; also see Torres et al. 2013 [two articles], and their lists of references.) People with autism, cerebral palsy, and other diagnoses describe a disconnect between their conscious intentions for what they want to do, for example, follow the direction given by a parent or teacher, and their bodies not responding to this intention. This can be true even for pointing at an item or a word or a letter. What is particularly frustrating for them is that, if there is an item of food within reach, a person will grab it and put it in her mouth, whether she wants it or not, whether she likes it or not. (One suggested explanation is that many people have been "overtaught" to feed themselves so will always respond to the stimulus of food. Another possibility is that we are biologically programmed to reach for food.) But if that person is told to pick up her shoes and put them on or to point to the blue circle, she can know what is wanted and desire to comply but be unable to make her body respond to her mind's intentions.

Lack of a Communication System Makes People Appear Incapable

For all of these reasons, people with sensorimotor challenges who do not have functional speech have experienced being judged as incapable of thought or learning before getting a communication system they could access. Sue Rubin, a woman who communicates by typing independently, wrote, "My own story starts with a very autistic child who was quite aggressive toward others—biting, pulling hair, throwing my head against someone's body, etc. I was also self-abusive—head banging, throwing myself against walls, biting, and quite ready to throw myself on the ground. I was so autistic I was in a separate world. When I was four my IQ was 50, but as I got older it went down so by the time I was 13 it was 24." (Gillingham & McClennen, Eds. 2008, 148).

Rubin continues by describing how her parents had always advocated for her to have some time in general education classes and how, at the age of 13, the possibility of communicating by typing was introduced. Rubin wrote, "The teacher typed with me at school everyday and my mom typed with me at home. I slowly progressed from single words to phrases and sentences and paragraphs. During this time it became apparent that I had been learning from the mainstream classes and my older brother's homework, and storing the information in my head. My brain was so disorganized it took months for me to be able to organize information and retrieve it. It took even longer for me to be able to clearly express original thoughts, not just short answers to homework." (Gillingham & McClennen, Eds., 2008, 149).

The next year, Rubin attended general education classes in high school toward a regular diploma. She wrote, "We chose honors and advanced placement classes to avoid taking classes with a lot of cooperative learning and behavior problems of non special ed students. We started with three classes and worked up to five classes each day. The transition to high school was very difficult for me and I often had to be removed from class. The psychologist was on call and often rushed to the high school when I was having a meltdown. I really believe that being in regular classes and having to spend hours doing homework everyday and on the weekends was what enabled me to overcome a lot of the autistic behaviors I was constantly battling. After a while it became easier and easier for me to stay in class. I became relaxed and spent less energy fighting autism. By the time I graduated high school I was a thinking person . . . quite aware of current events and aware of the thoughts and feelings of my peers and family. (Gillingham & McClennen, Eds., 2008, 149–150)

Following high school, Rubin attended Whittier College and earned a B.A. She wrote a documentary video, "Autism Is a World," which has been shown on television and was nominated for an Oscar. She wonders, in the chapter referenced above, why more people like her aren't given an opportunity to try alternative communication, including the possibility of typing, beginning with physical support. "Because of the way we move and our lack of speech we were assumed to be retarded. I was thought to be retarded (but) all this changed ... once I could type without support... (Rubin et al. 2001, 519)

Jenn Seybert had to wait until she was much older to get access to communication. Throughout her years of public education, she was relegated to segregated schools for people considered "severely retarded." In 2002, Jenn Seybert was a Keynote Speaker for the Maryland Coalition for Inclusive Education Conference. Here is part of her presentation, *Inclusion . . . Finally!!!*

> My life without communication was 24 years of a living hell. Imagine yourselves sitting in your seats and having your thoughts constantly interrupted by thoughts of terror, your own voice sounding like a thunder of garbled words being thrown back at you, and other folks screaming at you to pay attention and finish your task. You find your body and voice do unusual things, and you realize you aren't in control. People are screaming at you to stop the aggression and stick a raisin or lemon juice in your mouth, depending on your response. Now add to this that you cannot talk...maybe a few words...but nothing consistent with language. With all this in mind, welcome to the world of a person with autism who is also non-verbal.

> My life was always upside down. Nothing made sense. I kept trying to please but was not able to let anyone know what I was trying to say. We are a confusing lot. We are able to have intelligent brains, but our outward appearance is looked at as severely retarded. You are able to sit in your seats and have total control of your mind, voice and body. That isn't how we work. We are not in control all the time, and some of us folks, never. We want to comply, we want to please, but we can't make it work all the time.

> You see, for the first 24 years of my life, my behavior was appalling, and I was aggressive, very unhappy, and always frustrated. Seven years ago, I was introduced to facilitated communication and my world became unlocked in an instant. That is when my whole life opened up and the hell of being locked inside of myself disappeared. . .

> In the beginning I needed a lot of support, both emotional and physical. Like you, I will always want and need support from family and friends. My need for physical support, however, has been reduced to practically nothing at times. My thoughts are normal like yours, but my motor planning issue causes me to stall on each thought without the help of my facilitator to give me a gentle lift so I am able to get my next thought out.

> You can see from my appearance that I look retarded. The motor planning issue I have to live with makes me not respond immediately. When you are talking with me, I appear to drift off or am not listening. I utter involuntary sounds or words. These issues are part of my inward battle. These issues I have to struggle to keep in control so you, the audience, will believe in me as the author of my thoughts.

> These are issues that many people contend with every hour of their lives. To those who are caregivers, teachers, case managers, parents, and staff, think of those people you support who have difficulty with communication and productive motor planning. Maybe you hadn't thought of their problems in that light before. Maybe you just thought "retardation" or "behavior problem." (Gillingham & McClennen, Eds. 2008, 115–117)

Seybert began college by auditing one class for two semesters at Penn State, then began taking courses for credit. When her family moved to central New York, she (and her credits) were accepted at Le Moyne College in Syracuse, New York. After she earned a B.A., she was accepted into the graduate program in Disability Studies at Syracuse University and now has a Master's degree. Concurrent with working on this degree, she has achieved the motor control to type independently.

Unwanted Behavior

In addition to reading about the difficulties people with sensorimotor challenges have in trying to make their bodies follow the intention of their brains, you have also read about the challenges they have in trying to *not* engage in unwanted behaviors. With good intention, we encourage people to see behavior as communication.

Caregivers and teachers are taught to look for the intent of the behavior of a non-speaking person, such as protesting something the individual does not want or communicating a want or need, rather than assuming the behavior is meant to be aggressive or attributing another negative intention to it. But as some people tell us, even this does not go far enough in attempting to explain behavior that we do not understand.

Carly Fleischman, nonspeaking, diagnosed with severe autism and considered to be "severely mentally retarded," was provided with intensive therapy which included "hand-over-hand" typing on a keyboard. One day, with a therapist present but not touching her, she typed "hurt," then "hel," then vomited. With encouragement, she continued to express herself (with no physical support). Her ABC interview can be viewed on YouTube.

> "You don't know what it feels like to be me, when you can't sit still because your legs feel like they are on fire, or it feels like a hundred ants are crawling up your arms. . . People look at me and think I am dumb, because I can't talk."

When asked why she bangs her head, she typed, "Because if I don't, it feels like my body is going to explode. It's just like when you shake a can of coke. If I could stop it, I would, but it is not like turning a switch off. I know what is right and wrong but it's like I have a fight with my brain over it. . . I want to go to school with normal kids but not have them get upset when I scream or hit a table."

She typed about how her body will not do what her brain wants, about the noises she makes to drown out too much input that overloads her nervous system, and about many other things. "I take over a thousand pictures of people's faces when I look at them. That's why it's so hard to look at people."

To her Dad: "You've never been in my body. I wish for one day you could be in my body."

To everyone: "Autism is hard because you want to act one way, but you can't always do that. It's sad that sometimes people don't know that sometimes I can't stop myself and they get mad at me. If I could tell people one thing about autism it would be that I don't want to be this way. But I am, so don't be mad. Be understanding." (ABC News 2008)

D.J. Savarese gave his own "I Have a Dream" speech. Here is part of it:

> "...most people still perceive of kids with autism as bad and retarded. Instead of helping us, they hurt us. Instead of teaching us to read and write, they keep us in segregated classrooms of easy lessons. I have been justly treated but there are thousands of kids yearning to be free.

> "Autism is a neurological disorder that responsible people don't understand. They see us as fearful because we do strange things like flap our arms, clap our hands, bang our heads, and make strange noises. These behaviors very much are involuntary. We cannot control them. Autism just makes us look messed up, but inside all of us are the same.

> "From the involuntary movements we make, people respond. They get frustrated. They fear us. They voice thoughts of giving up on us. They also want us to be normal. When we can't be, they try to fear us. They say we're not as good as other students and they justify years of politely housing us in segregated classrooms. Other breathing hard kids with autism have created a website called Breaking the Barriers. They write that "we need people to understand that labels of autism and mental retardation are how people without disabilities try to label our experience—but really it is a label for your experience—what you see or experience a person doing. The label or what you see them doing tells you nothing about what they are experiencing or what they 'get' from their actions. This needs to be learned on a person-by-person basis." For example, when someone says hi to me, I might not start being able to respond until they've already moved on. They think I don't like them, but inside I'm thinking awesome kid just said hi to me. I yearn to invite them over to play.

What can we do to help these kids? Teachers can help these deserving kids to learn to read and write. If treat kids to care about respect both themselves and others, fear will disappear. You can help, too. Ignore my strange behavior but don't ignore me. Talk to me and wait long enough for me to respond. Write letters of support for inclusion to your politician . . . You'd headbang to (sic) if feared same fresh start wasn't available to you." (2006)

Typing to Communicate

Facilitated communication, commonly referred to as FC or supported typing, is a way to access communication for people whose sensorimotor challenges have made other approaches not possible. It requires a communication partner who provides physical and emotional support as the individual points or types on a keyboard. What type of support is provided depends on the needs of the individual. The goal is to work with the individual to reduce the support necessary. The transition from a great deal of support to very little (perhaps only the presence of a trusted person) may happen quickly or may take years. Being a good facilitator requires training. The Institute for Communication and Inclusion (ICI) at Syracuse University provides both training opportunities and referrals to trainers.

The transition from seeing incompetence to presuming competence has been difficult for some. They have questioned who is the author of the communication—the person with sensorimotor challenges or the facilitator. The ICI website provides a list of articles and books addressing all sides of the question. Professors and Speech/Language Pathologists David Beukelman and Pat Mirenda are two highly respected professionals. They stated in their Augmentative and Alternative Communication textbook, ". . . in regard to a small group of people around the world who began communicating through FC and are now able to type either independently or with minimal, hand-on-shoulder support . . . there can be no doubt that, for them, [facilitated communication] 'worked,' in that it opened the door to communication for the first time. . . For them, the controversy has ended" (Beukelman & Mirenda 2013, 327). Now, fifteen years later, many more people who were once thought to be incompetent and non-communicative are typing independently. Most of the people quoted in this chapter are typing independently or have validated their authorship. Professor June Downing, a highly-regarded educator, has noted, "When FC is done correctly, the facilitator does not move the student's hand to create the message but instead, follows the student's lead and only provides support as needed to allow the student access to the device. . . FC thus offers some individuals with severe and multiple disabilities an opportunity to express themselves and should be considered as a viable intervention option." (2004, 551–552)

What Can Teachers Do?

Some of the people reading this will become general education teachers and some will become special education teachers. In a book by Paula Kluth, Christi Kasa gives guidelines—relevant to all readers—for including a student who does not talk:

> Never talk about someone in front of them. Always acknowledge the person's presence. Some people may not be able to communicate through spoken words or body language that they understand what you are saying or that they are listening. Assume they are listening and interested in what you are talking about.

> Talk in an *age-appropriate* manner, using age-appropriate content. Using a sing-song voice or a tone similar to that used with a young child should be reserved for babies and toddlers. Be sure to check your tone of voice and the content you are talking about.

> While teaching, be sure to acknowledge the nonverbal student's presence often. You should not go an entire lesson without saying, "Sean I bet you'll like this part. I know you like to swim," or "Megan I see you smiling. I am sure you will like learning about volcanoes."

> If students use a yes/no communication strategy, be sure to use this during a lesson. You can do this during a whole group lesson by saying, "Do you all think that 5 + 5 = 10?" If they answer incorrectly, then you can say, "Oh, I don't think that is quite right. Does anyone have other ideas?"

> If the student uses an augmentative communication system, you need to be sure to have them utilize it across lessons.

> Use partners during lesson activities. Model and encourage peers to talk about topics with each other.

Take every opportunity to talk with the student. Talk about current events, age-appropriate interests, things you like to do, places to go, and events around school. Also, let them use their communication strategy to make LOTS of choices throughout the day.

Be sure to include them in the academic curriculum in the classroom. Assume learning is possible. (Kluth 2010, 131)

In this chapter there is space to include only some words of some people, but I want to emphasize that I am quoting from people who spent their childhoods, and sometimes well into adulthood, labeled as severely or profoundly intellectually impaired and treated that way. Yet here they are, having written and published and presented at conferences, discussing their own experiences eloquently. Taking the time to read what they say and truly hearing their words is fundamental to having the right attitude as a good teacher in inclusive education. Over the past 30 years this completely different way of looking at students labeled as severely intellectually impaired has emerged and what I am pointing out to you here in all likelihood goes against everything you will be told about "that kind of student." The difference in how we think about people that is represented in this point of view came about because some people with the label of "severe mental retardation" got the opportunity to have a communication system so that they could speak for themselves and enough people listened to them.

Please do not make the mistake of thinking, "The people quoted were exceptional." It takes work to shift perceptions and attitudes and how you see things, but the people who I am quoting are representative of the students you will see in your classrooms. Your job will be to understand that their sensorimotor challenges are getting in the way of their being able to demonstrate their intelligence. At the very least, talk to them just as you do their classmates, assuming that they understand and appreciate your giving them that respect.

If you are presuming competence and a student is doing anything that "he should know not to do because it's inappropriate, disruptive, etc.," there are two possible explanations. Either the student does not want to be doing it at all and needs your help to stop (not your admonishment) or it is serving a purpose, such as calming. In that case, the person needs your help in finding a better way to serve that purpose. The student does not need to be told that what he is doing is inappropriate. He already knows that. He does not need you to talk to him as if he should know better or needs a reminder. What he needs to hear from you is, "I'm guessing you don't want to be doing that but can't get your body under control or it's serving a purpose and we could find a better way."

While writing this chapter, I had an opportunity to talk with two women who have autism and Down syndrome. Neither was given an opportunity for inclusive education. I asked them what they would like to tell teachers. (Their names have been changed here.) Ann typed, "I am smart and so is gwen. just can't talk." Gwen typed, "be patient." I asked what would have made school better for them. Ann: "to type and get support." Gwen: "I wish people would have shared more books with me. I learn a lot from people reading." I asked, "Does your body sometimes do things you don't want?" Both responded yes. I asked what the teacher should do. Ann: "I can't help it. leave me alone please." Gwen: "i can't help it this is how I am. let me be me."

Here are a few more thoughts to keep in mind about interacting with students with sensorimotor challenges. As Ann and Gwen point out, characteristics that seem inappropriate or infantile—making weird noises, wearing diapers, jumping up while the teacher is talking, putting fingers in their mouths, staring out the window and flapping their hands, sticking out their tongues, or fiddling endlessly with toys—does not mean that students with sensorimotor challenges lack interest in learning. The presence of these characteristics does not negate their ability to learn the same material that is being taught to neurotypical students of their chronological age.

Furthermore, when a student has sensorimotor challenges, everything he is asked to do takes a huge amount of energy to make his body do what his brain wants. When the request does not have meaning, the student does not want to expend the energy. This is very understandable. For example, instead of working on pointing to the red block, work on pointing to the correct answer of two choices based on information from science or social studies.

Talk to students in a way that is respectful, not babytalk or babytone. If a student has struggled to do something meaningful and does it, "good job" is not a meaningful response. It says, "I'm not sure you are understanding why this is important, so I have to give you praise or reward for accomplishing it"; a more respectful approach is using language that lets a person know that you know she sees the importance of a task and is trying hard to accomplish it. "I see you trying really hard, and I believe in you."

Anne McDonald Gets the Last Word

Early in this chapter, you met Anne McDonald through her words and story. It ends with part of an address she delivered (using a device that spoke what she had typed) at Parliament House (in Australia) in 2008 when she was awarded the National Disability Award for Personal Achievement.

> "I spent my childhood and adolescence in a state institution for severely disabled children. I was starved and neglected. A hundred and sixty of my friends died there. I am a survivor. . . I wasn't exceptional in anything other than my good luck. I was selected for an experiment. Rosemary Crossley wanted a subject for her Bachelor of Education literacy project. She chose me . . . Rosemary found I could point to colours, then to words, and then to letters. She taught me to spell and to make my wishes known . . . I went to the Supreme Court and won the right to manage my own affairs.

> Unfortunately, that didn't mean that the institution offered the *other* residents the right to manage *their* own affairs. I was an exception. Through no desire of my own, I was out front in the struggle to get rights for people without speech. I tried to show the world that when people without speech were given the opportunity to participate in education we could succeed. . . I gave papers and wrote articles on the right to communicate. I set up a website to show that there was hope for people without speech. People thanked me for being an inspiration; however, they didn't understand why there weren't more like me. They continued to act as if speech was the same thing as intelligence, and to pretend that you can tell a person's capacity by whether or not they can speak.

> "*Please listen to me now*. . . If you let other people without speech be helped as I was helped they will say more than I can say. They will tell you that the humanity we share is not dependent on speech. They will tell you that the power of literacy lies within us all. They will tell you that I am not an exception . . . It should be impossible to miss out on literacy training, but thousands of Australians still do. As Stephen Jay Gould wrote, *We pass through this world but once. Few tragedies can be more extensive than the stunting of a life, few injustices deeper than the denial of an opportunity to strive or even to hope, by a limit imposed from without, but falsely identified as lying within.*" (McDonald, 2008)

Resources

Some Books by Professionals

Biklen, D. with Richard Attfield, Larry Bissonnette, Lucy Blackman, Jamie Burke, Alberto Frugone, Tito Rajarshi Mukhopadhyay, and Sue Rubin (2005). *Autism and the Myth of the Person Alone*. NY: New York University Press.

Donnellan, A., Hill, D. A., & Leary, M. R. (2010). Rethinking autism: Implications of sensory and movement differences. *Disability Studies Quarterly, 30*(1). Retrieved from http://dsq-sds.org/article/view/1060/1225

Kluth, P. (2010). *"You're going to love this kid!" Teaching students with autism in the inclusive classroom,* (2nd ed.) Baltimore, MD: Brookes Publishing Co.

Young, S. R. (2011). *Real people, regular lives: Autism, communication & quality of life*. Order from www.autcom.org

Some Books by People with Sensorimotor Challenges

Bascom, J., Ed. (2012). *Loud hands: autistic people, speaking* (sic). Autistic Self Advocacy Network

Blackman, L. (1999). *Lucy's Story: Autism and other adventures*. Brisbane, AU: Book in Hand

Gillingham, G. & McClennen, S., Eds. (2008). *Sharing our wisdom: A collection of presentations by people within the autism spectrum*. Order from www.autcom.org

Higashida, N. (2007) Translation copyright 2013 by D. Mitchell. *The reason I jump*. NY: Random House.

Marcus, E. & Shevin M. (1997). Sorting it out under fire: Our journey (pp. 115–134). In Biklen, D. & Cardinal, D., *Contested words, contested science: Unraveling the facilitated communication controversy.* NY: Teachers College Press

Mukhopadhyay, T. (2000). *Beyond the Silence: My life, the world, and autism.* London: The National Autistic Society

Rentenbach, Barb & Prislovsky, Lois. (2012). *I might be you: An exploration of autism and connection.* Knoxville, TN: Mule and Muse Productions

Some Websites

soe.syr.edu/centers_institutes/institute_communication_inclusion/

tash.org/

www.annemcdonaldcentre.org.au

www.autcom.org—Website of Autism National Committee; bookstore includes *Sharing Our Wisdom* and *Real People, Regular Lives,* both referenced in this chapter, as well as downloadable issues of *The Communicator* and some past conference presentations.

Questions for Discussion

► What are some of the ways in which sensorimotor challenges can mask intelligence?

► Why is it that certain kinds of behaviors tend to make us think that the person engaging in them is intellectually impaired (cognitively impaired, mentally retarded)?

► Describe a time when you had to work very hard to accomplish a new intentional movement. Explain this experience in terms of the body/brain activity you have read about.

► Why do teachers need to be careful about interpreting the behaviors of their students?

► What does it mean to "presume competence"? What do teachers need to do to show their students that they are presuming competence?

Section 3

How Is Disability Created and Maintained in Schools?

Chapter 19

A (Very) Brief History of Education in the United States

Phil Smith

How did we in the United States end up with the system of education that we have today? How did it come into being? This will be an incredibly brief story about how that happened—brief because it's not really the point of this book to describe it in any detail. The point of this particular section is to give you enough detail to understand how it is that we came to create a system of education for people with disabilities—one that is mostly segregated and separated from the system of education for everyone else in the United States.

In most places in what came to be the United States, before the Revolutionary War, there was no public education as we know it. Educational opportunities were available for those who could afford to pay for private school. This meant that mostly young men, from relatively wealthy backgrounds, and who were white, had the opportunity to go to school. Everyone else, generally, did not. Education was available along race, gender, and class lines, not unlike most things throughout U.S. history.

Those who wrote the Constitution, and who were active in the early political and cultural life of the United States after the Revolutionary War—people like Noah Webster and Thomas Jefferson—came to believe that establishing an educational system for all was an essential part of creating real democracy. Their early efforts made little headway, perhaps in part because there was little interest or need on the part of those who were in power (white, upper-class, men) to change things.

In the 1830s and 1840s, things started to change economically in the United States. Industry began to be an important driver of the economy. With the industrial revolution came the need to create workers who would be able to do the jobs needed in factories and other industrial settings. In some large degree, the industrial revolution created the need for what was initially called common education, in order to create workers with the skills and knowledge to perform increasingly technical tasks. Horace Mann was instrumental in promoting and creating this common school movement.

In common schools, education was still provided along racial and gender lines, generally denied to those who weren't seen as white or male. And higher quality, more advanced educational opportunities were still denied to those who were not wealthy.

Image © Geoffrey Kuchera, 2014. Used under license from Shutterstock, Inc.

Many have argued that a hidden curriculum has long existed in public schools in the United States, a curriculum designed to create obedient workers for industry. This curriculum, not overt in content being taught, but evident in the kind of behavioral and moral expectations of students, encouraged conformity and obedience (Mondale & Patton 2001).

Increasingly in the United States, by the latter part of the nineteenth century, and as a result of the common school movement, education was publicly provided and funded by taxes. School was increasingly taught by women, who were paid less than men, because their "natural" maternal instincts made them good at the work (Nielsen 2012).

The function of education in the early part of the twentieth century, with a huge increase in immigration, was in large measure to assimilate new arrivals into a culture dominated by white, upper-class, men—to ensure that new arrivals knew their place in society, and performed the roles expected of them.

After World War I, there was increased attention paid to tracking students—establishing appropriate educational experiences to ensure that they would have the kinds of jobs and life outcomes expected of them. Intelligence and other testing procedures were used to create and support these tracks.

By the middle part of the twentieth century, almost all children in the United States had access to school, although schools continued to be segregated along at least racial lines. And the quality of educational opportunities remained divided according to class and gender, limiting as it did so vocational options and life outcomes. After the *Brown vs. Board of Education* Supreme Court decision was handed down in 1954, racial segregation in schools, as mandated by law (de jure) ended, although it continues to the present time in the ways schools operate, are administered, and are funded (de facto) (Mondale & Patton 2001).

Change initiatives in education have been common throughout the twentieth century. John Dewey and the progressive schools movement was one. The 1983 report, "A Nation at Risk," spawned more reform. No Child

Left Behind legislation has had an impact on schools, too. These initiatives have been powerful; whether their effects on school and culture have been for good or ill is something that we need to explore and understand.

Many of you know the kinds of issues facing schools, teachers, students, and communities today: standardized testing, funding, school privatization, segregation, voucher programs, tracking, teacher accountability, school choice, and the application of a business model on education, to name a few. Continued issues related to race, gender, class, all reflecting what is going on in the wider U.S. culture, remain with us now.

The U.S. education business in the early part of the twenty-first century is worth hundreds of billions of dollars each year. Understanding what that means, and the effect of all that money on our society and culture, is an issue all by itself.

All of this has an impact on, and sets the stage for, the history of special education in the United States.

Questions for Discussion

▶ Why do race, gender, and class remain such contentious issues in schools? How has the history of education in the United States been affected by them?

▶ How has the general history of education in the United States affected the education of students with disabilities?

Chapter 20

Special Education's Journey: A Brief History

David C. Winters
Illustrations by Lloyd W. Meek

Understanding a field's past unlocks its present and influences its future. Although the field of special education has undergone rapid growth over the past few decades, the foundation for that growth was laid long ago.

Special education grew from a desire to help individuals who did not easily fit into society, so society considered them disabled. Throughout history, a person's culture has strongly influenced who is identified as a person with a disability and how society will treat that person. For example, in today's European and European-American culture, the ability to read and write has high value; therefore, those societies identify individuals who have difficulty with one or more of these academic skills as having a disability. Yet, when society and culture was primarily agrarian, individuals who had difficulty learning these academic skills often led successful, happy lives as farmers, ranchers, or other careers that did not heavily depend on reading and writing. Likewise, in the early 1700s, Venetian society highly valued the musicianship of young girls, and a girl who struggled to learn to perform music would have been treated as having a disability. In this way, disability and a society's values have a close connection.

While numerous cultural heritages have contributed to today's educational practices with children with disabilities, this chapter focuses primarily on the values and culture of European and European-American society, as they have had the greatest impact.

Before the 1500s

Imagine what life might have been like to be born with a disability hundreds of years ago. In ancient Greek society, Aristotle taught that a person born deaf was incapable of speech and, therefore, could not reason. He also taught that children with deformities should not be allowed to live (Safford & Safford 1996). Believing that children were the property of the state, the Greeks regularly examined children's fitness for citizenship, and those with significant, obvious disabilities were abandoned to the elements or thrown into a river to drown (Winzer 1993). The ancient Romans trained boys who were blind to become beggars, while they trained girls who were blind to serve as prostitutes. Before a child was three years old, a Roman father could throw his child into the Tiber River if he believed the child would be a burden to society (Winzer 1993).

Figure 1 Individuals with Disabilities before the 1500s

Illustration by Lloyd W. Meek

As the Catholic Church rose to prominence in the European Middle Ages, religious leaders considered children with disabilities as signs of parental sin or the direct work of Satan. For children born deaf, Augustine interpreted Romans 10:17 of the Christian Bible: "So then faith cometh by hearing, and hearing by the word of God" (King James Version) to mean that these children could not come to faith because they could neither hear nor read the Word of God (Winzer 1993). However, during this same time period, numerous Christian church leaders established hospices for persons with disabilities (Winzer 1993). In addition, many parents offered their children with disabilities to Christian convents and monasteries for a life of service to the church (Safford & Safford 1996). Often, children with intellectual impairment or physical disabilities became court jesters or fools kept by a wealthy family for amusement (Winzer 1993).

Interestingly, individuals who were blind during the Middle Ages did not always suffer such poor treatment. Society considered these persons to possess special powers and skills as a result of their blindness (Rosenberg, Westling, & McLeskey 2011). So these persons often received charitable help, including special hospitals for the blind such as the Hospital and House of the Three Hundred in Paris that was established in 1254 (Safford & Safford 1996).

The Renaissance and Age of Enlightenment

While conditions for individuals with disabilities were bleak through the Middle Ages, a new focus on humanistic principles arose during the European Renaissance, especially during the 1500s. This focus began a process to improve how society treated persons with disabilities, including dealing with their education. Efforts to teach these persons began with those who were deaf, then those who were blind. These efforts later spread to those who were intellectually impaired (Winzer 1993).

Figure 2   Pedro Ponce de Léon teaches boys who are deaf

Illustration by Lloyd W. Meek

In the mid-1500s, **Pedro Ponce de León** (1520–1584), a Benedictine monk in northern Spain, began to teach boys from noble and wealthy families who were born deaf (Safford & Safford 1996). Through systematic instruction, the boys learned to speak, read, write, and do math (Winzer 1993; Safford & Safford 1996). His approach began by having his students write the names of objects, followed by instruction and repeated drill of how to make vocalizations of the sounds that corresponded to the written characters. He also utilized a type of sign language that he and his fellow hearing monks used for communication in their times and places of required silence. Not only did Pedro Ponce de León demonstrate that people with a disability could learn, he also incorporated alternative sensory pathways in instruction (Winzer 1993), a strategy still used today.

Figure 3   Victor demonstrates his ability to match objects to drawings to Jean-Marc-Gaspard Itard

Illustration by Lloyd W. Meek

As the Western Renaissance gave way to the Age of Enlightenment that began in the mid-1700s, society began to seek better ways to educate individuals with disabilities as part of the goal to protect what were coming to be seen as people's natural rights. Challenged by the writings of John Locke, society came to believe that human function and nature had rational explanations (Winzer 1993). Such was the belief of a young physician in France, **Jean-Marc-Gaspard Itard** (1775–1850), as he took on the challenge, against the advice of experts, of teaching a 12-year-old boy who had been found foraging in a woods in south-central France (Safford & Safford 1996). Naming the boy Victor, Itard worked with him from 1800–1804 (Winzer 1993), believing that he could bring the boy back into society, since he felt that Victor's condition was largely due to his very limited contact with other human beings (Rosenberg et al. 2011). Itard focused on changing Victor's environment and used sensory stimuli to teach him practical skills, including speech. He developed five basic goals (see Figure 4), much like today's IEP annual goals, and used a specific set of instructional procedures based on the boy's individual strengths and weaknesses (Safford & Safford 1996). Although Itard felt his work with Victor was a failure, especially because the boy never really learned to speak or fit smoothly into society (Wizner 1993), current special educators often consider him to be the "Father of Modern Special Education."

	Figure 4 Itard's Five Goals for Victor
Goal 1	To interest him in social life by rendering it more pleasant to him than the one he was then leading, and above all more like the life which he had just left.
Goal 2	To awaken his nervous sensibility by the most energetic stimulation, and occasionally by intense emotion.
Goal 3	To extend the range of his ideas by giving him new needs and by increasing his social contacts.
Goal 4	To lead him to the use of speech by inducing the exercise of imitation through the imperious law of necessity.
Goal 5	To make him exercise the simplest mental operations upon the objects of his physical needs over a period of time, afterward inducing the application of these mental processes to the objects of instruction.
Source: Rosenberg et al. 2011	

Expansion and Refinement

During the 1800s through the mid-1900s, education of individuals with disabilities expanded throughout Europe and America, and people concerned with this population developed and refined instructional strategies and approaches.

In America, the rise of special institutions for the education of persons with disabilities paralleled the rise of the common school that came to provide a public education for all children (Winzer 1993). Therefore, while children with disabilities had more opportunities for education, their lives and education occurred separately from the free public education afforded to children without disabilities.

As with previous time periods, efforts to educate children with disabilities began with those who were deaf, followed by those who were blind, and then those who were intellectually impaired. The first institution established in the United States was a residential school for the deaf founded by **Thomas Gallaudet** (1788–1851) in

Hartford, Connecticut, in 1817 (Winzer 1993). Gallaudet, a minister, first became interested in teaching persons who were deaf because of one of his neighbor's daughters who was deaf. He agreed to travel to Europe to learn more about educating persons who are deaf and then became the principal of the school for the deaf.

Samuel Gridley Howe (1801–1876) was instrumental in establishing one of the first American residential institutions for the blind: the Perkins Institution and Massachusetts Asylum for the Blind, in Boston, Massachusetts, in 1832 (Safford & Safford 1996). Howe pursued a threefold approach in educating his students that included (1) incorporating the students' abilities and potential for contributing to the community; (2) providing a well rounded curriculum that closely resembled that of the regular schools, but with a special emphasis on handcrafts and music; and (3) preparing the students to be contributing members of their communities, including the social and economic aspects. He believed that his students could learn as much as students with sight (Rosenberg et al. 2011).

While Howe used a system of raised letters in order for his students to read and write, **Louis Braille** (1809–1852) adapted a military code consisting of twelve raised dots, six rows of two dots in each row (Winzer 1993) for reading and writing. Because Braille realized that this military phoneme-based pattern was too large for a single fingertip to feel, in 1834 he published his system based on three rows of two dots that represented letters. While this code was officially adopted in Paris in 1854, its adoption in the United States came much later. Not until 1917 did Braille become the accepted standard in America.

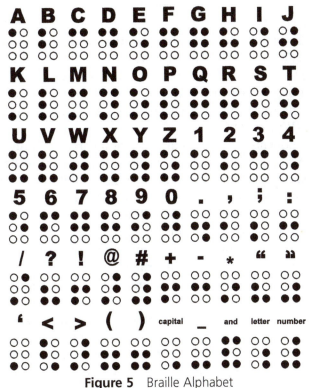

Figure 5 Braille Alphabet

Image © DeCe, 2014. Used under license from Shutterstock, Inc.

A contemporary and student of Itard, **Edouard Seguin** (1812–1880) expanded Itard's instructional strategies with students with intellectual disabilities. Seguin's influence extended to America when he emigrated to the United States in 1848. Seguin focused on specific sensory motor exercises and wrote one of the first comprehensive textbooks for the education of these students in 1866 (Winzer 1993). The components and strategies he developed continue to be used today, and include individual assessment; highly structured, systematic, and multisensory instruction; emphasis on self-help and daily living skills; and frequent use of games, music, and positive reinforcement.

In Italy, **Maria Montesorri** (1870–1951) incorporated Seguin's approach with the growing body of knowledge concerning child development (Winzer 1993). By using highly structured physical materials, she guided her students in their own self-education. While much work with individuals with disabilities came from a medical model perspective, Montesorri emphasized that intellectual impairment was an educational rather than a medical issue. In 1906, she established a program based on her educational strategies for children who were not disabled but lived in a Roman slum. Her success in educating these disadvantaged children led to a wide influence around the world, including the United States (Safford & Safford 1996). Montessori schools continue to provide an alternative approach to children's education today.

As educators worked to teach children with intellectual impairments, appropriate assessment, especially for identification, became an important issue. In 1904, the French government asked **Alfred Binet** (1867–1911) to develop an assessment instrument that would help identify children who might struggle to learn in school (Wizner 1993). Binet, with his assistant Théodore Simon (1873–1961), introduced the first version of his intelligence test in 1905. In the 1908 revision, he introduced the concept of mental age, which, when divided by a person's chronological age, yielded an IQ, or intelligence quotient (Safford & Safford 1996). A few years later, Henry Goddard translated Binet's test for use in America. Then, in 1937, Lewis Terman (1877–1956), the head of the psychology department at Stanford University, led an American revision of Binet's test that came to be known as the Stanford-Binet (Safford & Safford 1996; Winzer 1993).

While the use of intelligence tests helped bring a broader understanding of the cognitive aspects of intellectual impairment, they also became a chief tool in the **eugenics** movement, which was an outgrowth of Darwin's theories of natural selection (Winzer 1993). The eugenics movement began with the work of **Sir Francis Galton** (1822–1911). Galton, using the phrase *nature vs. nurture*, taught that a person's biological *nature* through heredity is almost totally responsible for a person's cognitive ability, while the role of the person's environment (*nurture*) has minimal impact. Therefore, a primary goal of the eugenics movement was to improve the human race through selective breeding (Winzer 1993).

One of the primary proponents of eugenics in America was **Henry Goddard** (1866–1957). Goddard was the research director at the New Jersey Training School for Feeble-minded Boys and Girls in Vineland, New Jersey. In 1912 he published a genealogical study of one of the students at the school. In his book, *The Kallikak Family: A Study in the Heredity of Feeble-mindedness,* Goddard asserted that he traced the girl's family back to the Revolutionary War to a soldier and a tavern girl and their 480 descendants. Of these descendants, 143 were feeble-minded and many had been criminals. This same soldier later married a respectable girl, and of those descendants, none were feeble-minded or had been criminals. From this information, Goddard concluded that feeble-mindedness and criminal behavior were inherited. Unfortunately, later review of Goddard's research methods and interpretations discredited much of his study of this family, but its impact on education and public policy was extensive.

While initial efforts to educate persons with disabilities focused on those with deafness, blindness, and intellectual impairment, a group of children who seemed to have adequate intellectual ability but had difficulty learning tool skills such as reading, writing, and math began receiving attention in the early 1900s. In 1925, **Samuel Orton** (1879–1948), director of the State Psychopathic Hospital in Iowa City, Iowa, began a program of mobile mental health clinics. At the clinic in Greene County, he met a 16-year-old boy who could not learn to read even though he seemed bright. Orton came to believe that this difficulty had a physiological basis.

Figure 6   Samuel Orton watches a 16-year-old boy (whom he called "MP") try to write

Illustration by Lloyd W. Meek

Besides spending much of the rest of his life researching this and other difficulties in learning and language, Orton and numerous colleagues developed instructional strategies. One of the best known of these colleagues was **Anna Gillingham** (1878–1964), a teacher at New York's Ethical Culture School. Integrating Orton's theories into a teaching approach for persons with difficulty learning to read and spell, often called *dyslexia*, she and Bessie Stillman (1871–1947) developed a systematic, sequential, multisensory approach based on the structure of written language.

Much of the knowledge and teaching strategies during this time period passed from a mentor to his or her students who then passed the knowledge to their students. Even though states established teacher education programs, originally known as normal schools, in the 1800s, these programs in the normal schools and state universities did not address how to teach students with disabilities. This situation began to change in 1914 when a program to train teachers for students with intellectual impairment was established at the Michigan State Normal School (now known as **Eastern Michigan University**) in Ypsilanti, Michigan. In 1924 this program developed into the first Department of Special Education in the country after the state legislature designated funds to school districts desiring to offer classes for children who were blind and deaf. In 1939, the university opened the Rackham School, the first building specifically designed for training teachers of students with disabilities (Halmhuber & Rocklage 2014). Currently the Department offers programs leading to endorsements in all of the special education categories offered by the State of Michigan.

A Matter of Civil Rights

Even though public attitudes and teaching strategies with individuals with disabilities had dramatically changed over the years, the majority of school-aged children with disabilities in the 1950s and 1960s did not receive appropriate specialized instruction in their local public school unless they were fortunate enough to live in an area with a strong special education program. And many of those who did receive their education in their local public school did so in separate classes apart from their peers who were not disabled (Winzer 1993). This situation began to change with the rise of the **civil rights movement**. While the origins of this movement involved the civil rights of African Americans, the precedents established through litigation and legislation as well as public opinion extended to other disenfranchised groups, including individuals with disabilities (Rosenberg et al. 2011).

The landmark 1954 Supreme Court decision in *Brown v. Board of Education (Topeka, Kansas)* struck down the idea that a separate education could be an equal education. While the immediate impact of this decision involved the struggle to racially desegregate schools, this principle provided the foundation for the integration of students with disabilities with their peers without disabilities two decades later (Winzer 1993).

One principle that arose from the *Brown* decision involved a child's right to treatment. One case involved the Washington, D.C., school district that had excluded a group of seven children with various disabilities from school based on the financial stress the school was experiencing. In the 1972 decision in *Mills v. Board of Education (District of Columbia)*, the federal district court ruled that a district's financial hardship was not acceptable grounds for denying an education to children with disabilities.

In another 1972 decision, *PARC v. Commonwealth of Pennsylvania*, the federal district court ruled that the state must provide a free and appropriate public education to all students, including those with intellectual impairment. This ruling also included due process rights and parental notice (Richardson & Powell 2011).

Another aspect challenged in court during this time period involved the use of assessment for special education identification and placement. Although the California State Constitution guaranteed equal educational opportunities for every citizen, nine Mexican American children aged 8–13 had been placed into classes for intellectual impairment based on intelligence test results. In the 1970 decision in *Diana v. State Board of Education (California)*, the court ruled that the intelligence tests were inherently biased against culturally and linguistically diverse children and, therefore, using them resulted in violating the children's right to a free and appropriate education (Richardson & Powell 2011). This precedent was extended to African American students in the 1972 *Larry P. v. Riles* case, which also used intelligence tests for identification and placement. As a result of this case, California eliminated the use of intelligence tests in the identification of African American students for all categories of special education except learning disability.

Change through Legislation

Through litigation and efforts of reformers, by the mid-1970s American society was ready for change in how it dealt with the education and treatment of persons with disabilities. As a result, between 1973 and 2001 four major pieces of legislation expanded educational opportunities for individuals with disabilities.

The first, **Section 504 of the Rehabilitation Act** (1973), protects individuals with disabilities from discrimination due to their disabilities in any organization that receives any federal financial assistance. This act is especially helpful for students who have a disability but are not eligible for direct services. For example, a student may have a 504 Plan that provides accommodations or modifications in the classroom such as extended time on tests or a quiet study location. College students with disabilities can also take advantage of this act to receive similar accommodations. However, because Section 504 is a civil rights act, it guarantees equal access but does not provide direct services.

While Section 504 provides civil rights protection, the passage of the **Education for All Handicapped Children Act (P.L. 94-142)** in 1975 mandated that public schools must provide for the education of all school-aged students. In the years since the original passage of this act, it has undergone several revisions and a name change. Currently known as the **Individuals with Disability Educational Improvement Act (IDEIA),** the most recent revision was in 2004. This piece of legislation has fundamentally changed American education (Richardson & Powell 2011). Seeking to provide as normal an education as possible, IDEIA requires that students with disabilities receive their education in the least restrictive environment rather than in segregated settings. (See Chapter 21 for a more extensive discussion.)

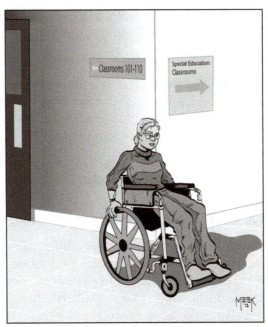

Figure 7   Even though P.L. 94-142 mandated a free appropriate public education for all children with disabilities, many schools segregated these students to special classrooms, sometimes whole wings of a building dedicated to special education

Illustration by Lloyd W. Meek

The impact of this legislation was far-reaching. As Winzer (1993) stated,

> Under this legislation exceptional children were, for the first time, accorded the right to a free and appropriate education in the least restrictive environment. Their parents or guardians were given the right of due process and confidentiality, and school boards were mandated to provide a range of educational services, an individual education plan for every exceptional student, and culturally fair testing. (382)

A third legislative act broadened the scope of access for persons with disabilities. The **Americans with Disabilities Act (ADA)**, passed in 1990, requires that all buildings be accessible to persons with disabilities (Rosenberg et al. 2011). The act applies to all segments of society, including recreation in addition to education and employment, although private schools and religious organizations are exempt. The act also provides other discrimination protection such as equal opportunity to participate and live independently in a community.

The fourth legislative act, the **No Child Left Behind Act (NCLB)**, passed in 2001, was actually the reauthorization of the Elementary and Secondary Acts (Rosenberg et al. 2011). While not an act dealing specifically with special education, it impacts all students, including those with disabilities. Although controversial, this legislation was an attempt to provide greater accountability for schools and educators. The main components of this act include

1. **Accountability for results** through state assessments. States use an *annual school report card* to describe these results on the basis of *annual yearly progress* (AYP) that is based on minimum benchmarks expected of each child. The law does allow schools to not assess 1% of students with disabilities and another 2% of students with disabilities may participate in an alternative assessment.

2. **Expanded flexibility and local school control** that allows school districts to distribute up to 50% of federal funds among a number of programs without getting prior federal approval.

3. **Teaching methods based on scientific research**, especially in the areas of literacy and mathematics.

4. **Expanded options for parents** that include the right for parents to transfer their children to a different school if the assigned school does not meet AYP for two consecutive years. In addition, if a school does not meet AYP for three consecutive years, the school must provide free tutoring and supplemental instruction. The law also provides expanded funding support for charter schools and Title 1 programs.

5. **Strengthened teacher quality** by requiring *Highly Qualified Teachers* that have appropriate licensure and are qualified to teach the core academic areas that they teach.

Current Education Trends that Impact Persons with Disabilities

A child with a disability entering school today encounters very different educational opportunities than even a few decades ago. Yet, despite the progress made, the education of children with disabilities remains uneven (P. Smith 2010). Efforts to provide more effective education to all students, not just those with disabilities, are currently centering around three trends: Inclusion, Response to Intervention, and Universal Design for Learning.

When PL 94-142 first became law, schools were required to integrate students with disabilities in general education classrooms as much as possible. Using the term *mainstreaming,* many students with disabilities were physically in the general education classroom but were not treated as an equal, integral member of the class. **Inclusion** involves much more than mere physical presence. In an inclusive classroom, all students are integral members, whether or not they have a disability. Inclusion demands close cooperation among all school staff, especially general and special education teachers. While many educators agree that inclusion is beneficial, translating that agreement into practice can be difficult. More information about inclusion is in Chapter 24.

Figure 8 Inclusion allows students with disabilities to be integral and equal members of a classroom

Illustration by Lloyd W. Meek

With the implementation of PL 94-142, the number of students with disabilities being served in their local schools mushroomed. In addition, people began to question the use of an intelligence/achievement discrepancy for identifying students with learning disabilities. In an effort to increase the accuracy of identification while giving students help without having to go through the formal identification practice, IDEA (2004) began to allow schools to use a **Response-to-Intervention (RtI)** approach. This three-tiered approach begins with high quality instruction for all students in a classroom at Tier 1. Teachers use universal screening to identify students who may be having difficulty. For these students, the teacher begins a special intervention within the classroom, often through group instruction, which is Tier 2. If a student does not respond to the Tier 2 intervention, he/she moves to Tier 3, which often involves one-on-one instruction, usually by a special education teacher. During Tier 3, a student may be formally referred for additional assessment or special education services. More information about RtI is in Chapter 28.

The third trend is the increasing use of **Universal Design for Learning (UDL)**, which uses multiple ways of presenting, assessing, and engaging the diversity of learners in a classroom. Based on principles originating in the field of architecture that integrates accessibility into original design rather than retrofitting, UDL allows teachers to present key information in multiple ways. For example, a teacher may use reading an article, watching a video, and presenting a slide show to teach the process of photosynthesis. More information about UDL is in Chapter 27.

Questions for Discussion

▶ What advantages do today's individuals with disabilities have over those born 50 years ago? 100 years ago? 500 years ago?

▶ Choose one or two of the people mentioned in this chapter and discuss how the work is or is not seen in today's American schools and society.

▶ In what way is education a civil right? Discuss how the civil rights movement has impacted both general and special education.

▶ Discuss why NCLB has been so controversial. What might be an alternative to NCLB?

Chapter 21

Individuals with Disabilities Education Act (IDEA)

David C. Winters

As noted in Chapter 20 the passage of the Education for All Handicapped Children Act (P.L. 94-142) in 1975 fundamentally changed American education (Richardson & Powell 2007), impacting both students with disabilities as well as those without disabilities. Since its original passage, the law has been reauthorized or amended in 1983, 1986, 1990, 1992, 1997, and 2004. As part of the 1990 reauthorization, Congress changed the name of the law from the Education for All Handicapped Children Act to the **Individuals with Disabilities Education Act (IDEA)*** (Rosenberg, Westling, & McLeskey 2011). Under the 2004 reauthorization, Part C of the Act provides services for children under the age of three and Part B provides services for children ages three through twenty-one (IDEA 2004).

By understanding the major components of IDEA, general educators, special educators, and families will be better able to work together to meet the needs of a child with disabilities. The seven major components of IDEA are (1) free appropriate public education (FAPE), (2) least restrictive environment (LRE), (3) zero reject, (4) nondiscriminatory evaluation, (5) parent participation, (6) procedural safeguards, and (7) the Individualized Education Program (IEP).

Free Appropriate Public Education (FAPE)

One of the fundamental changes brought to education by IDEA was the concept that every child has a right to a free appropriate public education (FAPE). While earlier governmental efforts encouraged states to provide education for their children with disabilities, the federal government did not require them to do so (Winzer 1993). That situation changed with the passage of IDEA, as the federal government now mandated that school districts provide an education for every child. This provision of FAPE ensures that the education of a child with a disability will be

- ▶ **Free**: Neither the child nor the child's family bears the cost for the child's education. The costs are the responsibility of the school district. To help school districts with the expense of educating children with disabilities, the federal government provides special education funding.
- ▶ **Appropriate**: The education the child receives must be appropriate for the child's disability and level of severity. The school must provide both direct and related educational services.
- ▶ **Public**: The child's local school district is responsible for the child's education. If the district cannot provide appropriate services for a child, it must pay for the child to receive those services elsewhere.

*From this point forward, this chapter will use *IDEA* when referring to the law originally known as the Education for All Handicapped Children Act and now known as the Individuals with Disabilities Education Act/Individuals with Disabilities Education Improvement Act.

▶ **Education**: The focus of IDEA is on a child's education rather than general life skills, although the two may be intermingled. Therefore, when determining eligibility for special education services, the multi-disciplinary team must show that a child's difficulty interferes with the child's learning in school. For example, if a child throws tantrums at home but not at school, the child would not be eligible for services under IDEA.

Least Restrictive Environment (LRE)

Closely related to FAPE is the concept of least restrictive environment. IDEA requires that a student's placement is to be as close to the typical general education setting as possible, while allowing services to be delivered in a setting that best meets the student's needs. When IDEA was first enacted, people used the term **mainstreaming** to describe LRE. For some students, mainstreaming meant that they were with their age peers during lunch or some other non-academic time. They might also sit in the general education classroom during an academic lesson but not participate in it. However, over the past several years, schools have begun giving a greater emphasis on **inclusion**, in which the student with disabilities is an equal and important member of the classroom community. While inclusion might be a worthy goal, over the years three types of placement for students with disabilities are common.

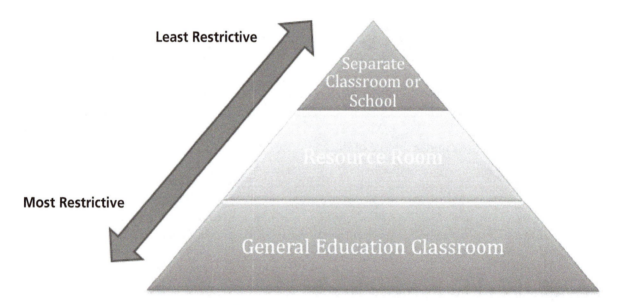

Figure 1 LRE Placements
Image courtesy of author

Zero Reject

School districts may not refuse to provide FAPE to any student with a disability, regardless of the level of severity of the disability. Therefore, IDEA does not allow a school to exclude a student because the child is considered uneducable, has significantly challenging behaviors, or has a communicable disease unless a threat to others' health exists. Even then, the school must provide educational services to the child.

Nondiscriminatory Evaluation

In addition to the provisions guaranteeing FAPE to students with disabilities, IDEA requires school districts to find and identify all children with a disability. They must determine if a child has a disability, and if so, whether the child needs special education and related services. A multidisciplinary team conducts this assessment. To ensure that assessment properly identifies children and does not discriminate against them by inappropriate assessment instruments or procedures, IDEA includes several requirements:

- ▶ Evaluation must be done in the child's primary language or mode of communication;
- ▶ A child cannot be identified on the basis of a single test or procedure;
- ▶ Assessment must include all areas of functioning related to the child's suspected disability;
- ▶ Only qualified personnel may conduct the assessment, and they must use validated tests;
- ▶ Tests and procedures must be unbiased, especially when assessing children who are culturally or linguistically diverse;
- ▶ Before assessment begins, schools must inform the child's parents or guardians and receive consent to do the assessment (Rosenberg et al. 2011);
- ▶ Children must be reevaluated every three years, unless both the parents/guardians and local school district agree.

The 2004 IDEA reauthorization also introduced the use of Response-to-Intervention (RtI) as an approach for the identification of children with learning disabilities. While IDEA does not require states to use RtI, it does require that states must permit school districts to use RtI instead of the traditional intelligence-achievement discrepancy criteria.

Parent Participation

Parents play a critical role in the assessment and educational planning for their child with a disability. IDEA requires that parents receive formal written notification

- ▶ When the school wants to evaluate a child
- ▶ For subsequent evaluations
- ▶ Before placing a child in special education
- ▶ Before exiting a child from special education (Turnbull, Turnbull, et al. 2011).

Because of IDEA, parents also have the right to participate in the decision-making process for their child. This right includes

- ▶ Being a member of the IEP team
- ▶ Participating in placement decisions
- ▶ Having access to their child's school records
- ▶ Participation on state and local special education advisory committees (Turnbull, Turnbull, et al. 2011).

Procedural Safeguards

IDEA also includes several procedural safeguards to protect children. IDEA includes these due process procedures to guard against (1) the exclusion of children, which is a violation of the zero reject provision, (2) misclassification, which is a violation of the nondiscriminatory evaluation provision, (3) denial of a genuine individualized education, which is a violation of the appropriate education provision, and (4) segregated placements, which is a violation of the least restrictive environment (Turnbull, Turnbull, et al 2011).

These procedural safeguards primarily include

- ▶ Providing adequate meeting notice to the parents/guardians
- ▶ Meeting at a mutually agreed-on time and place
- ▶ Notification when the school is considering changes in a child's educational programming or related services (Rosenberg et al. 2011).

If a child's parents and school cannot come to agreement about a child's eligibility, placement, or IEP, IDEA also includes a due process procedure. The first step in the procedure is for **mediation**. During the mediation step, an impartial, trained mediator works to achieve a successful resolution. If the issue remains unresolved, the second step is a formal **due process hearing**. During this step, both sides present their position and evidence to a due process hearing officer, who then makes a decision based on that information. If one of the parties does not want to accept the hearing officer's decision, the final step is to appeal the decision in **federal court** (Rosenberg et al. 2011).

IDEA also requires that all student information is confidential. Those working with this confidential student information must have training in appropriate records-management procedures. Additionally, parents have the right to inspect and review all information concerning their child (Rosenberg et al. 2011).

Schools have found that providing FAPE for children with severe behavioral problems can be difficult, especially when ensuring the least restrictive environment. A particularly troublesome issue involves student suspension or expulsion. IDEA requires that the school consider whether behavior that would normally result in a suspension or expulsion is a function of the child's disability. If it is a function of the child's disability, the school may not suspend the child for more than ten days. However, if the behavior involved bringing a dangerous weapon to school, selling or possessing illegal drugs, or causing serious bodily injury to someone either at school or at a school function, then the school may provide an alternative placement for up to forty-five school days. If the behavior is not a function of the student's disability, then the school may use the same disciplinary procedures as for all students. However, special education services for the child must continue (Rosenberg et al. 2011).

Individualized Education Program (IEP)

To ensure compliance with IDEA provisions and documentation of educational placement and planning for a child with a disability, each school-aged child eligible for services must have an **Individualized Education Program (IEP)**. Under Part C of IDEA, infants and toddlers to age 3 have their services documented in an **Individualized Family Services Plan (IFSP),** which is more family-focused. The following discussion will focus on the IEP.

Figure 2   The IEP consists of the child's parents, the child (when appropriate), general education teacher, special education teacher, someone who can interpret assessment such as a school psychologist, a local education agency representative, and other individuals who have knowledge or special expertise about the student

After a child's initial assessment, the IEP team meets to confirm eligibility for services, determine placement and related services, and plan progress and program goals for the coming year. Once a child begins receiving services, the IEP team meets annually to review and revise the IEP. While states and local school districts may develop their own IEP forms, IDEA requires the following components (Rosenberg, et al. 2011; Turnbull, Turnbull, et al. 2011; IDEA 2004):

▶ **Present Level of Academic Achievement and Functional Performance (PLAAFP).** The PLAAFP provides the rationale for a child's eligibility for services and the justification for placement, services, and annual goals. For a child to be eligible for special education services, the PLAAFP must discuss how the child's disability impacts performance in the general education curriculum. The PLAAFP includes data from various sources such as tests, observations, behavior reports, etc. Some children's PLAAFPs may focus on the child's academic achievement such as reading, writing, and math. Other children's PLAAFPs may primarily include information about functional performance such as self-help skills, attention, behavior, and oral language. Still other children's PLAAFPs may include both academic achievement and functional performance.

▶ **Annual Goals.** For each area of need identified in the child's PLAAFP, the IEP team develops annual goals. These goals must be measurable and appropriate for meeting the needs of the child for progress in the general curriculum. Annual goals should include
   • A measurable, observable behavior (Note: *Understand, thinks,* or *feels* are not measurable and should not be used in an annual goal)
   • The conditions under which the child will do the behavior
   • The criteria for determining whether the child has met the goal

Figure 3 Thinking About Activity	
For each of the annual goal examples below, determine if it is well written or not. Explain your reasoning. If it is not well written, suggest ways to improve it.	
Example 1	Jerry will correctly spell multisyllabic words containing closed, open, and silent-e syllables with 90% accuracy on a dictated spelling test.
Example 2	Weston will improve his spelling.
Example 3	Francine will use an assistive technology device to communicate her personal care needs at least four times each day according to a behavior checklist.
Example 4	Samantha will develop strategies for critical reading.
Example 5	Jackson will understand how to write an expository essay.

▶ **Short-term Objectives/Benchmarks.** Beginning with the 2004 reauthorization of IDEA, IEP teams only need to include short-term objectives or benchmarks for annual goals if the child participates in alternative assessment. Short-term objectives come from an analysis of the task/behavior contained in the annual goal. Using this task analysis, the IEP team determines intermediate steps that the child needs to achieve in order to meet the annual goal. Benchmarks are similar to short-term objectives but indicate specific time intervals.

▶ **Measurement of Annual Goals.** The IEP must include how progress on each annual goal will be measured. In addition, the document must state the manner, frequency, and to whom this progress is reported.

▶ **Special Education and Related Services.** The IEP must state the exact special education and related services, accommodations, and modifications that the child will receive as well as who will implement them. This statement also includes supplementary aids and services, such as assistive technology, occupational therapy, speech-language therapy, positive behavior supports, etc. Beginning with the 2004 reauthorization, IDEA requires the IEP team to consider assistive technology for every student eligible for services under the act.

▶ **Extent of Nonparticipation with Students without Disabilities.** To ensure that the IEP meets the IDEA LRE requirement, the IEP must include a statement of how much time, if any, the student will not participate with students without disabilities in the general education environment. This statement may include classroom, extracurricular, and nonacademic activities.

▶ **State and Local Assessment Accommodations.** The IEP must indicate what, if any, accommodations will be made for the child on state and local assessments. If the IEP team determines that the child is eligible for alternative assessment, this section of the IEP must provide justification why the child cannot participate in the regular assessment and why the alternative assessment is appropriate.

▶ **Projected Start Date.** The IEP must include the start date for the services included in it. This section also includes the anticipated frequency, duration, and location for each of the services.

▶ **Transition Planning.** If not earlier, beginning with the IEP following a child's sixteenth birthday, the IEP must include goals and services to prepare the child for postsecondary life. Like the rest of the IEP, the IEP team reviews and revises these goals each year. In addition, at least one year before the child reaches the state's age of maturity, which is often eighteen, the IEP must include a statement that the child has been informed of the rights under IDEA that will transfer from the parents to the child once he/she reaches that age of maturity.

For additional information about writing an IEP, an excellent resource is the *Guide to Writing Quality Individualized Education Programs* (2nd Edition) (2007) by Gordon Gibb and Tina Dyches.

Questions for Discussion

▶ What impact might IDEA have on you in your work, family, or community?

▶ Have students with disabilities been in your classes in elementary or secondary school? How did the school provide LRE for these students? What was the impact on your own education?

▶ Describe the difference between *mainstreaming* and *inclusion*.

▶ While many educators express concern about the amount of paperwork needed to complete the IEP, what might be the benefit to the student?

▶ What are the benefits of well-written annual goals?

Chapter 22

The Process of Labeling: Is Getting a Disability Like Catching a Cold?

Phil Smith

"... we don't want that label anymore ... You are experts in your field, but I am an expert too, in my own field. I lived in the institution, and I lived in a group home." (Monroe 1994, 9)

How is it that people are labeled as having a disability? That's been a question I've been asking for a long time. We "know" that some people have a disability just by looking at them—we can "see" the disability, and label them as having a disability because we see it. They're called visible disabilities. A person's appearance determines whether a person has a disability, and what disability they have. People who use wheelchairs are an example of visible disabilities. So are people who are missing body parts. Some people with very different facial characteristics are said to have visible disabilities, too. I've often wondered, though, what the dividing line is—how much difference "makes" a disability?

Other disabilities are invisible. Invisible disabilities are disabilities that people are said to have, but that you can't tell if someone has them just by looking at them. Sometimes psychiatric disabilities are invisible, as are intellectual disabilities. Multiple sclerosis is another example. So is muscular dystrophy. And learning disabilities.

The process by which people with disabilities are labeled as having a disability often happens in special education. The process of being assigned a disability label, and of being placed in special education is not a voluntary one. Students with disabilities—and often families—don't usually have a personal choice about whether or not they will receive special education services. And a great deal of stigma is attached to being in special education:

no matter what kinds of overt lessons are taught at the school about respect for difference or other such seemingly committed agendas with weak impact, the hidden curriculum, the stronger message, is that children in special education are different, incompetent and unsavory ... Expectations that the school, the disabled and nondisabled students, the parents, and the teachers have are inevitably lowered by these designations. Most damaging of all, the negative expectations are assimilated and internalized by the disabled children with devastating long-term consequences. (Linton 1998, 63)

The impact of getting a label of disability has negative effects on people, and on communities—we've known that for a long time. And yet it is something that we continue to do (P. Smith 1999). Why? There must be something about labeling people with disabilities that benefits at least someone. Who benefits? And how?

Stigma

Image © Sam72, 2014. Used under license from Shutterstock, Inc.

What is stigma? The word comes from the ancient Greek, and meant, back then, a mark on the body. In those long-ago times, someone who did something wrong, or was felt to be morally wrong, would be marked in some way, by a brand perhaps, or some other permanent mark on the outside of the body. This marking was done to let others know what the person had done that was wrong. Later, naturally-occurring marks (birthmarks, for example) were taken to be a kind of stigmata—that is, a mark indicating something about a person's moral nature or character.

A disability, at times, was (and is) seen as this kind of physical marking, indicating that a person might have done something wrong before they were born, or that the person's parents or ancestors did something wrong. In a way, this kind of physical marking of a person's body was (and still is) seen as a kind of punishment for some wrong-doing.

Erving Goffman wrote fifty years ago what is taken to be the most important work about this topic, in a book called *Stigma: Notes on the Management of Spoiled Identity* (1963). He describes the idea of stigma in this way:

> While the stranger is present before us, evidence can arise of his possessing an attribute that makes him different from others in the category of persons available for him to be, and of a less desireable kind—in the extreme, a person who is quite thoroughly bad, or dangerous, or weak. He is thus reduced in our minds from a whole and usual person to a tainted, discounted one. Such an attribute is a stigma, especially when its discrediting effect is very extensive; sometimes it is also called a failing, a shortcoming, a handicap. (3)

The idea behind this is that we make assumptions about how people should act, should look, should dress, in our culture. We make these assumptions unconsciously, without thinking about them. Those assumptions are based on our own background, including race, class, gender, and so forth, and where we fit (or not) in those categories. And we go around in the world carrying those unnoticed assumptions with us. When others that come into our lives fit into those categories in the ways that we assume they should, all is well. When someone doesn't fit into those categories—doesn't meet the assumptions we have about them—in the ways that Goffman describes, then we say that such a person is impacted by stigma, that their identity is stigmatized. And as Goffman indicates, people with disabilities typically experience stigma.

I should point out that stigma is a pretty relative idea, and is a function of how our culture looks at people, and what our individual place in the culture is. A person with an identified disability might not see another person with a disability as stigmatized, depending on the disability of each person. A person from the upper-, rich class might see someone living in poverty as being stigmatized by that poverty. Another person, from a different class position, and/or a different idea about the meaning of class, and/or from a different culture, might perceive such a person differently.

Goffman identifies three basic kinds of stigma:

> First there are abominations of the body—the various physical deformities. Next there are blemishes of individual character perceived as weak will, domineering or unnatural passions, treacherous and rigid beliefs, and dishonesty, these being inferred from a known record of, for example, mental disorder, imprisonment, addiction, alcoholism, homosexuality, unemployment, suicidal attempts, and radical political behavior. Finally there are the tribal stigma of race, nation, and religion, these being stigma that can be transmitted through lineages and equally contaminate all members of a family. (4)

Interestingly, Goffman describes people who do not perceive themselves as stigmatized as "normals" (5). What counts as normal, and what counts as stigmatized, are clearly culturally maintained and organized identities. And the stories we tell ourselves about what normal is, and who normal is, as well as what and who is stigmatized—these stories are ideologies.

The Hardening of Disability Labels

Once a disability label is assigned to a person, a process begins that is called reification. Reification means to reify something—to make it concrete. The words reification and reify come from the Latin word re, for thing—in a sense, the word reify means to "thing-ify"—indicating that the word means to make what was an idea into a thing.

What does that mean, and what's it got to do with disability labels? Remember that disability is socially constructed—it's something that our culture has made up, or constructed. Disability is an idea that our culture brought into existence. By labeling people as having a disability, we assign the idea of disability to groups of people, and to individuals, within our society. In a way, through the process of reification, the disability idea, the disability label, becomes real in the body and mind of the person who has been labeled.

And people who know that a person has been labeled as having a disability assume that the disability label is real and true—that the person certainly and definitely has that thing. Going a bit further, the person and the disability become one thing, the same thing. The person is the disability, and the disability is the person. Everything that the disabled person does is a reflection of their disability. We can't see the person, can't understand who they are and their place in the world, except through the lens of disability. They become the disability; they are the disability made flesh in the world.

Who Benefits from Being Labeled as Having a Disability?

So who benefits from a disability label? Common sense would say that it is the disabled person—as a result of getting a disability label, they will receive specialized services in the school, medical field, and in the community. They will become employed, live a good life, because they get the supports they need.

I wish that was how it worked. But it isn't. People with disabilities mostly live in poverty, have high rates of unemployment, are segregated at school, are more likely to end up in prison, experience high levels of violence and abuse in their lives. In other words: their lives suck.

Who benefits from the labeling of disabled people? Mostly, its people without disabilities. An entire multi-faceted disability industry has been created for people with disabilities, an industry that makes billions and billions of dollars in the United States, money that goes to professionals, administrators, and business people. Professionals get a lot from this disability industry: teachers, doctors, nurses, rehabilitation specialists, employment specialists, social workers, professors—they earn degrees, write books (like this one), get decent jobs with good pay, and are praised by society for being "patient" and "doing good deeds"—all on the backs of people with disabilities.

This is partly the result of something called commodification—the process by which a socio-cultural identity, issue, or problem gets turned into a commodity, something that can get bought and sold, something that makes money. In this case, disability is turned into a commodity—a commodity that makes lots of money, for lots of people, just mostly NOT people with disabilities. The disability that some people in our culture are said to have is turned into something that requires supports and services for them to live their lives, supports and services that are provided by a wide range of professionals and support workers that earn good wages in roles that are widely respected in our society. People with disabilities get no social benefit from the commodification of their so-called impairments (P. Smith 1999; 2006).

Overrepresentation

People are labeled because of the ways we think about people, and the roles they have (and are allowed to have) in our culture. People are labeled as having disabilities because of the stigma that we apply to particular body shapes and sizes; particular ways of acting and thinking; and particular groups that exist in our culture.

People from different groups, and their actions, behaviors, thinking, and ideas, have been widely medicalized in Western culture. That is, people whose behavior or thinking has been seen as stigmatized have been formally diagnosed as having a disability. For example, psychiatrists use a book called the DSM, or the *Diagnostic and Statistical Manual of Mental Disorders*, published by the American Psychiatric Association, as a way to decide who has what psychiatric disability, and what the symptoms are. For many years, homosexuality was described as a mental disorder in the DSM. It's only relatively recently that it is no longer seen as a mental disorder.

In somewhat the same way, people with social identities that are stigmatized by the dominant elements in U.S. culture have been given disability labels in part because their cultural position is seen to be outside what is normal. Sometimes, the word overrepresentation is used to describe this phenomenon—a group is said to be overrepresented in a particular disability category when the percentage of people from that group who are said to have a particular disability is greater than would be expected.

I'll give you an example. African Americans, particularly African American young men, are more apt to be labeled as having intellectual disabilities, than whites—in fact, they are three times as likely to get that label as whites. African American young men are more apt to be labeled as having emotional disabilities than are whites. African Americans, African Caribbeans, and South Asians are more apt to be labeled as having psychiatric disabilities when compared to the general population. And once identified as having a disability—Down syndrome, for example—people from racially marginalized groups are more apt to die earlier than are whites. In this context, African American young men are overrepresented in the disability category of intellectual disability, and also are overrepresented in special education (Smith 2004).

What appears to be true is NOT that African American young men are more likely to be intellectually inferior to whites (although that is a story that is told by some educators and modern eugenicists—see Herrnstein and Murray's infamous book, *The Bell Curve: Intelligence and Class Structure in American Life*, published in 1994). Instead, because of racist perceptions of some racial and ethnic groups, founded on racist ideology that is inherent and foundational to U.S. culture, people from those groups are seen as inferior in many ways, including intellectually and emotionally, to dominant groups (Smith 2004).

Questions for Discussion

▶ Who benefits from the overrepresentation of African Americans with labels of intellectual disabilities and emotional-behavioral disability?

▶ Have you ever experienced stigma in your life? What did it feel like?

Chapter 23

The Segregation of People with Disabilities

Phil Smith

"The oppressive silencing of even one voice through any form of segregation eliminates that set of experiences from our collective conversation and diminishes the culture of the community." (Kliewer 1998, 5)

People with disabilities, particularly those said to have significant disabilities, including those with intellectual, developmental, and psychiatric disabilities, have been segregated from the rest of Western society for a long time. Many think that this intentional segregation has long since ended, but this is far from being the case. People with disabilities—children in schools, as well as adults—continue to be systematically excluded from the mainstream of civic and educational communities. Much of this is a result of the discrimination, oppression, and marginalization that people with disabilities experience daily (P. Smith 1999). While legally (de jure) racial integration has been in place for a few decades (although it can be argued that such integration is not complete in fact, or de facto), the segregation of people with disabilities remains something that is permitted, even sometimes required, in the United States and elsewhere in Western societies.

Civic Segregation

The segregation of people with psychiatric disabilities has a particularly long history in Western culture. In England, the most notable institution for people with psychiatric disabilities was a place called Bedlam, by all reports an awful, horrible place to live. The word Bedlam itself has entered common English and American vernacular, indicating a situation of some chaos and disorder.

At the beginning of United States history, responsibility for impoverished or homeless persons was the responsibility of local communities. They were typically provided for in so-called poorhouses (often in more urban environments) or poor farms (typically in more rural settings). There, inhabitants often engaged in labor in partial compensation for housing and support provided to them. Many such impoverished or homeless persons included people that we would recognize now as having psychiatric or developmental disabilities. While families were seen as being responsible for providing support to people seen as having significant disabilities, sometimes families (for a variety of reasons) were unable to provide that support, and so their support devolved to local communities (Nielsen 2012).

In the early part of the nineteenth century, progressives sought to teach people with intellectual and developmental disabilities, often in places away from the mainstream of civic communities. They did so with an eye toward providing them the skills needed to return to their local communities able to live in ways in which they contributed to the needs of those communities.

At the same time, other progressive groups (notably the Quakers) established small communities in which people with psychiatric disabilities might spend short, relatively defined amounts of time recovering from periods we might recognize now as a psychiatric break. These communities offered people said to have psychiatric disabilities good food, music, art, and other cultural activities, in an atmosphere of low stress, in which they might gain the strength (emotional, mental, and physical) to return to their home communities. The expectation—as well as the reality—was that people could and would recover on their own, and return to being productive members of their community. Such thinking is, of course, contrary to modern thinking of much of the medical community, in people with significant psychiatric disabilities are seen as never being able to recover, to get better (Whittaker 2001; 2010).

In the latter part of the nineteenth into the early part of the twentieth century, in the United States, partly under the influence of the so-called eugenics movement, increasingly large numbers of people identified as having psychiatric and developmental disabilities were sent to large state-run institutions for their support and care. Along with people that we would identify as having disabilities, people perceived at the time as being of low moral character were sent to such institutions. These included people from racial and ethnic minorities, people living in poverty, and even women who were mothers of children born out of wedlock.

Again, all of this was under the influence of the eugenics movement, which sought to create a better society by removing from it people seen to harm the social and genetic good (as portrayed by white, middle- and upper-class men). As part of this forced segregation as directed by eugenicists (many of whom were perceived as being quite progressive at the time), large numbers of people with psychiatric and developmental disabilities (as well as people outside of the dominant social groups) were legally prevented from marrying, and forcibly sterilized against their will, or without their knowledge or consent.

This system of forced segregation and institutionalization began as an effort to protect people with disabilities from a society that some thought would harm them. With the coming of the eugenics movement, people with a wide range of disabilities were forcibly institutionalized in order to protect the mainstream of society, the belief being that they would harm the fabric of social and genetic good in the United States. Later, any real rationale for their institutionalization was lost—they were just locked up, that being simply what was done (Wolfensberger 1975).

Throughout much of the twentieth century, the number of people with psychiatric, intellectual, and developmental disabilities who were institutionalized in large, state-run institutions rose steadily and consistently. Their numbers peaked as late as in the early 1970s, when they slowly began to fall. The so-called deinstitutionalization movement began to gather steam in the 1960s. Senator Robert Kennedy, whose brother John became President of the United States, and who had a sister with intellectual disabilities living in an institution, visited institutions and found horrific conditions (Shapiro 1993). A critical exposé was undertaken by Syracuse University Professor Burton Blatt and photographer Fred Kaplin. They published a book, *Christmas in Purgatory*, in 1966 (1974), which included a series of photographs with accompanying text describing life and conditions in institutions for people with developmental disabilities in the northeast U.S. A few years later, journalist Geraldo Rivera made a for-television film exposing conditions at an institution on Long Island, called Willowbrook.

Since that time, the number of people with developmental, intellectual, and psychiatric disabilities institutionalized in large state-run (and funded, at least partially, by the federal government) institutions has declined. A number of states have completely closed their large institutions for people with intellectual and developmental disabilities. The first of these was New Hampshire, followed closely by Vermont, and then (not in this order) Alaska, District of Columbia, Hawaii, Maine, Michigan, Minnesota, New Mexico, Oregon, and West Virginia (Larson, Salmi, et al. 2013).

As of this writing, however, most of the fifty states—thirty-nine at last count—still run large institutions for people with intellectual and developmental disabilities, and many tens of thousands of people throughout the country are still forced to live in them. Even in the states in which large institutions are closed, people remain institutionalized. In Michigan, for example, which closed its Mount Pleasant Center in 2009, some people labeled as having intellectual and developmental disabilities continue to live in institutions with as many as fifty so-called residents. All states have at least some group homes. Only one state has congregate-living settings no larger than six people (Vermont); all other states have at least some settings larger than that.

And some analyses assert that the number of people receiving residential supports outside of their home has actually grown. For people with intellectual and developmental disabilities, that number was a bit less than 250,000 in 1977. By 2009, it had grown to almost 450,000, coming very close to doubling in a little more than twenty years (Larson, Lakin, et al. 2010).

For people with psychiatric disabilities, the situation is even more grave. Only one state (again, Vermont) has closed its state-run facility for people with psychiatric disabilities. The other forty-nine states have at least one such institution. And the system of community services for people with psychiatric disabilities in every state is a complicated and confusing mess, which often leaves at least some people falling through the cracks. At least partly as a result, jails and prisons have become the social service system of last resort for many (P. Smith 2005).

Even where people with disabilities are physically integrated into civic communities, they remain socially segregated. They may live *in* communities, but are often not a part *of* them. This is especially true for people with intellectual and developmental disabilities, who often do not have the kinds of social connections that people not labeled with disabilities take as a matter of course (Newman et al. 2009; Siperstein, Kersh, & Bardon 2007).

Wherever people live, whether they have a disability or not, having a choice about where to live is something many of us take for granted. Whether it is inside or outside of an institution, being able to choose where one lives, and with whom, seems such a basic and inherent condition, even a right, that it is rarely spoken of. Yet for people with developmental disabilities, not even half report that they choose where to live, and even fewer say they choose with whom they live (National Association of State Directors of Developmental Disabilities Services 2010).

Where one lives is only one element of the ways in which people with disabilities are segregated and excluded. In the area of employment, as one example, only 21% of working-age people with disabilities are employed (Kessler Foundation/National Organization on Disability 2010). That means that 79% are unemployed. As you read this, compare that number to the number of overall people in the United States who are unemployed, and you can't help but see a huge, monumental disparity in life experiences between people with and without disabilities.

Impossibly, it gets worse. People with intellectual, developmental, and psychiatric disabilities are sometimes employed in so-called sheltered workshops. By federal law (Section 14(c) of the Fair Labor Standards Act), sheltered workshops can pay people less—sometimes much, much less—than minimum wage. One-quarter of people working in sheltered workshops make less than $1 an hour—again, I want to emphasize that all of this is *sanctioned by federal labor law*. Only one state has closed down all of its sheltered workshops for people with developmental disabilities—can you guess which one (Rogan & Rinne 2011)? Given that, the use of the term "employment" in relation to sheltered workshops seems quite a bit more than just a little ironic—they constitute what many would argue are state-sanctioned sweatshops, even slave labor. Such conditions, if they occurred in countries like China, India, or other foreign countries, would give rise to calls for ending flagrant civil and human rights abuses.

Employment is only one way that people with disabilities are segregated from others in the United States, no matter where they live. Similar arguments, just as, if not more egregious, could be made in regards to access to health care (quality or otherwise), lifespan, leisure activities, wealth (or more accurately, its lack), freedom from violence and abuse—the list goes on and on, and the statistics start to become almost numbing in their intensity and volume. Perhaps it should not be surprising that, in all of these areas, including in residential and employment segregation, people coming from racially and ethnically diverse groups, experience substantially worse outcomes, although given the horrific nature of overall outcomes for people with disabilities, that might almost seem impossible that there could be worse ones. One area of particular note, however, is the segregation of students with disabilities in education.

Educational Segregation

"All disabled children, not just those who can be more readily assimilated in mainstream society, should be learning together" (Linton 2006, 163).

Into the 1970s (long after huge and sometimes violent civil rights actions, in which schools were forced to be racially integrated), school systems were not required to educate students with disabilities. And especially for those with so-called significant disabilities, school systems in large measure chose not to do so. It was not until the mid-1970s with the passage of the federal law initially called P. L. 94-142 (now known as the Individuals with Disabilities Educational Improvement Act, or IDEIA), that schools were required to meet the educational needs of students with disabilities. In one sense, given that so many students with disabilities were completely left out of the system of public education, the fact that there is a system of safeguards, rules, regulations, and laws in place to guarantee their right to learn in public education, seems like a huge gain. And in many ways it is; I don't want to imply the opposite in what follows.

But the fact remains, for anyone who takes more than the merest cursory glance at the realities of education at the beginning of the twenty-first century, that the "segregation and marginalization of disabled children are still the norm" (Linton 2006, 62). The facts are plain, simple, and undeniable. The truth is that most students with disabilities spend at least some of their time outside of general education classrooms. This is true not just in the United States; it is a global phenomenon. As a result, because they do not have access to the general education curriculum, compared to students without disabilities, they experience negative social as well as academic outcomes (Janus 2009; P. Smith 2010; World Health Organization 2011).

Perhaps the most horrific example is that of students with intellectual disabilities. Only a bit over 11% of students with intellectual disabilities, nationally, spend most (not *all*, but *most*) of their time in general education classrooms—they are said to be "fully" included (although, given the way that these things are counted, that means that they may spend as much as 20% of their time away from general education classrooms, not a small amount of time). That means that more than 79% of students with intellectual disabilities spend very substantial amounts of time away from the general education curriculum (P. Smith 2010).

In many states, the number of students with intellectual disabilities who are "fully" included is much less than 11%. In Michigan—which ranks 43 in the country for the inclusion of students with intellectual disabilities—only about 5% of students with intellectual disabilities are "fully" included. There are, perhaps obviously, some states with numbers much worse than that (P. Smith 2010).

These numbers are played out in other disability areas as well. Around the country, less than one-third of students with emotional/behavioral disabilities are "fully" included. And 4.2% of students receiving special education supports and services, of whatever disability type, do so completely outside general education settings, in institutional or residential placements (P. Smith 2010).

OK, so those numbers aren't terrific. In fact, they're pretty bad. But given that *most* students with disabilities didn't receive necessary supports and services in general education settings before the mid-1970s, that's still an improvement, right? For students with intellectual disabilities, from nothing to 11%, that's still a pretty decent improvement, correct? Slow but steady wins the day, some might say.

But that's not the whole story. Sticking with students with intellectual disability labels, the picture is more grim than that—much more. Because while the percentage of such students included in general education grew from the 1970s through the 1990s, it appears that the percentage of students "fully" included since that time has, at best, leveled off. And there is some indication that the percentage is actually reversing itself, going back down. We may have seen—and now passed—the peak of inclusion. Woot.

What are the reasons for this change for the worst? It's complicated. Reasons seem to differ from state to state. The so-called federal No Child Left Behind Act is probably implicated. But a central and foundational reason for the continued, wholesale exclusion of students with disabilities in schools is that

The whole institution of special education may have been founded on a desire to assure disabled children access to education, but I believe its continuation rests, in part, on an unconscious wish to contain and control children considered undesirable. (Linton 2006, 159)

And although Linton implies that continued exclusion is unconscious, I'd suggest that it's not JUST unconscious—that there are many teachers, administrators, families, and community members who seek intentionally to "contain and control." There are some students who are just not welcome in districts, schools, and classrooms.

Fortunately, not all states are doing so poorly as I've indicated here—a couple of states (but just, almost literally, a couple) have *substantially* higher rates of inclusion (although they have, in at least one case, also shown the greatest decrease in their rates of inclusion). But as a social and educational goal, moving toward inclusion is not something that schools and communities in the United States, as a whole, are leaping to embrace (P. Smith 2010).

Race has a LOT to do with segregation for students with disabilities. Students from minority backgrounds are much more likely to be segregated than are whites (LeRoy & Lacey 2010). Simply: "segregation and marginalization of disabled children are still the norm" (Linton 2006, 62).

What is the solution? Well, it's probably a set of solutions, and to do the discussion justice would probably take another book. Revising IDEIA would be one step; eliminating No Child Left Behind would be another.

Training teachers differently would be another important change. Instead of offering only one course focused on disability issues for pre-service teachers—that's the norm around the country, by the way (P. Smith 2010)—requiring additional course work would be a step in the right direction (including course work in classroom management/community building). And "let's train all teachers to utilize a flexible repertoire of approaches to teach a broad range of learners" (Linton 2006, 162). Providing inservice and preservice educators with the knowledge and skills they need—including co-teaching, collaboration, and creative problem-solving—to work in inclusive schools is essential. Understanding how to deliver appropriate curricular modifications and accommodations is important. Eliminating the boundaries—some call them silos—in teacher education programs, between general and special education, will be critical. Putting disability studies (like the content in this book) and critical theory at the foundation of teacher preparation is a change worth implementing (P. Smith 2010).

Finally, we'll need to begin a conversation—probably initiated by grassroots teachers, and people like you, in which special education is "reconceptualized as a set of services that are available to children who need them, without the need for a disability label" (Harry & Klingner 2006, 175). This will require dismantling special education as we know it—really, *education as a whole* (P. Smith 2010). Big changes; big work. And absolutely essential.

Conclusions? What can we know and understand about the lives of people with disabilities given this discussion? From the beginning of life to its end; from early childhood, through school, and on through adulthood, people with disabilities in the United States continue to experience dramatic, sometimes horrifying and unconscionable degrees of segregation, regardless of disability label, and across a plethora of life domains. Such segregation remains almost entirely invisible to people without disabilities, unless they have a friend, colleague, or loved one with a disability. Even then, such segregation is simply accepted as the status quo, the way things are, how it's supposed to be, even in twenty-first-century America. When compared to other minority groups, such segregation is at minimum striking; at most, it shines a laser-targeted spotlight on the values and public policies of a country held up by some to be the most free, the most democratic, of any in the world.

Chapter 24

Inclusion— From Societal Influences to Classroom Realities

Janet Fisher

On a daily basis, we are bombarded by stereotypes, labels, standards, norms, and many other linguistic concepts that perpetuate the marginalization of individuals. As a result, high potential people are kept from many opportunities to contribute their talents to communities and society at large. A very prominent example of this kind of labeling is "disability." A variety of sources provide definitions which perpetuate the idea of inadequacy. According to the Oxford Dictionary, a disability is "a physical or mental condition that limits a person's movements, senses, or activities; a disadvantage or handicap, especially one imposed or recognized by the law." The Bing Dictionary defines disability as: "restricted capability to perform particular activities: an inability to perform some or all of the tasks of daily life" and includes synonyms such as: "incapacity, infirmity, frailty, debility, ill health." Mosby's Medical Dictionary describes the etymology of the Latin origin being "*dis,* opposite of, *habilis,* fit; and the loss, absence, or impairment of physical or mental fitness." The prefix "dis" is currently used as slang and means to "treat disrespectfully … criticize somebody or something" (Bing Dictionary). Synonyms include: "insult, affront, disrespect, belittle, disparage, denigrate, lessen, put down" (Bing Dictionary)."

The word disability may actually defeat or at least delay positive outcomes by imposing a mindset that a problem needs to be fixed. A more helpful way of replacing "disability" might be correlated with something every human being possesses—that of meeting needs.

Image © iQoncept, 2014. Used under license from Shutterstock, Inc.

Merriam-Webster defines need as: "necessary duty; obligation; a lack of something requisite, desirable, or useful; a physiological or psychological requirement for the well-being of an organism; a condition requiring a supply or relief; lack of the means of subsistence: poverty." We all have needs resulting from many factors including:

age,　　　　gender,　　　families....　　　　　　　　　　　　　　　　　　genetics,

health,　　　　accidents,　　　life-choices,　　　temperaments,　　　learning styles,

Images top row: © grum_l, Nina Buday, Monkey Business Images, Andy Dean Photography, Nina Buday, mathagraphics, 2014. Used under license from Shutterstock, Inc.
Images bottom row: © everything possible, Zern Liew, Kesu, alphaspirit, iQoncept, 2014. Used under license from Shutterstock, Inc.

developmental levels, experiences, addictions, etc. Meeting needs through maximizing strengths while supporting challenges can help us embrace a new normal when helping students with special needs to realize their optimal potential.

The following chart represents how we can conceptualize disability in contrast to meeting a human need which expresses action and hope while disability simply describes an undesirable condition.

Disability Condition Reactive/Controlling *Assumed Deficits*	**Meeting a Human Need** Action Proactive/Supportive *Presumed Competence*
A physical or mental condition that limits a person's movements, senses, or activities (Oxford Dictionary)	Necessary duty (Merriam-Webster)
A disadvantage or handicap, especially one imposed or recognized by law (Oxford Dictionary)	Obligation (Merriam-Webster)
Restricted capability to perform particular activities (Bing Dictionary)	Lack of something requisite, desirable, or useful (Merriam-Webster)
An inability to perform some or all of the tasks of daily life (Bing Dictionary)	A physiological or psychological requirement for the well-being of an organism (Merriam-Webster)
Incapacity, infirmity, frailty, debility, ill health (Bing Dictionary)	A condition requiring a supply or relief (Merriam-Webster)
Opposite of fit (Mosby's Medical Dictionary)	Require something in order to have success or achieve a goal (Bing Dictionary)
Loss, absence, or impairment of physical or mental fitness (Mosby's Medical Dictionary)	Be necessary: used to indicate that a course of action is desirable or necessary (Bing Dictionary)

Image courtesy of author

Presumed Competence vs. Assumed Deficits

The emphasis on presumed competence in students encourages educators to believe that all students are capable of learning the general education curriculum in the general education classroom (Donnellan 1984). Changing our attitude promotes a current as well as future quality of life to which all students are entitled.

Donnellan (1984) proposed the criterion of least dangerous assumption for educators to consider when planning education programming and outcomes for students confronted with learning difficulties. This philosophy encourages educational decisions that challenge students to reach levels of learning that may not be reached if we become complacent and let perceived deficits limit our expectations for individual student achievement.

A number of key factors show the benefits of the inclusive approach to education.

Inclusion Considerations

Intelligence tests do not measure what students can do with appropriate educational supports.

Successfully helping people to communicate has opened a whole new world to those who otherwise were seen as incapable of learning (i.e., Helen Keller).

Our job is to determine what supporting interventions are needed to break down any communication and learning barriers.

Talk less and wait longer. Give students a chance to learn and tell us what they know at their own pace. How many times have we interrupted their hidden brilliance?

Be their cheerleader!

Encourage every approximation of behavior toward the eventual

Capitalize on their strengths—let them shine in front of their peers by using their talents.

We each possess a desire to belong (Maslow, Frager, & Fadiman 1997; Glasser 1999) and a unique capacity to contribute to society. To insure every individual is afforded the opportunity to make their contribution, strengths need to be recognized and talents must be developed. When the deficit model is replaced with the strength based model, people are encouraged and given the freedom to find new enjoyment in learning and self-expression of capabilities.

Garcia and Guerra (2004) and Valencia (1997) addressed the "deficit thinking model" as experienced by students at the classroom level:

Teachers attribute student failure in school to the student's own deficiencies including ability, linguistic challenges, or parents and families rather than to school policies or specific teacher treatment. Teachers who are guided by this deficit perspective will often misunderstand causal factors contributing to a student's failure.

Image © Zurijeta, 2014. Used under license from Shutterstock, Inc.

The "deficit thinking model" places responsibility on the person who is in need of being "fixed," while disregarding the school environment in which students are often being confronted by physical, cognitive, and emotional triggers that can circumvent the learning process.

In contrast, inclusion should be preferred as a model for educating students because it provides the necessary supports to help them achieve their potential. Educational inclusion is a method of instructing students with specific learning and/or behavior needs in the general education classroom.

Proponents of inclusion maintain that the general education classroom should be the starting point for students. Additional educational supports and adaptations deemed necessary are provided to all students and emanate from this foundational opportunity to co-exist and learn with peers.

Image © Batshevs, 2014. Used under license from Shutterstock, Inc.

An earlier held concept known as mainstreaming determined that many students with various learning needs were placed in a special setting allowing them to enter the mainstream only when they could "fit in" to the prevailing activity.

Image © 2jenn, 2014. Used under license from Shutterstock, Inc.

Students with learning and behavioral challenges have traditionally had the most transitions within a school day as they made their way from the special education to the general education classroom and back again. This attempt to help students gain social and academic time with their peers has been complicated by this disruptive daily migration. The benefit of routine and a predictable environment has often been elusive to the very group of students who need it the most.

Image © khz, 2014. Used under license from Shutterstock, Inc.

Currently held practices of inclusion in some schools have given students the opportunity to spend all of their day in the general education classroom. Optimal use of the general education setting allows special education supports and services to be provided without the constant disruption of moving the student from one classroom to another. In addition, students aren't teased by their peers or made to feel different because they have to leave the classroom.

Providing for student needs by adapting school environments and learning situations is at the heart of the evidence-based practice known as positive behavior supports (PBS). "Positive behavior support is a general term that refers to the application of positive behavioral interventions and systems to achieve socially important behavior change" (Sugai et al. 2000, 133). When teachers understand student needs, then the student is not perceived as a problem, but a person with dignity who can be given suitable support in order to excel in the inclusive classroom. An example of this kind of aid may be seen in a carefully observed case study.

A Real Life Case Study

Image © titov dmitriy, 2014. Used under license from Shutterstock, Inc.

Image © Juriah Mosin, 2014. Used under license from Shutterstock, Inc.

In December, Michael (not his real name) stopped completing his class work. As a second grader, he was being sent to the office almost daily for disrupting the classroom by wandering throughout the aisles and making a moderately loud whining noise when he was frustrated. Diagnosed with Pervasive Developmental Disorder—Not Otherwise Specified (PDD.NOS), Michael possessed some characteristics of Asperger's and High Functioning Autism. His neurological uniqueness introduced a variety of strengths and challenges represented in the chart below.

Michael's STRENGTHS	Michael's CHALLENGES
3rd grade independent reading level	Sensitive to noise levels; hated time limits
Strong science vocabulary including: white/red blood cells, molecules, hydrogen, brain cells, germs, and magnets	Worried a lot; confused by verbal expectations; weak muscle control in his hands; disliked writing
Verbal, friendly, wanted to please	Upset by changes in routine; tired easily
Had a sweet tooth and did chores at home	Distracted by objects, people, and noise

Michael was included in the general classroom all day. Even though he was scheduled to go to the resource room at the end of the day, he refused saying he didn't want to miss anything in his classroom.

Image © Junial Enterprises, 2014. Used under license from Shutterstock, Inc.

This was Mrs. Brown's (not her real name) first experience with a student on the autism spectrum. After teaching early elementary for thirty-four years, she was at a loss and frustrated that she could not engage him in the lessons.

Mrs. Brown needed help to provide Michael with what he needed to be successful in her classroom. A support team was formed to determine his needs and appropriate strategies.

Image © Africa Studio, 2014. Used under license from Shutterstock, Inc.

Once positive behavior supports were introduced and adaptations were made to assignments and the learning environment, Michael began to soar in the classroom! Key skills such as: work production, peer interaction, reading level, spelling, on-task behavior, math, staying in the classroom and out of the office, raising his hand, and performing to ability went from not evident to emerging to evident within eleven weeks.

Once Mrs. Brown saw his classroom performance increase, she re-gained her self-efficacy in successfully teaching Michael. She was so excited for him and never gave up her pursuit to discover new ways to provide the support he needed to actively engage in classroom tasks and demonstrate his ability to perform within the general education curriculum. Mrs. Brown's own words tell the story of how her attitude changed as a result of meeting Michael's needs in her classroom:

► "I don't know if general education is appropriate; he doesn't produce much at all; he can't read at second grade reading; can't get things done in a certain time; when we push him, he loses control; if we don't push, he will sit 70 percent of the time; oppositional defiant disorder (ODD) behavior back and forth with parapro; will get up and walk around and then wants to talk to the teacher; what works in a.m. won't work in p.m.; noise at lunch bothers him; the more you encourage him, the more he avoids; he doesn't show what he knows; very hard to get him to raise his hand; is not social—not confident of self and doesn't know how to interact with others" (January)
► "We are finding out answers that we haven't found out" (February)
► "I feel like we are going onward and upward; you've got to give up your power, you've got to understand where they are coming from; I just got it into my head, he doesn't have to do all the home links; everything is going so incredibly well; I like [Michael] a lot, especially since we (the team) started working together and I understand him much better" (March)
► "Maverick Mind class helped me jump over from general education thinking. You can't expect the same things out of these kids as others; reassure the teacher that she's doing a good job—he is learning; I'm going to do the best I can—I never thought this would happen (re: student performance); I had to tell myself—don't you give up—keep trying new things; you may not see the differences" (April)
► "Intelligence is so there; sensitive; tender, he teaches me and the students a lot" (May)(Fisher 2013)

In summary, we have seen how the current meaning and use of "disability" may be contributing to a mindset that makes us think of fixing others rather than meeting their needs.

Rather than focusing on deficits, significant others are encouraged to look at assets.

Image © donatas1205, 2014. Used under license from Shutterstock, Inc.

Image © Tyler Olson, 2014. Used under license from Shutterstock, Inc.

This frame of reference may also be hindering successful inclusion into the general education environment where peers and curriculum can be accessed.

Image © B & T Media Group Inc., 2014. Used under license from Shutterstock, Inc.

Presumed competence inspires us to search deeper to find the strengths and capabilities each human being possesses. Once these positive attributes are uncovered, a unique motivation for teaching and learning can be unleashed. Michael's story is a living example of how one boy's life was enhanced by a team of people who believed in his capacity to attain a more quality life.

Image © Rafal Olechowski, 2014. Used under license from Shutterstock, Inc.

Educators, parents, counselors, therapists, friends, and families have the distinct opportunity and privilege to positively affect the trajectory of a student's school and adult life. Empowering others to overcome the pain, frustration, and loneliness of societal challenges by walking alongside and providing support is one of the greatest gifts a human being can impart to another.

Chapter 25

Multiple Intelligences

Jennifer Desiderio

Over the centuries, there have been numerous theories and definitions of intelligence with equally numerous attempts at measuring this abstract concept. Everything from head circumference to reaction time has been used to quantify something that is essentially intangible. Remarkably, what constitutes "intelligence" has remained relatively unchanged since the beginning of the 1900s. Although several models exist at present, most conceptualize intelligence as a blend of verbal facility (e.g., vocabulary, analogies, acquired general knowledge, mathematical reasoning) and nonverbal/spatial reasoning (e.g., puzzles, visual sequencing, matching, patterning, identifying missing parts).

Figure 1 How the view of intelligence has changed over the centuries, from observing physical characteristics such as head circumference and facial features to measuring verbal, spatial, and memory capabilities to recognizing that there may be many types of intelligence that cannot be assessed by traditional means. Perhaps the question we should be asking is not "How smart are you?" but, rather, "How are you smart?"

However, in the 1980s, developmental psychologist Howard Gardner proposed a revolutionary new vision of "intelligence." Based on research in fields as diverse as neuroscience, genetics, anthropology, and psychology (among others), Gardner asserted that everyone possesses seven different types of intelligence (later amended to nine), though in uniquely different combinations so that no two people in the world have exactly the same profile. These *multiple intelligences* allow individuals not only to solve day-to-day problems but also to find creative solutions for larger issues that impact their world. By extension, the assorted aptitudes contribute to one's ability to offer a product or service that is valued in a given society. In Gardner's view, environmental factors contribute to both development and expression of the various abilities. Therefore, it is crucial for schools to be mindful of multiple intelligences in order to diversify and differentiate instruction as well as to cultivate students' talents.

So What Exactly Are the Multiple Intelligences

Intelligence	Description	Sample Classroom Activities	Possible Careers
Verbal-Linguistic	Well-developed verbal skills and sensitivity to the sounds, meanings, and rhythms of language[1]	Read stories aloud, write poetry, create an infomercial or radio broadcast for a given concept, debate, publish a class newspaper	Poet/writer, journalist, editor, teacher, lawyer, politician, translator
Logical-Mathematical	Ability to think conceptually and abstractly as well as the capacity to discern logical or numerical patterns[1]	Solve logic or number puzzles, create a budget, make predictions, create a secret code	Scientist, engineer, computer programmer, accountant, mathematician
Spatial	Ability to think in images and pictures; to visualize accurately and abstractly[1]	Incorporate drawing and collages, diagram sentences, make maps, build 3-D models, use concept maps and graphic organizers	Sculptor, artist, inventor, architect, mechanic, engineer
Musical	Ability to produce and appreciate rhythm, pitch, and timbre (tone quality)[1]	Create songs or raps about key concepts, listen to music from different historical periods, perform experiments about sound and vibration	Singer, composer, musician, conductor, DJ
Bodily-Kinesthetic	Ability to control one's body movements and to handle objects skillfully[1]	Reenact historical events, act out concepts as a group (e.g., the solar system), play charades, play Simon Says	Dancer, athlete, gym teacher, firefighter, actor

	Description	Classroom Application	Careers
Interpersonal	Ability to detect and respond appropriately to the moods, motivations, and desires of others[1]	Small group projects, cooperative learning, peer tutoring, role playing	Therapist, salesperson, business owner, teacher, politician, clergy, nurse
Intrapersonal	Ability to be self-aware and in tune with inner feelings, values, beliefs, and thinking processes[1]	Journaling, independent projects, self-reflection, goal-setting, write essays from the perspective of a literary character or historical figure, provide choices	Researchers, theorists, philosophers, novelists
Naturalist	Ability to discriminate among living things (both plants and animals) as well as sensitivity to other features of the natural world (e.g., weather, rocks)[2]	Collect items from nature, care for a class pet, cultivate plants or a class garden, participate in park clean-ups or recycling drives	Geologist, biologist, environmentalist, botanist, gardener, farmer, animal trainer, chef
Existential	Sensitivity and capacity to tackle deep questions about human existence, such as the meaning of life and death[1]	Critical thinking exercises, class discussions, debates, mock trials, journaling, examine current events (especially those with a humanitarian focus)	Scientist, philosopher, theologian

1. Educational Broadcasting Corporation, 2004
2. Public Broadcasting Service, n.d.
Images © Nastia Larkina, DKalderon, Morphart Creation, Lorelyn Medina, Morphart Creation, VLADGRIN, Chistoprudnaya, beboy, Yoko Design, 2014. Used under license from Shutterstock, Inc.

Table 1 A summary of Howard Gardner's nine currently-held intelligences, how they can be enhanced in the classroom, and how particular strengths can manifest in one's choice of vocation. Keep in mind that Gardner believed intelligence is evolving, not fixed. Therefore, as the Naturalist and Existential intelligences were added within twenty years of the original framework, other distinct types may be identified in the future.

For more information on multiple intelligences, check out these web resources:

▶ Multiple Intelligences for Adult Literacy and Education (contains a quiz as well as activities and resources)
  http://www.literacyworks.org/mi/assessment/findyourstrengths.html

▶ Integrate to Differentiate (brief descriptions of all nine multiple intelligences as well as classroom activities and technological support)
  http://farr-integratingit.net/Trainings/Differentiate/styles.htm

▶ Birmingham Grid for Learning Multiple Intelligences quiz
  http://www.bgfl.org/bgfl/custom/resources_ftp/client_ftp/ks3/ict/multiple_int/what.cfm

Additional web resources for classroom activities based on multiple intelligences:

▶ Scholastic—Clip & Save Checklist: Learning Activities that Connect with Multiple Intelligences
  http://www.scholastic.com/teachers/article/clip-save-checklist-learning-activities-connect-multiple-intelligences

▶ Multiple Intelligences (Concetta Dotti Ryan, M.A. for Edupress)
  http://www.unco.edu/cebs/psychology/kevinpugh/5-7320/ITcomponents/Multi_intel.htm

▶ LoveToKnow Kids—Classroom Activities for Multiple Intelligences
  http://kids.lovetoknow.com/wiki/Classroom_Activities_for_Multiple_Intelligences

Chapter 26

Learning Styles

Jennifer Desiderio

Another way teachers can diversify and differentiate instruction is by considering students' learning styles. Although similar to multiple intelligences, they are nonetheless different constructs and should not be used interchangeably. While the idea of multiple intelligences has been applied to learning contexts, it was chiefly developed as theory of one's *ability* to acquire and subsequently apply knowledge and skills. On the other hand, learning styles generally refers to "*the way* [emphasis added] in which each learner begins to concentrate on, process, absorb, and retain new and difficult information" (Dunn, Denig, & Lovelace 2001, 11). In other words, learning styles represent one's preferred mode of learning independent of ability/aptitude or content area. For example, a student with a kinesthetic learning style learns new and difficult information best through whole body movement and involvement. However, he or she may not demonstrate the excellent eye-hand coordination, dexterity, and physical control indicative of strong bodily-kinesthetic intelligence.

In addition, learning styles often address far more elements of learning than does multiple intelligences. In fact, there are many models of learning styles, but the original and most comprehensive is the one created by Kenneth and Rita Dunn in the late 1960s. Contrary to other learning styles schema, they identified twenty unique elements along five dimensions for K–12 students and twenty-five elements in six domains for adults.

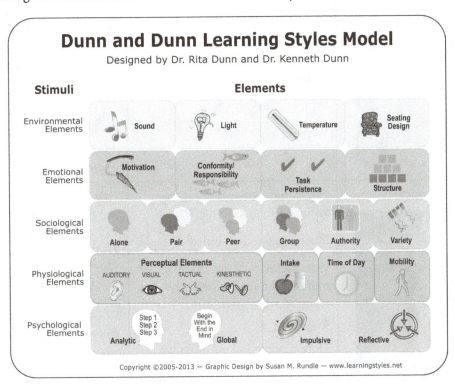

Copyright ©2005-2013 — Graphic Design by Susan M. Rundle — www.learningstyles.net

The Five Domains of the Dunn and Dunn Learning Styles Model...Explained!

Domain	Elements Included	Additional Explanation
Environmental	Quiet—Sound Low light—Bright light Warm temperature—Cool temperature Formal seating—Informal seating	Do you have a preference for the room in which you are learning new and difficult information? For example, some people find it difficult to concentrate unless they are seated at a traditional desk with a hard chair, while others work better while lying on the floor or sitting with their feet up on a table. Some need absolute quiet, while others prefer music or background noise.
Emotional	Internally motivated—Externally motivated More conforming—Less conforming Single-task persistent—Multi-task persistent More structure—Less structure	Consider your self-direction as a learner. Do you prefer choices and options? Do you like specific rules and guidelines? Are you able to work on several things at once or only one thing at a time?
Sociological	Alone Pair Small group Large group With an authority figure With variety	When learning something new, do you learn best by yourself? In a group? With only one other person? Is it better for that other person to be a peer or an authority figure like a teacher or a parent? Some people have specific preferences for what works and does not work for them; others actually learn best when they can learn new information in a variety of ways.
Physiological*	Perceptual elements (auditory, visual, tactual, kinesthetic) More intake—Less intake Preferred time of day (early morning, late morning/early afternoon, late afternoon, evening) More mobility—Less mobility	These elements are considered to be more biologically-based. For example, some people need to eat or drink for maximum understanding and retention. Others learn better at certain times of day. Some people learn best when they hear information. Others need to read it. Still others need graphics, charts, and other images.

Psychological 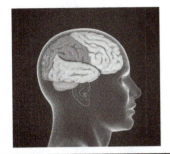	Analytic—Global Impulsive—Reflective	This domain is focused on processing. Are you more left-brained (sequential, analytical) or right-brained (whole-to-part, global)? Similarly, some people jump in right away, while others take time to think things through and plan.
*For the adult assessment of learning styles, the perceptual elements become their own domain with six perceptual learning styles: visual word, visual picture, auditory, auditory verbal, tactual, and kinesthetic.		

There are currently four different formal assessments developed by the Dunns and subsequent collaborators, with questions and interpretation determined by age. For each item, an individual might show a strong preference, slight/moderate preference, or no preference at all ("it depends"). Some elements typically have a greater influence on one's learning than others; therefore, it is important to identify which elements truly have an impact so they may be accommodated either within the classroom, outside the classroom (e.g., studying at home), or both. When mismatches exist between a student's learning style(s) and the teaching style of the instructor, that student may become bored and inattentive in class; score poorly on tests; get discouraged about school…and themselves; and, in severe cases, drop out of school altogether. Yet, because there are any number of learning styles present in a given classroom, teachers should strive for a balance of instructional and assessment methods (see: Universal Design for Learning). If balance is achieved, all students will be taught *partly in a manner they prefer*, which leads to an increased comfort level and willingness to learn, and *partly in a less preferred manner*, which provides practice and feedback in ways of thinking and solving problems with which they may not initially be comfortable. Each person is born with certain inclinations toward particular styles, but culture, experience, and even biological development influence these preferences.

For further information on learning styles, check out these web resources:

▶ International Learning Styles Network (home of the Dunn and Dunn model; includes the BE adult learning styles assessment)
http://www.learningstyles.net/en/about-us

▶ Index of Learning Styles Questionnaire
http://www.engr.ncsu.edu/learningstyles/ilsweb.html

▶ The VARK Questionnaire
http://www.vark-learn.com/english/page.asp?p=questionnaire

Chapter 27

Universal Design for Learning

Jennifer Desiderio

Imagine Washington Middle School. Of the 700 students enrolled...

▶ 252 students (36%) are African American, 196 (28%) are White, 182 (26%) are Hispanic/Latino, 56 (8%) are Asian, and 14 (2%) are "Other." (Figure 1)

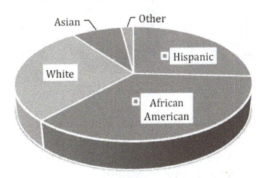

Figure 1
Image courtesy of author

▶ 406 (58%) receive free or reduced lunches. To qualify for *free lunch*, families of students like Shelby must have income at or below 130% of the poverty level; through July 2013, this means earning $29,965 or less per year for a family of four. Shelby's mom is a single parent supporting three children by working full-time as a grocery store cashier and part-time as a bartender. As the oldest, Shelby often has to care for her younger siblings. For *reduced lunch*, families must fall between 130% and 185% of the poverty level, which means Eric's grandmother, who has

been the legal guardian for Eric and his brother since they were removed from their mother's custody six years ago for abuse and neglect, can earn up to $42,643 for their family of four. Although sixty-seven years of age, she cannot retire as she is the family's sole source of income since her husband had a stroke that limited his mobility.

▶ 42 (6%) are English Language Learners, as diverse as Danuta from Poland and Alejandro from Mexico. Danuta has only been in the United States since the start of the school year. Her family moved here to obtain a better education for her nine-year-old brother, who has autism. Danuta speaks Polish and German along with some English. Alejandro's father came to the United States five years ago looking for better work. Three years later, his wife and four children, of which Alejandro is the second eldest, joined him. Alejandro's father is currently employed at a meat-packing plant, while his mother provides housekeeping services for a local hotel.

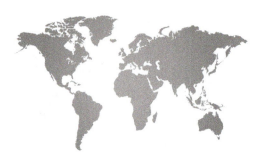

Image © Stephen Marques, 2014. Used under license from Shutterstock, Inc.

▶ Still others are first generation Americans with strong cultural and religious traditions. These include Anjali, who is bilingual in Hindi and English; Dineh, a Muslim who speaks Persian, Arabic, and English; and Ji, who must regularly translate for his parents who only speak Mandarin.

Images © dedek, Aleks Melnik, Igor Shikov, 2014. Used under license from Shutterstock, Inc.

▶ 112 (16%, higher than the national average, according to the U.S. Department of Education, 2012) receive services for a disability under IDEIA. This includes students like Dakota, who has an IEP for an Other Health Impairment due to Attention Deficit-Hyperactivity Disorder; Meagann, who has a learning disability in basic reading skills and written expression; and Jerome, who has cognitive, communication, and motor delays related to Down syndrome.

Image © Khalima, 2014. Used under license from Shutterstock, Inc.

▶ 35 (5%) are identified as Gifted and Talented, like Rashid and Anastasia. With an IQ of 148, Rashid was classified as intellectually gifted in elementary school. Independent and self-motivated, he is widely perceived as a leader and is well-liked by his peers. Although Rashid is successful in all academic areas, he is particularly interested in science. Anastasia's giftedness, on the other hand, was not recognized until the end of her first year in middle school. She excels in divergent thinking and openly challenges traditional assumptions, which often frustrates her teachers. Anastasia also possesses exceptional talent for drawing.

Image © VLADGRIN, 2014. Used under license from Shutterstock, Inc.

▶ On the state proficiency test, 476 (68%) of 8th graders are *not proficient* in reading, 560 (80%) are *not proficient* in writing, and 511 (73%) are *not proficient* in math.

Of course, most students share several of the above characteristics. Beyond those demographics, there are numerous other variations of interests and abilities which affect learning and social relationships. In fact, the way people learn is as unique as their fingerprints (Center for Applied Special Technology, n.d.)!

Image © Keith Bell, 2014. Used under license from Shutterstock, Inc.

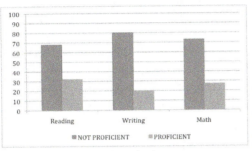

Image courtesy of author

Now picture all of these students in one classroom. The historical approach to education, especially in middle school, high school, and college, emphasizes lectures, textbook readings, worksheets, written reports/papers, and tests. These methods best serve those who have visual (print) and auditory strengths, who excel at writing, and who prefer to work alone. Even then, there is little connection between the content and real-world application. These perennial practices create obstacles for a sizeable percentage of students. Therefore, it is no wonder that we hear teachers lament students' lack of motivation, poor retention of information, deficient critical thinking skills, inattention, and carelessness. Predictably, many students also express negative opinions about school; they often feel bored and detached and do not see the value of what they are being taught.

Is it really possible to meet the needs of such diverse learners?

Images © eurobanks, michaeljung, Zurijeta, eurobanks, michaeljung, Chepe Nicoli, Golden Pixels LLC, Lisa F. Young, michaeljung, michaeljung, Real Deal Photo, Lisa F. Young, Lisa F. Young, wizdata, center; Carlos Caetano, 2014. Used under license from Shutterstock, Inc.

Yes! Just as the universal design movement in architecture made buildings and tools for living accessible to everyone and provided alternatives (e.g., automatic doors, ramps, common symbols on signage), so Universal Design for Learning (UDL) aims to give all students equal opportunities to learn. UDL is a curricular framework targeting engagement, instructional strategies, and authentic assessment by considering the varied needs, strengths, and interests of students. It is founded in large part upon research that has shown that several brain networks are involved in the learning process. It starts with the recognition networks: your senses must first take in information and categorize what you are experiencing. It follows that we then have to *do* something with that information; how we organize and express our knowledge is the responsibility of the strategic networks. This whole process is optimized by the affective networks, which stimulate us and help us stay engaged. UDL was conceived to operate with the "what," the "how," and the "why" of learning through flexible approaches unique to each individual's talents, limitations, and preferences.

After years of development, the Center for Applied Special Technology (CAST) first unveiled its three core principles of UDL in 1998. Instead of a one-size-fits-all philosophy of teaching, they advocated multiple ways of (1) presenting content, (2) allowing students to express their knowledge, and (3) exciting and animating the learning process. Let's look more in-depth at these principles in practice.

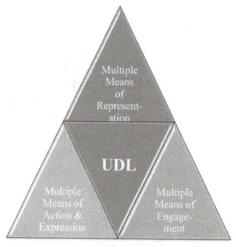

Image courtesy of author

Multiple Means of Representation

As noted earlier, in a typical classroom (especially at the middle school level and higher), the teacher shares information through lectures (auditory emphasis) and assigned independent readings and practice worksheets (visual-print emphasis). While some students can master information using these methods, we erect barriers for at least half of their peers due to varied learning styles, sensory or learning disabilities, language differences, or cultural differences. Moreover, solely using such means turns students into passive pupils. Although students often believe this is the most effective way to teach, research has shown that employing a variety of techniques, including active strategies in which students are challenged to make meaning from the content, leads to deeper, longer-lasting outcomes.

Check This Out!

▶   Imagine learning science this way—either by viewing this video or by actually performing it yourself!

http://www.ted.com/talks/john_bohannon_dance_vs_powerpoint_a_modest_proposal.html
(also check out Dance Your Ph.D. at http://gonzolabs.org/dance/)

First and foremost, we cannot assume that everyone has the same contextual knowledge or realizes which experiences are relevant to the current subject. Therefore, teachers must first activate (or supply!) vital background. It is also essential to clarify the meanings of words and symbols, translating significant terms into multiple languages, as warranted. Teachers must further provide opportunities for and assist students in finding the "big idea," discovering patterns, and making connections to concepts both in and outside of school. Since accessibility is fundamental to UDL, all of this should be done through multiple channels. This means options for different modalities (e.g., graphic organizers, concept maps, and word clouds; comics and graphic novels; online videos; 3D interactive websites; cooperative learning groups; demonstrations with real-world objects; exercises involving whole body movement) as well as formats that can be adjusted to meet a given student's needs (e.g., the size or font of text, transcripts, closed captioning, audiobooks).

Check This Out!

Cool online dictionaries:

- ► Visuwords—dictionary, thesaurus, and (mobile) concept map all in one (http://www.visuwords.com)

- ► Shahi visual dictionary—provides definitions along with pictures from Google, Flickr, and more (http://blachan.com/shahi/)

Image © Tribalium , 2014. Used under license from Shutterstock, Inc.

Multiple Means of Action and Expression

When it comes time for students to "show what they know," this, too, is usually limited in the conventional classroom. Much of the focus is on the written word through tests and reports. Furthermore, these evaluations frequently focus on the lower levels of the cognitive domain of Bloom's Taxonomy, namely basic remembering and understanding, rather than higher levels of thinking that involve applying, analyzing, evaluating, and creating. As a result, there is often little connection between the content and how it is being assessed.

Students differ considerably in the way they make meaning and best demonstrate their comprehension. Therefore, it should not be surprising that a central tenet of the UDL framework is to provide choices for students to communicate what they have learned. Moreover, these assessment checks should occur not only at the end of a unit but also frequently throughout the lesson. Sometimes these options are designed to break down barriers, such as the use of Speech-to-Text programs (e.g., Dragon Naturally Speaking), touch screen overlays for computers, and specialized

What is Bloom's Taxonomy?

Benjamin Bloom (1913–1999) was an educational psychologist who believed that learning involved the head, the heart, and the hands. He divided the cognitive domain (the "head") into six categories, represented by a pyramid. The higher up on the pyramid, the more critical thinking is involved. The categories were modified slightly in the 1990s (see below) to better reflect 21st century learning demands. This framework is designed to help teachers create more well-rounded learning objectives and experiences.

DOMAIN	QUESTIONS
Remembering	Can the student recall or remember the information?
Understanding	Can the student explain ideas or concepts?
Applying	Can the student use the information in a new way?
Analyzing	Can the student distinguish between different parts?
Evaluating	Can the student justify a stand or decision?
Creating	Can the student create a new product or point of view?

keyboards and "mice." Other options are intended to inspire creativity and tap into students' strengths. For example, instead of writing a paper, a student could produce a video using live objects or animation (e.g., iMovie, Xtranormal, Animoto). Similarly, a student could design an interactive poster using Glogster, with the opportunity to embed sound and video. Another student might craft his or her own simple comic strip illustrating a specific concept (see below for an example) or a whole book using traditional paper media or technology such as the CAST UDL Book Builder or Kerpoof™. Someone who prefers to work with peers might collaborate to write and perform a skit.

Used by permission of author and site creator Bill Zimmerman. This comic strip was created at MakeBeliefsComix.com; go there to create your own.

With all the variety of activities, UDL proponents remind teachers that many students are still developing such executive functions as goal-setting, planning, organization, and persistence. It is, therefore, important to furnish both guidance and the tools necessary for them to truly express their knowledge. This could be as simple as providing models, checklists, rubrics, and prompts or using programs such as Webspiration Classroom™.

Multiple Means of Engagement

Emotion is a crucial element in learning. Just as anxiety, confusion, boredom, or indifference negatively impacts a student's ability to learn, so curiosity, enthusiasm, and pride enhance the educational experience. Noted previously, activating (or providing) background knowledge, introducing material in different ways, and offering choices in assessment additionally serve to stimulate and maintain student interest. It is also imperative to show the relevance of content through authentic activities. Nevertheless, because a given class consists of varied ethnicities, cultures, socioeconomic statuses, genders, and aspirations, it is erroneous to assume that what is relevant to one is relevant to all. Even the same individual's inclinations and preferences will change over time as he or she develops new skills and encounters unknown people and environments.

Once again, the UDL theme of options comes into play. Teachers should vary instructional strategies and sources of information, involving students themselves in exploring, experimenting, and reflecting on the content in an environment that minimizes threats and distractions. Working with peers in pairs and small groups not only further creates a community of learners dedicated to a common goal in the present but also fosters collaborative skills that will benefit students for years to come. Another element for promoting engagement is immediate feedback that is constructive and based on mastering specific objectives that can be achieved through effortful practice.

The word cloud created by the author from three UDL principles and their components, summarizing and emphasizing major ideas and terms. Word clouds can be used in the classroom to highlight important concepts from reading or lecture materials to assist with comprehension.
Created at www.wordle.net

Although UDL is not yet explicitly codified in any national laws related to K–12 education, the U.S. Department of Education unambiguously endorsed UDL as part of their rationale for changes to the upcoming reauthorization of the Elementary and Secondary Education Act (referred to as "No Child Left Behind" when it was last revised in 2001) in a section targeting "other diverse learners." This group includes students with disabilities, Native Americans, English language learners, homeless and migrant children, and neglected or delinquent youth (U.S. Department of Education 2010). For all of these students, the federal government seeks to:

> …ensure that teachers and leaders are better prepared to meet the needs of diverse learners,…and that more districts and schools implement high-quality, state- and locally-determined curricula and instructional supports that incorporate the principles of universal design for learning to meet all students' needs. (20)

While it may be challenging for teachers to incorporate all of the UDL principles into every single lesson plan, they nonetheless provide a philosophy and structure for teaching that will ultimately benefit a greater number of students.

Reflection

Reflecting on your own educational experiences, did you have any teachers who seemed to follow the UDL framework in any part of their teaching at the elementary level? Middle school? High school? College?

If so, was there a specific subject where you experienced more alternatives?

Did those alternatives occur more with Representation, Action and Expression, or both?

Image © Sergey Furtaev, 2014. Used under license from Shutterstock, Inc.

Challenge

Imagine you are a 7th grade social studies teacher with the following goal for your students, based on your state's standard:

> Learn and explain how the purposes served by government affect relationships between the individual, government, and society as a whole as well as the differences that occur in monarchies, theocracies, dictatorships, and representative governments.

Your class of 26 includes Shelby, Danuta, Anjali, Dakota, Meagann, and Rashid, depicted at the beginning of this section. Many of your students struggle with reading and writing and find politics and government "boring."

Considering differences in skill level, language proficiency, culture, background experiences, interests, perceptual learning styles (visual, auditory, tactual, kinesthetic), and sociological learning styles (individual, pair, small group, large group, with an adult)...

► Describe 3–5 different ways of stimulating and maintaining engagement with the topic.
► Describe 3–5 different options for students to learn about the different types of governments and their impacts on societal relationships.
► Describe 3–5 different options for students to demonstrate their new knowledge. Please include activities to check understanding during the unit (formative) as well as at the end (summative).

Image © NEGOVURA, 2014. Used under license from Shutterstock, Inc.

For more information on UDL, check out these web resources:

► The IRIS Center for Training Enhancements' Module on Universal Design for Learning
http://iris.peabody.vanderbilt.edu/module/udl

► Center for Applied Special Technology
http://www.cast.org/

► National Center on Universal Design for Learning
http://www.udlcenter.org/

► Teaching Every Student
http://www.cast.org/teachingeverystudent/

Additional web resources mentioned in this chapter:

Animoto	http://animoto.com/
CAST UDL Book Builder	http://bookbuilder.cast.org/
Dragon Naturally Speaking	http://www.nuance.com/dragon/index.htm
Glogster	http://www.glogster.com/
Kerpoof	http://www.kerpoof.com/
Make Beliefs Comix	http://www.makebeliefscomix.com/
Tagxedo	http://www.tagxedo.com/
Webspiration	http://www.mywebspiration.com/
Xtranormal	http://www.xtranormal.com/

Chapter 28

Response to Intervention

Jennifer Desiderio

The philosophy behind UDL merges with the Response-to-Intervention (RTI) movement as they are both founded on high-quality instruction tailored to the individual in the general education environment. However, even when all three UDL principles are applied, some students will likely require additional support to maximize their learning. Further, the intensity of support necessary for that student to be successful may indicate the presence of a disability. A different process should be engaged to document and guarantee services to such individuals.

In brief, RTI addresses early identification and intervention for students with academic or behavioral concerns. But wait! Isn't this an assumed responsibility of those who work within the education system? Why is there a special endeavor focused on what would seem to be a "given"? Certainly, adjusting and differentiating instruction for the benefit of each child is advocated by many professionals, but years of experience and research have shown a disconnection between beliefs and consistent practice.

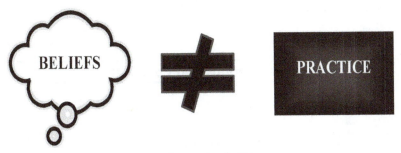

Image courtesy of author

As a result, many students graduated high school functionally illiterate or did not graduate at all because they dropped out. Still others were categorized as "disabled," when they were merely victims of a system that did not fulfill their needs. However, being classified with a disability was often considered preferable to the alternative since it was typically the only way students could receive additional help. Yet, special education services were not necessarily any more effective; not only did many students achieve only minimal gains in skills, a great deal showed declines in self-esteem and other social-emotional variables. The problems with special education as practiced since 1975 were well-articulated in the 2002 President's Commission on Excellence in Special Education, especially in *Finding 2*:

> The current system uses an antiquated model that waits for a child to fail, instead of a model based on prevention and intervention. Too little emphasis is put on prevention, early and accurate identification

of learning and behavior problems, and aggressive intervention using research-based approaches. This means students with disabilities don't get help early when that help can be most effective. Special education should be for those who do not respond to strong and appropriate instruction and methods provided in general education. (7)

Image © metrmetr, 2014. Used under license from Shutterstock, Inc.

The Commission further confirmed the overrepresentation of minorities in special education, something that might be avoided with early screening and intervention. As one can see from the above quote, the Commission did not limit their analyses to students with academic difficulties; they maintained that children "at risk for [emotional and behavioral] difficulties could also be identified through universal screening and more significant disabilities prevented through classroom-based approaches involving positive discipline and classroom management" (23). Many of the resulting recommendations appeared in the reauthorization of the Individuals with Disabilities in Education Act in 2004 and echo the ideals of RTI.

Like UDL, RTI is a framework based on a specific philosophy of education, not a single, defined program. In fact, several standards of RTI have been developed over the years in response to decades of research in the fields of both education and psychology (problem-solving and standard protocol are the most common). Though its roots took hold as far back as the 1960s, more systematic application did not begin until the early-to mid-1990s, most notably in Iowa (Heartland Area Education Agency), Minnesota (Minneapolis Public Schools), and Ohio. It was not widely known by its current moniker until the early-2000s, primarily due to the reauthorization of IDEA when it was explicitly referenced as an alternative scheme for identifying learning disabilities. Because of this, many people assume not only that RTI is a "special education initiative" but also one that pertains solely to suspected learning disabilities. Both of these could not be further from the truth. The components of RTI can be applied to all aspects of a child's education, from academic instruction and behavior management to communication and functional skills. Moreover, the goal of RTI is actually to reduce the necessity for special education by addressing concerns early and systematically, thereby increasing the likelihood that only students with true disabilities will warrant labels.

Although RTI has been carried out in a variety of ways, all share common underlying assumptions and core concepts (NRCLD 2007):

RTI Assumptions and Core Concepts	
	✓ Students receive high quality instruction in their general education setting.
	✓ General education instruction is research-based.

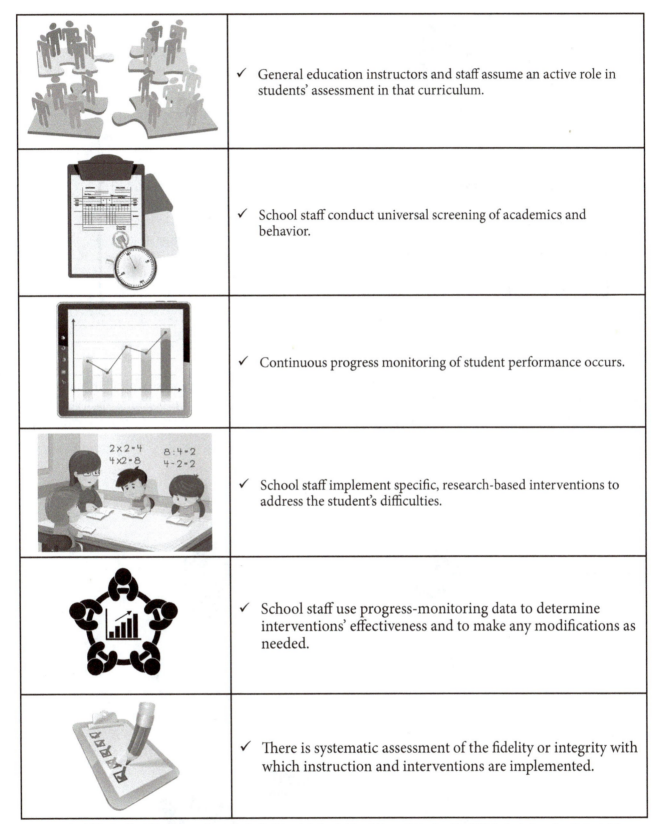	✓ General education instructors and staff assume an active role in students' assessment in that curriculum.
	✓ School staff conduct universal screening of academics and behavior.
	✓ Continuous progress monitoring of student performance occurs.
	✓ School staff implement specific, research-based interventions to address the student's difficulties.
	✓ School staff use progress-monitoring data to determine interventions' effectiveness and to make any modifications as needed.
	✓ There is systematic assessment of the fidelity or integrity with which instruction and interventions are implemented.

Umm, what exactly does "research-based interven- tion" mean?

Also sometimes referred to as "scientifically-based," this was defined in the No Child Left Behind Act of 2001. They are generally understood to be instructional practices that have statistically significant evidence of concrete, observable changes in student performance based on rigorous data analyses. Ideally, the studies demonstrating effectiveness have been replicated at least once, across various implementers, populations, and settings. Such studies have generally been accepted for publication in reputable, scholarly journals and/or have been reviewed by an impartial panel of experts.

Regardless of its name, since its inception RTI has consisted of a circular process with four fundamental steps: (1) Define and Analyze the Problem (which includes hypothesizing why the problem exists, a crucial step that must not be overlooked or shortchanged), (2) Plan the Intervention, (3) Implement the Intervention, and (4) Evaluate the Intervention.

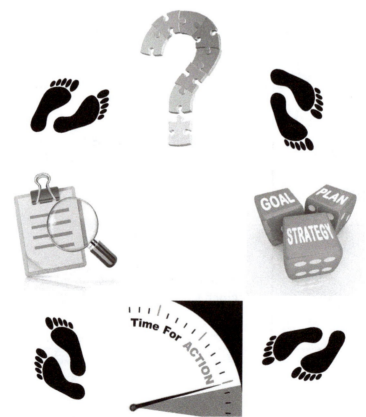

Many examples of RTI in practice describe levels or tiers of service; the higher the level, the more intense the intervention. As the core concepts noted in Table 1 reveal, much of RTI actually occurs within the general education setting. Because it is grounded in prevention of more severe problems, the heart of RTI is high-quality instruction in the regular classroom; this includes a research-based course of study using methods that have demonstrated effectiveness, differentiated to accommodate a variety of needs (remember UDL!). In other words, students should not be singled out for assistance because they are "instructional casualties." In a tiered approach, this is Tier 1. In addition to universal screening or checkpoints (analogous to annual wellness exams from your doctor), there should be ongoing monitoring of progress so that struggling students can be readily identified and provided with more targeted evidenced-based interventions. This usually indicates a shift to Tier 2.

While those students continue to be instructed in the core curriculum, they are also given more intensive small group or even individualized intervention that has documented evidence of effectiveness focusing on their identified needs. Progress is now monitored more often (bi-weekly or weekly) so the teacher may modify each student's program as necessary. Success at this level generally justifies fading of the intervention to return to the less restrictive Tier 1.

A smaller percentage of students typically require even greater support (either still Tier 2 or possibly Tier 3, depending on the system); such students may need more time with the intervention (i.e., minutes per day or days per week) or may need an even smaller group or one-on-one instruction. Assessment remains frequent (at least once/week) in order to track growth and make changes to improve the student's rate of progress. Since the fundamental goal of RTI is to achieve student success, school staff must continually specify and analyze the problem(s) at hand, set realistic yet challenging goals, reliably implement evidence-based interventions, objectively monitor the effects of those interventions, and make educational decisions based on the data. Given those steps, it should be noted that it is entirely possible to go directly from Tier 1 to Tier 3 if there is a significant, immediate need for more intensive intervention, just as it is possible to go from Tier 3 back to Tier 1 if the student demonstrates continued success and growth in the absence of more rigorous instruction.

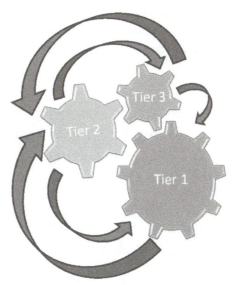

Image courtesy of author

In RTI, decisions about students are made collaboratively by those with a "stake" in the child's education. This includes principals, general educators, special educators, related services personnel (e.g., school psychologists, counselors, speech/language pathologists), and, most importantly, parents/guardians. Although precisely who is involved, when they are involved, and how they are involved varies by school district, satisfactory implementation of RTI necessitates that multiple stakeholders have a common goal and truly share responsibility, resources, and accountability. It is important to have a decision-making "team" because their combined talents, energies, and efforts produce better results than any one member working alone. Each team member brings unique and varied experiences, perspectives, and expertise and is valued for those contributions. Ultimately, RTI requires a diverse, flexible, organized, and integrated system in order to be successfully executed.

Image © Orla , 2014. Used under license from Shutterstock, Inc.

In Luke's case (on following page), the Team did not suspect a disability was contributing to his reading difficulties. However, that question is raised for about 5–10 percent of students served through RTI. Depending on the system, some additional assessments may be performed for a more comprehensive evaluation, or the Team may base their eligibility decision solely on the information accumulated during the various levels of intervention, analyzing the child's history, information collected from the child's parents/guardians, the types of interventions utilized, and the progress monitoring results. In RTI, whether or not a child is determined to have a disability is ultimately based on three main considerations: (1) low level of performance relative to peers (or an identified standard), (2) slow rate of progress relative to peers, in spite of evidence-based interventions reliably employed, and (3) an adverse impact on educational performance necessitating the need for special education in order to progress in the general education curriculum. Therefore, when deliberating eligibility, the following questions are posed:

Luke: An RTI Success Story

Luke is a 2nd grader. In mid-November, his teacher referred him to the Student Assistance Team (a group who met monthly, consisting of the student's homeroom teacher, the school's guidance counselor, the school psychologist, the school's "literacy coach," the principal, and the student's parents) for reading concerns. He had already been identified by his teacher and the guidance counselor for some additional intervention through the school's universal screener. As a result, Luke was receiving Title I remedial reading services twice a week for twenty minutes with three other students who had similar reading concerns.

According to numerous criterion-referenced assessments, Luke showed a great deal of inconsistency with correct usage of long and short vowels as well as with word endings. In general, Luke's reading skills fell in line with end of 1st grade expectations. In fact, when given 2nd grade curriculum-based oral reading fluency measures, he was only reading 32 words correct per minute (wcpm), which was not only considerably below the fall benchmark of 52 wcpm or greater but also fell below the district's "cut score" indicating significant concern (36 wcpm).

Following *the problem-solving model* of RTI, the Team hypothesized that Luke had a skill deficit that required more targeted practice. Consequently, the plan was for him to work with the school psychology intern twice each week with a combination of two specific evidence-based interventions called Listening Passage Preview and Repeated Readings. These involved first reading aloud a short passage to Luke while he followed along (the preview), then having him read the same passage three times in a row (the objective is for the student to read with an increased pace and greater accuracy each time). Luke's progress would be monitored using the curriculum-based oral reading fluency method once each week with a goal of reading at least 44 wcpm in 2nd grade material by the end of **January.**

Treatment fidelity was monitored through random observation checks by the school psychologist. The intern did meet with Luke twice each week (on Tuesdays and Fridays) and faithfully followed the scripts for each intervention. Weekly progress monitoring revealed a decrease in errors, but Luke did not meet his goal for words correct per minute (weekly scores ranged inconsistently from 25 to 41). Since he had mostly improved over his original score of 32 wcpm and was close to his goal, the Team decided to continue the intervention for another six weeks but add an extra day during weeks when the intern was able to meet more frequently.

Based on his current performance, Luke's new goal was 48 wcpm. When the Team reconvened in **March,** the intern indicated that she had continued to meet with Luke only twice each week, with the exception of one week. Even without the increase in time, Luke's progress was very encouraging (weekly scores ranging from 40 to 59). Although he had met his short-term goal, he remained far from the spring benchmark of 85 wcpm and, unfortunately, still fell below the "at risk" cut-off (64 wcpm). Additionally, Luke was observed in multiple environments to be more interested in "speed reading," which often caused him to make mistakes on small words and sight words he clearly knew in isolation.

The Team did not suspect a disability since Luke was less than a year behind his peers, and he *had* made progress. Nonetheless, they knew they needed to change the intervention in order to better model appropriate reading rate and prosody (intonation, rhythm, and emphasis given to words and sentences) as well as to effect greater change. Although Luke was improving, he was more or less making growth parallel to his peers; at that rate, he would never close the gap. Thus, the Team decided on another evidence-based, scripted intervention called Paired Reading. Again, he would work with the intern school psychologist two to three times each week, with a goal of 70 wcpm.

The results reported in May were astounding! Over the course of the intervention, Luke's oral reading fluency in grade-level material went from 63 to 86 wcpm with one or fewer errors. To see if his progress could be maintained in the final four weeks of the school year, the intervention was withdrawn, and he was returned to regular classroom activities only. Remarkably, by the end of the year, he consistently achieved oral reading fluency scores between 85 and 90 wcpm (recall that 85 wcpm was the spring benchmark). His teacher further noted his excellent performance on both 2nd grade *and* 3rd grade Running Records (another type of reading assessment). Luke's mother continued to focus on reading over the summer so he could begin 3rd grade on target…which he did!

Questions to consider when discussing special education eligibility in an RTI model.
Image courtesy of author

Contrary to common understanding, the purpose of RTI is **not** to show that a student did not respond positively to increasingly intense evidence-based interventions, per se; rather, in a true RTI approach, the school is charged with continuing intervention until the student *does* respond ("successful response" being defined by the educational professionals working with the target student). If what works for the student is so intense and specialized that it "looks like" what might be provided as special education services (e.g., specialized instructional materials, including technology; curricular modifications; expertly trained teachers), that is a strong indication that the student has a disability.

Advantages of RTI

- It is an ongoing process available to support *all* students.

- It identifies students for significant intervention *before they fall too deeply into a hole*.

- It identifies students who might otherwise be missed, while at the same time reduces "false positive" identification (i.e., labeling a student who does not, in fact, have a disability).

- It yields more thorough and instructionally/educationally relevant information. If a student is deemed eligible for special education, this leads to better IEP goals and objectives.

- It promotes shared ownership of the student's education and provides for the flexible use of resources.

- It promotes resolution of concerns rather than focusing on the student as deficient.

Some Challenges of RTI

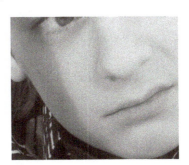

▶ Delivering high-quality, research-based instruction as part of the core curriculum

▶ Learning evidence-based group and individual interventions

▶ Implementing evidence-based group and individual interventions with fidelity

▶ Offering a flexible continuum of supports

▶ Having enough resources (personnel, time, etc.) to be effective

▶ Making decisions based on sound data instead of verbal reports and "gut" feeling

CAN YOU THINK OF OTHER CHALLENGES??

For further information on RTI, check out these web resources:

▶ *National Center on Response to Intervention*
   http://www.rti4success.org/

▶ *National Dissemination Center for Children with Disabilities*
   http://nichcy.org/schools-administrators/rti

▶ *RTI Action Network*
   http://www.rtinetwork.org/

Websites for evidence-based interventions and assessment:

▶ Dynamic Indicators of Basic Early Literacy Skills
   https://dibels.uoregon.edu/

▶ Intervention Central
   http://www.interventioncentral.org/

▶ National Center on Student Progress Monitoring
   http://www.studentprogress.org/

▶ What Works Clearinghouse
   http://ies.ed.gov/ncee/wwc/

Section 4

How Does Disability Intersect with Other Social Identities?

Chapter 29

The Intersection of Disability and Race

Pamela Colton

The Final Frontier

In the 1960s, *Star Trek* was noted for pushing the boundaries on social issues. Show creator Gene Roddenberry consciously created a culturally diverse cast for the starship's most visible crew members—including an African woman as communications officer and a Japanese man as the ship's helmsman. The episode "Plato's Stepchildren" (1968) featured the first interracial kiss broadcast on television in the United States, staged between black actress Nichelle Nichols and white actor William Shatner. Network executives worried that such characters and storylines would alienate the audience. Progressive viewers criticized Roddenberry and his writers for not going far enough. Issues related to gender, sexual orientation, and disability were generally ignored or portrayed as monstrous. Even in *Star Trek,* space was not really the "final frontier."

In November 1986, Roddenberry told an eager audience of over two thousand fans, "It's time that we're really about diversity." David Gerrold, one of the writers and producers for the *Star Trek: The Next Generation* series, says that Roddenberry "decided we had to have a disabled character." There was talk about a character with Down syndrome who used a "brain augment," but the most important consideration was how a character's disability would work in the context of the show. Roddenberry settled on the concept of a ship's engineer who was blind and used a prosthetic device to simulate sight. African American actor, Levar Burton, was cast in the role. Referring to the fact that a person from a so-called "minority" racial group would portray a person with a disability, one concerned executive at Paramount Studios sent a memo to Roddenberry that asked, "Why are you giving this character *two* disabilities?" (Gerrold 2013).

If Paramount's executive had been pressed to revisit the wording of his question, he might have laughed at the slip of the tongue, waved a hand, and said, "You know what I mean." And really, we do know what he meant.

Otherness

He was asking, "Why are you giving this character two categories of *otherness*?" Otherness in the United States is created in relation to "normal" meaning the same thing as white, able-bodied, income-earning, and male. When you hear general terms like person, manager, worker, chairperson, scientist, actor, technician, etc., the first images you probably have in your mind are of white, able-bodied men. An eye-opening conversation at a feminist book reading meeting went something like this:

"When you wake up in the morning and look in the mirror, what do you see?" she asked.

"I see a woman," replied the white woman.

"That's precisely the problem," responded the black woman. "I see a black woman. To me, race is visible every day, because race is how I am not privileged in our culture. Race is invisible to you, because it's how you are privileged. It's why there will always be differences in our experience."

… I was startled, and groaned… Being the only man in the room, someone asked what my response had meant.

"Well," I said, "when I look in the mirror, I see a human being… As a middle-class white man, I have no class, no race, and no gender." (Kimmel 2002).

Kimmel's realization that he had "no class, race, or gender" was an admission that labels of otherness are imposed upon these groups by the self-declared standard for normal.

What students can see a block away from their schools and outside
their homes on the north side of Flint, Michigan.
Image courtesy of author

Race, Gender, *and* Disability Are Not Biological

It is relatively easy to explain, but difficult for people to understand or accept, that race is not biological. Race is socially constructed to categorize individuals in relation to White culture. Genetically, there are more differences between individuals within the same supposed racial categories than between people across all racial groups. For example, a "Black" person from Micronesia would be much more likely to find a compatible donor for an organ transplant among White Europeans than among native West Africans, even if in skin color this person closely matches people from West Africa. Likewise, "African American" golfer Tiger Woods would be better off looking for genetically compatible donors in Asia, since he is primarily of Asian heritage.

It is less easy for most people to understand that gender is socially constructed. Gender is a performance of social expectations that begins at birth when biological sex is determined (or in cases of ambiguous genitalia, "assigned"). At first the performance is played by parents dressing their children in blue or pink, and picking gender-appropriate toys. Later the performance becomes internalized, and society only notices when people perform their genders differently than is expected of them (Butler 1990).

The idea that *disability* is socially constructed can be much more difficult for people to grasp. Evidence lies in the fact that not all cultures consider the same conditions to be disabilities (Kudlick 2003). Still, disability in educational settings in the United States is described in terms of tangible inadequacies, pathologies, and inabilities. In fact, to qualify for special education accommodations and services, these inadequacies, pathologies, and inabilities must be described and documented in unavoidably insulting terms on a legal document—the student's IEP. This legal language serves to precisely define whether or not a student meets certain criteria for a disability label. The official nature of this language distracts from the fact that these criteria are constructed to describe what is *socially* unacceptable in the general education setting, and *not* what is impossible to accommodate.

Physical, sensory, intellectual, and psychological variations are real in how they can impact the ways in which individuals interact with their environments. *However, these are not disabling until society refuses to accommodate and include people with these differences.* For example, a student whose vision can be corrected with glasses or contacts is not considered disabled on the basis of visual deficit even though they rely on man-made corrective lenses, because these are well-accepted (normal) tools for accommodating vision. No one would ever deny a student's right to wear glasses in the classroom.

Labels of otherness are socially constructed. Privilege is invisible. But both otherness and privilege have very real-world consequences.

Uncovered drainage hole on an elementary school playground with
a broken beer bottle and discarded child's school work in Flint, Michigan.
Image courtesy of author

Twice "Othered"

In the United States, American Indian and Alaska Native students are almost twice as likely to be identified as having specific learning disabilities, and more than three times as likely to be labeled with developmental delay (Reschly 2009). African American students are three times more likely to be labeled with intellectual disability (cognitive impairment, or mental retardation depending on the state), and almost two and a half times more likely to be identified with emotional impairment or emotional disturbance than any other group (Ladner 2009). Hispanic students are 20 percent more likely to be identified with specific learning disabilities, and slightly overrepresented nationwide in the categories of hearing impairment and intellectual disability. However, school districts with a predominantly White population have Hispanic students placed in special education programs at rates 47 percent higher than do high minority school districts (Monroe 2009). White non-Hispanic students are 60 percent more likely to qualify for special education services for "other health impairments"—the category under which ADHD/ADD is generally placed (Gould 2009). Asian Americans and Pacific Islander students seem to be affected by "the model minority stereotype" (United States Commission on Civil Rights 2009, 19), as they are notably *underrepresented* in all subjective special education eligibility categories (Zamora 2009).

The incidence of overrepresentation and underrepresentation among ethnic groups in special education is referred to as "disproportionality" (Artiles, Kozleski, et al. 2010; Blanchett, Mumford, & Beachum 2005; O'Conner & Fernandez 2006; Skiba, Poloni-Staudinger, et al. 2005; Sullivan & Bal 2013). Disproportionality has been an issue in American education for as long as the United States has had compulsory school attendance laws (Dunn 1968; Hollingsworth 1923). For nearly as long, many educators have recognized that special education has been used as another way to impose racial segregation. In fact, special education disproportionality for Black students increased after 1954, when the *Brown v. Board of Education* Supreme Court decision made segregation on the basis of race alone (officially) illegal (Algozzine 2005; Dunn 1968).

Today, sixty years later, African American students with disabilities are still more likely than any other group to be placed in restrictive (segregated) educational settings, such as self-contained classrooms and separate facilities for students with intellectual or emotional disabilities. Over one-third of African American students with disabilities are in restrictive educational environments for more than 60 percent of the school day; whereas 15 percent of White students with disabilities are in restrictive class settings (Monroe 2009).

Door at elementary school in Flint, Michigan.
Image courtesy of author

During the nineteenth and twentieth centuries, thousands of Native American and Alaskan Native children were sent to involuntary residential schools designed to force assimilation to Euro-American culture and language. Today, overrepresentation of Native American and Alaskan Native students as "learning delayed" and learning disabled, may underscore the cultural bias in special education labels. The language, concepts, and information valued in American schools reflect a worldview based on linear thinking and placement of information in order according to a determined hierarchy. Jamake Highwater (1995) outlined the fundamental problem American Indian students can face when trying to adapt to White American schools:

> But there are no methods by which we can translate a mentality … when an English word is descriptive—like the word "wilderness"—I am often appalled … How perplexing it is to discover two English synonyms for Earth—"soil" and "dirt"—used to describe uncleanliness, *soiled* and *dirty*. And how upset-

ting it is to discover that the word "dirty" in English is also used to describe obscenities! Or take the word "universe," in which I find even more complicated problems, for Indians do not believe in a "*uni*-verse," but a "*multi*-verse." Indians don't believe that there is one fixed and eternal truth; they think there are many different and equally valid truths (206–207).

Many school psychologists might find it a daunting task to test a student who insisted upon answering with "many different and equally valid truths."

Disproportionality in special education is not unique to the United States, but the results of cultural bias look quite different in different countries. In Australia and New Zealand, Indigenous peoples and Pacific Islanders are most overrepresented in special education, are most likely to be educated in restrictive settings (especially separate facilities), and are most likely to face expulsion. Black Caribbean (*not* African), Pakistani, Irish-Traveller, and Gypsy/Roma students are overrepresented in special education in the United Kingdom, and they are more likely than other ethnic groups to be educated in restrictive environments. The United Kingdom's Irish-Travellers and Gypsy/Roma students experience the greatest degree of disproportionality, being significantly overrepresented in several categories related to intellectual and behavior disabilities. Gypsy/Roma students also experience the greatest degree of overrepresentation in special education and restrictive settings in the Czech Republic, where they are more than twenty-one times more likely to be identified as having mental retardation. In the Czech Republic city of Ostrova *over half of all* Gypsy/Roma students are restricted to separate special education schools (Reschly 2009).

Elementary school building on the north side of Flint, Michigan.
Image courtesy of author

International comparison of disproportionality suggests the problem is something much more sinister than coincidence made worse by isolated cases of bigotry and cultural misunderstanding. Ethnic groups experiencing the most marked educational discrimination and segregation are the same groups which have been subjected to histories of systematic persecution—forced relocation, ethnic cleansing, and genocide. So when we speak in terms of Least Restrictive Environment, and decide that segregated self-contained settings can be justified for some, we should consider the historical implications. These are among the "facts that remain difficult to ignore anymore" (Algozzine 2005).

Graffiti in Flint, Michigan.
Image courtesy of author

Institutionalized Racism in Schools

Just as ableism is at the foundation of U.S. culture, so is racism—it is at the base of all U.S. social institutions. And so it is that people who are white, middle or upper class, male, heterosexual form the dominant group in American society. Racism plays out unintentionally and often unknown in U.S. schools. Tools used by schools to dominate groups that are Other rely on special education to segregate them, ensuring that they never achieve the opportunities taken for granted by many. It doesn't matter that those tools are unseen and unknown by those who hold power (they are unseen and unknown *because* they hold power)—they serve to keep dominant groups, and Othered groups, firmly in their places (P. Smith 2004).

Questions for Discussion

▶ Why might White students be overrepresented under the category of "Other Health Impairment," and not for intellectual or behavioral disabilities? Consider that a student with an Other Health Impairment label may have the same test scores and behavior problems as a student identified with mild cognitive or emotional disability.

▶ Segregation based on disability can be used to perpetuate racial segregation. Does knowing this make you think differently about inclusion?

▶ Were you surprised that Pacific Islander students are considered a "model minority" and underrepresented in special education in the United States, but then overrepresented in special education in New Zealand and Australia? What about the difference in disproportionality among African students in the United States versus the United Kingdom?

Chapter 30

Gender, Sexuality, and Disability: AJ's Story

William Milburn and Michael Peacock

Hi!

I'm AJ. I'm a 24-year-old student at Deveraux College. Before you read my story, take a good look at me. I am a person with a disability, although my life does not revolve around my disability. You may not even be able to tell that I have a disability just by looking at me. Is a disability even visible? What makes a disability a *disability*, anyhow? My story may give you an idea of how disability has made an impact on my life, but no matter how much of my story I tell you, I'm still the expert on my own life. You're the expert on how you interpret my story. So, don't worry—you're not completely powerless!

Images © Anchiy, 2014. Used under license from Shutterstock, Inc.

When I was a kid, my dad and I used to go on long-distance rides. I remember a time when we got stuck in a terrible storm. We had to stop riding our bikes and set up camp for the night. What would be a stressful situation for anyone, ended up as the best time we ever spent together. That was ten years ago.

When I was 17 my dad came home from work early and caught me in my room looking like this:

Image © Anchiy, 2014. Used under license from Shutterstock, Inc.

For any normal teenage girl that wouldn't have been an issue, or at least one that would not have had the implications I faced. My dad didn't think his teenage son should look like that. He called me "disgusting" and said I was an embarrassment to the family. His words hurt more than the bruises on my ribs. I was literally kicked out of my house and had nowhere to go. Lucky for me, I was still in a jeans and t-shirt. I washed the makeup off my face in my neighbor's pool and ran to my friend Eric's house.

Connections

▶ In the U.S., 40% of homeless youth identify as lesbian, gay, bisexual, transgender, or queer.

▶ 26% of youth who come out experience parental rejection and are kicked out of their homes.

Additional Resource: Kicked Out by Sassafras Lowery

Six months later I got my first apartment and registered for my first college classes. Initially, I struggled with figuring out financial aid and the means to pay for school. My relationship with my father became very strained and complex as he was no longer an option to turn towards for support. I would often sit by the phone wanting to call him. I would sit there for hours feeling helpless, even depressed at times.

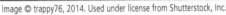

Image © trappy76, 2014. Used under license from Shutterstock, Inc.   Image © Aletia, 2014. Used under license from Shutterstock, Inc.

Connections

"Lesbian, gay, bisexual, transgender, and queer/questioning (LGBTQ) people are likely to be at higher risk for depression. The reason for these disparities is most likely related to the societal stigma and resulting prejudice and discrimination that LGBTQ face on a regular basis, from society at large, but also from family members, peers, co-workers and classmates"

Additional Resource: National Alliance of Mental Illness: Depression and LGBTQ Community Fact Sheet

http://www.nami.org/Template.cfm?Section=Depression&Template=/ContentManagement/ContentDisplay.cfm&ContentID=88883

College started and I took my first steps into the world as a woman. I began dressing in women's clothing and wearing make up; it felt natural and allowed me to feel true to myself. However, the gaze of my classmates and the anxious feeling of going against expectations led me to feel a knot in my chest. This was the beginning of many panic attacks during my first semester of college. I would later come to find out that depression and anxiety were components of my life that needed to be addressed.

Connections

A person's sexual orientation is not directly related to one's gender identity. For example, a transgender man may identify with a heterosexual orientation as much as a cisgender (typically-gendered) man would.

For more information visit: http://www.glaad.org/transgender

The panic attacks became worse and intensified throughout my first semester of college. If you never had a panic attack before, then you've probably never felt like you're having a heart attack—unless you've had a heart attack. I couldn't breathe or talk, and would be drenched in sweat when they would subside. The first one happened while I was in my biology class. I sat there feeling like the world was caving in on me while my classmates took notes and followed along with the lecture. I was invisible.

Image © Intellistudies, 2014. Used under license from Shutterstock, Inc.

Image © hikrcn, 2014. Used under license from Shutterstock, Inc.

My second semester was better; I declared a major and began seeking friends and ways to feel more connected on campus. I had always been interested in theater and people had always mentioned that I was witty and had a decent sense of humor. I saw an ad for an open mic night with the campus Improv Club at a local coffee shop and thought I would give this a try. I instantly knew I had found something for me. People were laughing along with me, and not at me. It had been a long time since I had felt this comfortable in a social situation and I thought that perhaps I had turned a page in my life. My panic attacks became fewer and farther between, and I felt energy in my life that had been missing since the incidents with my father.

Image © Condor 36, 2014. Used under license from Shutterstock, Inc.

Image © AlienNation, 2014. Used under license from Shutterstock, Inc.

I began hanging out with an upperclassman from the Improv Club named Lucille. She would come over to hang out and would bring a bottle of cheap vodka to share. We could be doing the simplest things but would have the greatest time together. I didn't like the taste of vodka at first but getting drunk was worth it. Everything and everyone around me was more fun when I was drunk. I had never had a panic attack while I was drunk. There were a few times I woke up puking and didn't quit for six hours. There is nothing pretty about seeing your own bile, but I kept drinking anyways.

Image © Marcio Jose Bastos, 2014. Used under license from Shutterstock, Inc.

Connections

▶ An alcoholic is a person with a **disability** and is protected by the Americans with Disabilities Act.

▶ Seeking help for anxiety, depression, or substance abuse from one's primary health care providers can be a challenge in and of itself for LGBT people. "Health care providers are in a position to respond to suicidal behavior in youth even if young people do not readily volunteer information about these problems. Unfortunately, LGBT people report hostile treatment and substandard care as well as **denials of care** by health care providers."

www.ada.gov and http://www.sprc.org/

I began developing a crush on Lucille, and felt the feelings were being reciprocated. One night Lucille and I got really drunk and fell asleep together on my bed. I woke up to her arm around me. I had always thought that Lucille may be a lesbian like me, and heard rumors in our Improv Club that this was the case. This didn't matter to me. I enjoyed it but also felt a sense of tension inside of me that I couldn't quite explain. The more time we spent together the stronger my feelings developed. Lucille became the person I could confide in, to vent to, or simply to share a laugh with.

Connections

A *homoromantic* person who is romantically attracted to a member of the same sex *or gender*. Homoromantic asexuals seek romantic relationships for a variety of reasons, including companionship, affection, and intimacy, but they are not necessarily sexually attracted to their romantic partners. The sexual counterpart to homoromantic is homosexual. Most homosexuals are also homoromantic.

For more information visit: www.asexuality.org

One night after a great show, Lucille and I went to a cast party. Everyone there drank more than they should have. I had to have gone through ten red plastic cups. At about 3 A.M., our friend Braden offered Lucille a free shot if she kissed me. I didn't know she was going to kiss me, but when she did, I didn't know what to do. People laughed and cheered, Lucille got her shot, and I started feeling the pangs of a panic attack. I ran into the bathroom to be alone. I couldn't stop crying and shaking. Lucille knocked on the bathroom door about five minutes later asking me if I was alright. I didn't answer, she barged in, and closed the door behind her. She stayed there silently until I stopped crying. She suggested we should head back to my apartment.

I forgot my driver's license on my coffee table before I left the house earlier that night. When we got to my apartment I went straight to the bathroom to throw up. When I came out of the bathroom, Lucille was gone. She didn't return my calls or texts the next day. I guess she didn't know what to do after she found out that my real name is Anthony Jablonski.

I stopped going to class and I never went back to the Improv Club. Losing Lucille as a friend made me feel embarrassed and as abandoned as when my father kicked me out of the house when I was 17.

After my financial aid stopped coming in, and I had spent all my money on cheap vodka and rent, I realized I had to get a job so I wouldn't end up on the streets. Getting job interviews wasn't the hard part. Their expectations didn't meet reality when I walked through the door. They were expecting to see Anthony when AJ came in for the interview. Interview after interview, I never got called back.

Connections

Most people develop a gender identity that matches their biological or anatomical sex. For some, however, their gender identity is different from their biological or assigned sex.

For more information visit: www.genderspectrum.org

Image © asiana, 2014. Used under license from Shutterstock, Inc.

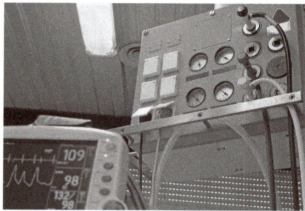

Image © smart.art, 2014. Used under license from Shutterstock, Inc.

I was two weeks late paying my rent when I finally got a job. Rather—Anthony got the job. AJ was back in the closet, lonelier than ever. Having to hide my identity again made me feel that whoever I thought I was, was deviant, and that something must be wrong with me. The panic attacks became more frequent and severe, lasting longer, and interfered with my job. I showed up to work drunk from the night before more than once. I got fired after having come into work late for the third time. I couldn't help myself from the panic attacks. I wanted to work, but I didn't want to be who everyone else thought I should be.

The depression subsumed me. I was unable to deal with the world around me. My shame had transformed into utter disgust and hatred toward myself. No one should ever feel this way. Later that night I drank myself into oblivion. Somehow I managed to make it to Lucille's apartment. She barely knew who I was, as she had never met Anthony before. The next thing I knew I was lying in the emergency room with a tube up my nose. If you've never had a stomach pump, then imagine a garden hose being shoved up your nose, through your sinus cavity, and into your throat. Liquid charcoal gets pumped into your stomach to absorb the alcohol. That same hose has to come out of your face, along with the residual liquid charcoal, mucus, and blood.

Connections

A study of transgender people over the age of 18 found that 32% had attempted suicide.

For more information read:
Clements-Nolle, K., Marx, R., & Katz, M. (2006). Attempted suicide among transgender persons: The influence of gender-based discrimination and victimization. *Journal of Homosexuality, 51*(3), 53–69.

This wake-up call pushed me to change and take control of my life again. I started seeing a counselor on campus to deal with my depression, anxiety, and alcoholism. I started cycling again. I found an outlet that helped me through times of frustration that was healthy and not destructive. I know that dealing with depression and anxiety will be a component of my life and it will never completely go away. Now I have ways to be in more control and to take on these challenges.

Image © Anchiy, 2014. Used under license from Shutterstock, Inc.

Image © Kryvenok Anastasiia, 2014. Used under license from Shutterstock, Inc.

Reflection

What we can learn from AJ's story is that there are many aspects of our lives that are completely invisible. Or, there are things we take for granted and just assume about people we don't know. Even the people closest to us have parts of their identity that we may never get to know.

AJ's sexuality and gender identity are only two aspects of AJ's life, yet you and your classmates may have the least difficult time recalling those aspects of her identity as you share her story with your friends. Which aspects of AJ's life do you think may present the most challenges in her life? Which aspects of her life may afford her the most privileges? As you think about your response, consider what evidence you can gather from AJ's story regarding her race, ethnicity, social class, disability status, gender, sexual orientation, age, mental health, physical well-being, social/support network, political views, education level, and family upbringing.

Sure, it's easy to make assumptions about one person or another based on how they look or what kinds of friends they have. You might think that having an identity is what helps us distinguish *ourselves* from *others*. Have you ever thought that maybe your identity is a collection of generalizations that *others* use to describe *you*?

Section 5

How Do We Imagine a Society in Which People with Disabilities Are a Part of All Communities?

Chapter 31

Creating Community

Phil Smith

Loneliness is the only real disability. (Mount, in Morgan, 2009)

In this book, we've looked at how the United States is an increasingly diverse society. Diversity is a good thing—whether it's in the wider environment, represented by biodiversity, or in our culture, represented by social diversity. Biodiversity in the natural world ensures that *all* beings live and thrive. In a world in which living things are connected synergistically (the total is actually greater than the sum of the parts), we cannot remove any single piece of the puzzle without putting the whole at risk. Instead of planting cropland to a single plant (monocultural farming), some argue that we gain much more by planting farms that produce a great variety of plants (polycultural farming)—the soil, the environment, and ultimately human health and well-being. Watersheds and bioregions benefit from a wide diversity of plant, animal, and landscape features. Lacking these, the environment—and we—suffer.

The same is true in the social context. Diversity in our culture gives us richer conversations, richer contexts, richer communities, at macro and micro levels. We all learn and grow and benefit from the participation and engagement of multiple ethnic, racial, sexual, religious—and, yes, ability—groups.

So it makes sense that, rather than shunning or eliminating diversity in our social communities, we should embrace it, and enhance it. How do we do that? What does this have to do with disability? And what do we mean by the notion of community?

In schools, we've known for some time that all students, including those without disabilities, benefit both academically and socially when students with disabilities are fully included in the general education curriculum (P. Smith 2010). When we create inclusive environments in educational communities, everyone benefits.

It makes sense that the same should be true in civic communities—the communities of neighborhoods, streets, villages, towns, cities, states, countries, and the globe. Big or small, however they are constructed or understood, communities benefit from socio-cultural diversity. This is tough sometimes in a society like the United States (and many other modern Western societies) which have roots firmly entrenched in racism, classism, sexism, ableism, and heterosexism (to name just a few). What will be required, then, is a kind of cultural shift—changing the culture in which we are embedded. No small task. And all needing to be done by breakfast time tomorrow. Phew! No pressure, right?

The work is made more difficult by another feature of U.S. culture, which holds the notion of independence as a quality to which we should all aspire. Our forebears put it into words at the very beginning of this country, in the *Declaration of Independence*. The rugged, pioneering individualism of our ancestors has, unfortunately, brought us all (and by us, I include all sorts of groups who are otherwise disenfranchised and oppressed in the

United States) kinds of trouble and difficulty, harming us in ways big and small, seen and unseen. I think a quality more appropriate to a diverse society, one that will bring us greater benefit, is that of interdependence—discovering and honoring the connections between us, seeing that we need each other, with all of our strengths and weaknesses, assets and deficits. This will mean that we need to focus on establishing and tightening the connections between us, of supporting each other. We'll need to create and enhance ways for us to truly belong. O'Brien and O'Brien talk about the importance of becoming "members of each other":

> People recognized as members benefit from everyday exchanges of support that create opportunities to play socially valued roles and chances to form personally significant relationships. People excluded from membership risk loneliness, isolation, and powerlessness. (1996, 5)

We all benefit from receiving support, and from providing support. Encouraging and creating opportunities for everyone to be members of civic and educational communities.

There is a danger here though, a trap, for those offering support to others. The trap is what Norman Kunc calls the "politics of help." Sometimes, people offering or providing support and help to others do so in order to make themselves feel good: "I helped someone today, so I'm a good person." The help or support they provide benefits *them*, and not the person who is helped or supported (Van der Klift & Kunc 2002).

There is only one way out of this mess, and it goes back to the idea of interdependence. Interdependence is a two-way street, not one-way. It implies not only that we need to *give* help and support, but we also have to *receive* it. The notion here is one of reciprocity—relationships need to be two-way, reciprocal. Both parties to a relationship need to get something out of it, not just one. Only when the helper becomes the helped, and the helped becomes the helper, will the relationship be truly reciprocal, and reflect real interdependence (Van der Klift & Kunc 2002).

Belonging

You've probably seen Maslow's hierarchy of human needs. An essential element for self-actualization is that of belonging.

Basic human Needs

Image © SCOTTCHAN, 2014. Used under license from Shutterstock, Inc.

Yet too often, people must earn the right to belong, because they are too far outside the range of what is considered normal in our culture. Everyone deserves the right to be part of our communities. Belonging creates the opportunity for creating real human diversity, and real community (Kunc 2000).

One of my colleagues, Deborah Gallagher (2010), suggests (and I think she's right) that the whole notion of inclusion for people with disabilities is not a great idea. She says that because people with disabilities don't truly belong in our communities, our institutions, and our culture. Because they don't belong, when we try to include them in educational communities, and civic communities, people are always questioning whether they should really be there—whether they *can* really be there. What she's implying, I think, is that what we need to work on is not so much inclusion for people with disabilities, but belonging—and, of course, not just for people with disabilities, but for all of us.

Keeping People Safe

Because people with disabilities don't belong (or at least, they haven't) in our communities, they've been segregated, kept out. At least one rationale for segregating people with disabilities, either in institutions or in separate schools and classrooms, was the notion that it was the only way to keep people safe. The idea was that people with disabilities, especially those with significant, developmental, and psychiatric disabilities were at great risk of violence and abuse. It is absolutely true that people with disabilities are at extraordinary risk for experiencing harm, physically, emotionally, and psychologically, in our society (P. Smith 1999; 2001; 2005). What we have come to know and understand, though, is that people with disabilities are not safer in segregated settings. In fact, the reverse is true—given our experience with institutions in the twenty-first century in the United States, we know that people are more likely to experience violence and abuse in those settings.

Instead, "the only real protections for a person are other people" (Schwartz 1992, 166). Neighbors, colleagues, friends, family members: those are the kinds of folks who keep each of us safe, keep all people safe. Again, the real work for people with disabilities may not be trying to include people into communities, but to create and enhance communities so that everyone truly belongs.

How Do We Build Community? Circles of Support

We all need help to do what we want in our lives, whether or not we describe ourselves as having a disability. Interdependence and reciprocal relationships are essential for us to meet our needs and achieve our dreams. One way to get that started is through a circle of support (Aichroth et al. 2002; P. Smith 2010). A circle of support can be described as

> an intentional, invited, facilitated group of friends, neighbors, co-workers, family members, and support persons who gather to provide natural support, advice, and friendship for a focus person who does not otherwise have unpaid supports in their life. (Aichroth et al. 2002, 21)

Image © Antonov Roman, 2014. Used under license from Shutterstock, Inc.

Many people have lots of different kinds of people in their lives. Imagine, if you will, a set of nested, concentric circles, in which the people we rely on reside. In the innermost circle is ourselves, and perhaps one or two loved ones without whom we could not imagine living our lives. In the next circle out is our family and close friends (however you define family and friendship for yourself). In the circle surrounding that one are people that we might describe as associational—groups to whom we belong, such as churches, youth groups, volunteer organizations, hobby groups, and the like. In the final circle are people who are paid to be in our lives—physicians, lawyers, tax preparers, dentists, and the like.

Many people who are vulnerable for whatever reason, including people with especially significant disabilities, have fewer people in their inner circles. Most of the people in their lives are in their outer circles. Some people, perhaps the most vulnerable, only have people who are paid to be in their lives. Imagine what your life would be like if you had only those kind of folks around you—no family, no friends. Imagine how you might feel about your life, about your future. While people who are paid to be in our lives are important, and can offer us much—can even care deeply about us—nothing can replace the kind of care and support from people who are *not* paid to be in our lives.

For circles of support to be successful, especially when the focus person has only paid people in their lives, a person to facilitate the circle is essential. Their role is to organize the participants, to invite people to participate, to ensure that the circle doesn't fall apart. They may set up meetings for the circle (food can be an important and useful tool to pull people together). The facilitator does not need to be paid in order to fill the role. They do need to ensure that the focus person's needs and wishes regarding the circle and its activities are met.

Circles of support will not solve the problems of support, reciprocity, and interdependence for people with disabilities. They are only the first step toward developing real friendship and community for vulnerable people—they do not, in and of themselves, constitute friendship and community. But, sometimes, taking that first step is an essential thing to undertake.

The Power of Self-Advocacy

There's a lot that professionals can do in our lives. We all rely on them—my dentist makes sure my teeth are in good shape; my physician helps me when I have the flu. But there are some things professionals can't give to us: real friendship is one. Unfortunately, "real gains in empowerment and choice for persons with … disabilities have been made in spite of the work of professionals rather than because of it" (Aichroth et al. 2002, 24).

For a long time, people with disabilities—especially those with intellectual, developmental, and psychiatric disabilities—have been denied opportunities to make decisions for themselves, and to speak for themselves. They've long been perceived as being mentally incompetent—unable to manage their affairs in ways that others think are appropriate.

The self-advocacy movement began in the 1960s alongside the disability right's movement. It became more formalized in 1991, with the establishment of a national organization, Self-Advocates Becoming Empowered (SABE), with active chapters across the United States. Supporting self-advocacy and the self-advocacy movement is a critical move toward ensuring that people with disabilities play an active role in all of our communities.

Image © Mark Baldwin, 2014. Used under license from Shutterstock, Inc.

Asset Based Community Development

One approach to developing inclusive communities is called Asset Based Community Development (ABCD). Developed by Mike Green, Henry Moore, and John McKnight, it proposes that all communities have a set of assets that, if located and understood, can help communities figure out what they need to do in order to solve their problems. Rather than focusing on the problems that a community has, ABCD seeks to map out the cultural, physical, and other resources or assets that exist in and alongside communities. The approach is democratic, and citizen-centered, based in developing reciprocity, interdependence, care, and support at community levels. It relies on unpaid community leaders rather than paid professionals. It can be a powerful tool for changing culture and society from the grassroots (Green, Moore, and O'Brien 2006).

Questions for Discussion

▶ What could you do to work toward creating inclusive communities? What would you do in your own community?

▶ How do the ideas discussed here translate into what you do on a daily basis, in your own neighborhood?

Chapter 32

Disability and Faith Communities

Rhonda Vander Laan Kraai

"To assume that spirituality is irrelevant to a person simply on the basis of a label of intellectual disability or autism is among the deepest forms of prejudice." (Carter 2007)

Introduction

Community and spirituality takes many forms and is as diverse as the individuals who desire to access both. Although many barriers in public places have been removed because of the Americans with Disability Amendments (ADA) of (1990 and 2009), the ability to fully participate in one important aspect of community remains limited, that of communities of faith. Many agencies are supportive in their efforts to encourage the idea that anyone with or without a disability should be able to find an inclusive congregation in order to practice their faith and be supported by a congregational community. From the White House (2001), The New Freedom initiative states, "Every effort should be made to ensure that Americans with disabilities have the opportunity to be integrated into their communities and welcomed into communities of faith" (23). *TASH*, an international advocacy association of people with disabilities gives their statement of affirmation: "supports the right of individuals with disabilities to participate in spiritual expression or organized religion as they so choose and promotes the provision of any and all supports needed by people with disabilities to so participate (2003). The National Organization on Disability (NOD), (2010), found that 57 percent of people without disabilities in the United States said that they attended a place of worship at least once a month compared to 43 percent of people with significant disabilities. The gap may seem insignificant, however, until you explore perhaps why there is a gap.

Congregational Response: A Study

With those inclusive resolutions in mind, Kraai and Snyder (2010) (unpublished findings) conducted a study that included interviewing face-to-face, forty-seven different Christian church staff members, to determine their ideas about their roles in serving people with disabilities. Findings indicated that most churches were not attuned to the need for inclusion (thirty of forty-seven Midwest churches), with larger churches no more likely than smaller ones to have made physical access improvements or to offer special services or programs. In response to the reasons that they don't provide access, the most stated response was that "there wasn't a need or not enough interest." However for those churches that did have inclusive access, there was a high correlation between starting the disability ministry and there "being a need" for programming. The most frequent types of opportunities for those with disabilities were: Sunday school, special activities, worship support, and support groups. Follow-up interviews revealed that most of the pastoral staff did not have any training or knowledge in the area of providing inclusive access for people with disabilities, and they felt that it would be helpful to be more knowledgeable about inclusive practices for faith communities. Senior leadership in the church were often quoted as, "we didn't learn anything about disabilities and church life in seminary." It was reported by respondents that some of the strongest, most well-developed inclusive congregations began programs to help those with disabilities because there was a need in the congregation, and then as they presented inclusivity, their numbers grew in terms of volunteers and those whom they served promoting an attitude of belonging to all who wished to worship.

Barriers to Inclusion

During conversations with interviewees, many felt that having wheelchair access and hearing aid devices were the extent of access to their congregations. Physical access is of course, a prerequisite for those with physical disabilities to enter and move around the facility without difficulty. However, there are many other ways that churches may have roadblocks to inclusion that they might not have even considered.

Carter (2007) has identified barriers that push people away or prevent people from participating in communities of faith. Those barriers include more than the usual elevator provided or an assistive listening device for hearing in the pew. He suggests there are other issues that prevent full inclusion for those with disabilities that include architectural, attitudinal, communication, program offerings, and the type(s) of participation needed during a worship service.

Levels of Acceptance

Hubach (2006) in her book, *Same Lake, Different Boat: Coming alongside people touched by disability*, describes her family's first Sunday in their congregation after their son was born.

> "Timothy Robert Hubach was born last Sunday morning. Fred and Steph have asked me to let you know that he was born with Down syndrome." At that point the audible gasps of our church family could be heard around the sanctuary, giving voice to the raw pain in our own hearts. "But Fred and Steph also want you to know that your condolences are not expected. Instead, they want you to celebrate with them the life of this child of the covenant." Greeted after the service by the congratulatory hugs of our teary-eyed friends, we could not imagine a more wonderful way to introduce Timmy to his church family.

People who desire to join in a community of faith, should be able to find an inclusive environment in which to participate that doesn't provide barriers to inclusion, but actually supports and nourishes their spiritual development and desires. Ideally, this environment provides an outlet to support spiritual growth as well as a place for them to use their gifts in the development and service of others in and outside of the community of faith.

Faith communities can create their own attitudes about disability. The culture of the congregation can either be supportive, non-supportive, or lukewarm to the idea of those with disabilities being included in their congregation. Vander Plaats in his *5 Stages, the Journey of Disability Attitudes* (Elim Christian Services & Vander Plaats, D. 2012), suggest that there are stages of acceptance of those with disabilities in the culture of a church setting. Similar in sequence to other journeys of acceptance of other issues, each stage is a step toward full inclusion of everyone in the congregation where everyone is seen as an equal partner in the mission of the congregation.

Perhaps on your own walk of acceptance for those with differing challenges, you find yourself somewhere on a continuum of acceptance of people who are not typically included in the mainstream of your social circles. Somewhere from just being aware to advocating for those with special needs, or falling somewhere in between.

the 5 stages
changing attitudes

STAGE 1: IGNORANCE

Weaknesses and disabilities are a sign that God either does not care or is not able to fix the situation. In fact, they may be a result of sin or a lack of faith. God is not involved in the life of someone with a disability, because He can't use people who are so broken. I do not know people with disabilities, nor do I know anything about disabilities. I have no interest in getting to know them or to know more about their life.

STAGE 2: PITY

I feel sorry for people with disabilities. It's too bad, really. I am blessed by God and I can help others. I am grateful that my children are not disabled. People with weaknesses and disabilities obviously need someone like me to help them and give them meaning, due to their troubles. I really don't see any meaning or purpose to their lives.

STAGE 3: CARE

Like me, people with disabilities were created in God's image. By that virtue alone they have value. I hope that someone will take the time to show them God's love, and I will happily support such an effort. In fact, I think we need to find ways to help those people. Maybe we should start a special church education class, or respite care for the sake of the parents.

STAGE 4: FRIENDSHIP

I have come to know and spend time with a friend who has a disability. This person has value in God's sight, but also in mine, and I know that my life is better for having known this person, and as much as I have helped her, she has also blessed me. In fact, I now like to initiate relationships with people who have disabilities. God brings many different people into my church and community, including people with disabilities, and we all benefit as we grow in friendship with each other.

STAGE 5: CO-LABORERS

If God has called each of us to serve and praise Him with every fiber of our beings, then He has done the same for our brothers and sisters in Christ with disabilities. I think ministry should not just be to people with disabilities, but with or alongside people who have disabilities. Together, we will encourage and equip each other, with and without disabilities, into every good work to respond to God's call on our lives. We can all give and we can all receive.

BUILDING AWARENESS   PROVIDING ACCESS   INTEGRATING   ENGAGING

"5 STAGES: THE JOURNEY OF DISABILITY ATTITUDES" IS COPYRIGHT © 2014, ELIM CHRISTIAN SERVICES AND DAN VANDER PLAATS WITH THANKS TO DISABILITY CONCERNS CRC, DISABILITY CONCERNS RCA, JONI AND FRIENDS, AND MANY OTHERS

ELIM

SCAN THIS CODE OR GO TO WWW.THE5STAGES.COM FOR MORE INFORMATION AND RESOURCES.

IMPORTANT SCRIPTURES

John 9:1-3, 2 Corinthians 11:30, 2 Corinthians 12:9 — God uses a life with disabilities to display the power of Christ.

1 Corinthians 1:27, 12:14, 18, 22-25 — We need one another in the body of Christ.

Luke 14:13-14, 21-23 — Christ calls us to include everyone.

Psalm 139:13-14, Ephesians 2:10 — God designed each person for his express purpose in this world.

2 Timothy 3:16-17, 1 Thessalonians 5:11 — God has called and equipped all His children to serve His Kingdom.

— thanks to Wendie Benton for her submissions.

THEOLOGICAL FOUNDATION

We are all disabled, but we are also not all disabled — we are all broken, yes, but some of us truly do face more difficulty, need more help, etcetera.

Disability is not a curse, but it is also not a blessing — God somehow works His will despite and sometimes even because of, a disability.

We are not valuable because of what we accomplish (because we are able) or simply because we are different (because we are disabled). **We are valuable because we are created in God's image, and because of His work in, through, and around our lives.**

OTHER RESOURCES

Same Lake, Different Boat
Stephanie Hubach

GLUE Training Manual
Barb Newman

Inclusion Handbook
Mark Stephenson and Terry De Young

Including People with Disabilities in Faith Communities
Dr. Erik Carter

TALKING POINTS - PRESENTING THE "CHANGING ATTITUDES" JOURNEY

The following are general guidelines to help you prepare your own presentation of the 5 Stages. These guidelines were prepared by Mark Stephenson and Terry De Young, directors of the Disability Concerns ministries of the Christian Reformed Church of North America and the Reformed Church of America, respectively.

INTRODUCTION

Becoming a congregation where everybody belongs and everybody serves is not an action but a journey.

Define disability: "Persons with disabilities include those who have long-term physical, mental, intellectual, or sensory impairments which in interaction with various barriers may hinder their full and effective participation in society on an equal basis with others." (U.N. Convention on Rights of Persons with Disabilities)

Highlight what your own church has done to become more inclusive of people with disabilities. Give specific examples including building accessibility (ramps, bathrooms, etc.), communication accessibility (large print bulletins, hearing loops, etc.), ministries (Friendship, inclusion of children with disabilities in youth programs, etc.), and involvement in ministry (make a general reference to people with disabilities on committees and serving in ministry in a variety of ways).

TRANSITION

Invite people to look at the diagram on the front tat moves from "Ignorance" to "Co-Laborers."

SELF-ASSESSMENT

Invite people to assess their own relationship with people who have disabilities by asking themselves questions like these: How do I feel when I am with someone who has a disability — fear, pity, disgust, concern, appreciation, enjoyment, admiration? How do I treat this person — ignore, greet, interact and engage? What have I done to make our church more welcoming to people who live with disabilities?

CHURCH ASSESSMENT

Encourage members to think about where their church is at on this journey. If someone with wheelchair came to our church, could she get in, use the bathroom, sit in the sanctuary with her family? If a boy with autism and behavior issues came to our Sunday School, would leaders ask his parents not to bring him back, or would they work to find out how they can best include him? How often do our members visit or phone members who do not attend church because of depression or some physical disability? What do we need to do next to continue on the journey of disability attitudes: build awareness, provide access, encourage integration, or engage people with disabilities?

CONCLUSION

Sixty-seven percent of families affected by disability have left a church because they did not feel welcome. Of that 67 percent, one third of them not only left their congregation, but also left their faith tradition. Do we want to be a church that drives away people affected by disability, or that engages them as co-laborers in the work of God's Kingdom?

Where do we go from here?

Awareness of the freedoms that need to exist for all is an important first step. Opening the doors of all institutions, whether they be community, recreational, private, or faith institutions so that all may enter, was a tenant of the basis of the creation of America. Inclusionary practices for faith communities is more than a passing thought of kindness. Many congregations have created respite services, after-school programs, long-term care homes for people in their congregations with disabilities. All types of avenues of support are being created. On the flipside, many other congregations are only beginning to consider what could be done to open their doors to everyone who wants to worship in their faith communities. Many resources are available to help congregations think about being inclusive and what that may look like for their particular type of mission. Full inclusion for people with disabilities in faith communities is definitely in the evolution stages. It appears that the shift to full inclusion will take a launch into re-thinking about how people with differing abilities can sit under the same roof and worship the same God in a graceful and peaceful community of believers.

Chapter 33

The Role of the Family

Sally Burton-Hoyle

Introduction

"Family" refers to two or more people who regard themselves as a unit and perform the functions that are typically completed in order for the family to maintain a sense of balance. Does this definition fit your family? "Family" may look differently depending on your age, race, and culture. "Family" may be what is thought of as traditional with a Mom and Dad or it could be a group of adults who possess a strong connection and work toward a common outcome for their identified members. The goal of each family is to successfully launch their child or children into the community so that they can become self-determined adults. There are obstacles for all families, but when a family member has a disability, challenges may seem insurmountable.

In 2011, researchers at the Centers for Disease Control studied the prevalence of persons with developmental disabilities. They found that there were 1.8 million more children with developmental disabilities in 2006–2008, as compared to a decade earlier. The prevalence of autism has increased 289 percent, and ADHD has increased 33 percent. See additional data from the study in Table 1 (Boyle et al. 2012).

TABLE 1   Autism: Rates of Occurrence
► Males have twice the prevalence of any DD than females and more specifically had higher prevalence of ADHD, autism, learning disabilities, stuttering/stammering and other DDs;
► Hispanic children had lower prevalence of several disorders as compared to non-Hispanic white, and non-Hispanic black children, including ADHD and learning disabilities;
► Non-Hispanic black children had higher prevalence of stuttering/stammering than non-Hispanic white children;
► Children insured by Medicaid had nearly a two-fold higher prevalence of any DD compared to those with private insurance; and
► Children from families with income below the federal poverty level had a higher prevalence of DDs.
(Boyle et al. 2012)

When we consider these numbers, it is important to remember that each person with a disability is part of a family. Families will invariably experience difficulty when a child is diagnosed with a disability. The impact on things like marriage and finances may lead to divorce and/or other familial problems. Families may also struggle to find adequate resources to support a disabled child in their home, school, and community (Ivey 2004). There is also variability in the overall socialization and communication ability of each child or individual. This can challenge a family's approach to managing their son's or daughter's future. The family's perception of disability in general may also influence how negatively or positively they react to a diagnosis. Some families may view a disability as a catastrophe, while others look upon the experience as "difficult but manageable." This chapter will cover the cognitive adaptation and functions of the family and the shared responsibilities of school and community that are necessary in raising a child or children with a disability to become self-determined adults.

How do families adapt to a disability?

Cognitive adaptation is defined as the factors that impact how families cope with the stress of living with a child with a disability. The stages of cognitive adaptation include the following:

▶ **Search for Meaning**—When families are faced with the information that their child has a disability they may first ask themselves "Why?" As they search for the cause of a disability, and why it happened to their child, many families will ask, "Is it the fault of the environment?" "Vaccines?" "Is it genetic?" "Is it a result of sin?" Families may have a difficult time understanding the disability and may not be able to stop searching until they discover a cause that makes sense.

▶ **Searching for Mastery**—This part of the process may include speaking with experts, gaining additional diagnoses from other doctors and specialists, going on special diets, embarking on treatments which claim to cure the disorder, attending conferences, or speaking with other families. A plan for the remediation of the disorder may provide families with a sense of satisfaction for the time being. They may approach the disability differently, at a later date, but a treatment plan or regime for the time being is helpful for the family.

▶ **Search for Acceptance**—This occurs when the beliefs and experiences of a family are shared and used to support and strengthen all family members. Families may begin to attribute new friendships, connections, and events, which are positive in nature, to having a child with a disability. They accept who their child is and what services and supports will be necessary, at this stage, for the child's future (Turnbull, Summers, & Brotherson 1986).

How a family perceives a disability will either be positive or negative based on how they adapt cognitively to the information. Cognitive adaptation impacts the family system and its approach to fulfilling the roles and responsibilities that all families must contend with.

Family Systems and the Functions of the Family

Family systems theory is based on the idea that all families operate as a system. There are external as well as internal forces which impact the success of the family. Within the family, there are subsystems which include siblings, parents, marital, and extended family. Each of the subsystems has roles and responsibilities that also influence how the family operates.

TABLE 2   Roles of the Family
▶ Parents are in charge of their children.
▶ A marital subsystem is two parents who are married and have a loving and intimate relationship.
▶ Brothers and sisters will nurture, support, and socialize with each other over the lifespan.
▶ Extended family is made up of grandparents, aunts, uncles, cousins, and close family friends.

Image © atikinka, 2014. Used under license from Shutterstock, Inc.

However, with a 50 percent divorce rate, family systems may operate in a manner that does not lead to self-determined children; this often results in dysfunction and disorder in the family. Schools and communities must support families so they can carry out the important roles and responsibilities involved in raising their children. If a family lacks the resources and skills to carry out their optimal roles and responsibilities, then each subsystem fails to support the balance of the unit.

Family systems theory also includes the concepts of flexibility and cohesion. Families must possess the ability to be flexible and adaptive to the new situations and circumstances that arise when a child or family member is diagnosed with a disability and, at the same time, remain cohesive and bound together as a strong family unit. If the family is too adaptable then there are no boundaries and the typically developing siblings may have an inordinate amount of freedom. This may result in truancy, substance abuse, and other signs of family disorder and distress. The benefit of family cohesiveness is evident in traditions valued by the family such as holidays, vacations, and religious events. Alternately, excessive cohesion may lead to increased discipline and overall rigidity to rules. This may have a bad outcome, and certain subsystems within the family may engage in activities that help them avoid or escape the family unit. As a family grows and adapts, it is important to understand the functions and tasks that each subsystem must perform in order for the overall system to work.

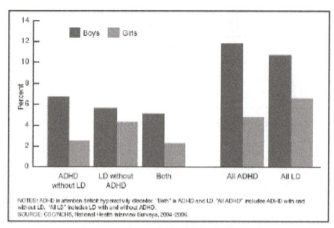

(http://www.cdc.gov/ncbddd/adhd/data.html)

Functions and tasks of the family

Providing for the needs of typically developing children is difficult enough. However, when a family member is diagnosed with a disability, planning for self-determination, while managing the rest of the household, may be overwhelming. Whether there is difficulty or not, the goal of parenthood is to raise children who are productive, self-determined community members. The path toward self-determination is difficult and each family has tasks that must be undertaken; they include:

► **Affection**—Each member of the family must feel appreciated and loved in order to return affection within their own family and to others.

► **Self-esteem**—Families find ways, through their members and the subsystems, to foster feelings of positive self-worth.

► **Spirituality**—This refers to how people find meaning in their lives and how they "perceive the connections between themselves, others, and the universe." How spirituality is instilled in each family is unique, but should be present in some capacity.

► **Economics**—Financial responsibility requires that there is enough money to pay for groceries, rent, and medical expenses. These expenses are typically covered by the adults in the family unit.

► **Daily Care**—Time and proactive planning are needed for the daily care of the family. Simple functions like brushing teeth and showering are just a few of the daily tasks that families must carry out.

► **Socialization**—Each family member must have adequate opportunities to learn the act of being social. This may occur through good role models in the family and neighborhood, as well as a values-based education.

► **Recreation**—In order to maintain balance in the family, recreation should be a year-round component. Opportunities for recreation encourage good self-esteem, socialization, and daily care but may be hard to provide if a family lacks sufficient financial resources.

► **Education**—It is the job of each family to secure maximum educational opportunities for each of its members. This is more time-consuming when there is a child with a disability.

Image courtesy of author

While it is critical for families to engage in all tasks, emphasis cannot be on all areas at all times. Families with children diagnosed with a disability need support from their schools and communities if they are to be on equal footing with other families and students. Overall affection in the family enhances self-esteem and helps children grow successfully into adulthood. The concept behind from "roots to wings" implies that when children are given a stable childhood, they will enter adulthood ready to pursue their life according to their strengths and needs (Turnbull & Turnbull 1996).

Case Study

When they divorced, Dr. and Mrs. Brown had three boys aged nineteen, seventeen, and four. Dr. Brown was a professor who had written several books. Mrs. Brown was a corporate attorney. Their oldest son was diagnosed with autism but successfully attended college. The family made arrangements for academic and social supports for their eldest son, but the cost was quite expensive. Although the financial responsibility yielded a positive outcome, it drained their savings. The two-income couple had always maintained college funds for each of the children, but these funds were in jeopardy due to the divorce and the anticipated marriage of Dr. Brown to his new fiancé. The exit of Dr. Brown from the family home and the new arrangement with his fiancé caused the oldest son to act out with challenging behavior at a local mall. He was ultimately charged with assault and asked to leave the store and the family had to hire an attorney for his defense. The middle son, who had been an honor student, began experimenting with alcohol and other illegal substances; he was arrested in his school parking lot. Not to be outdone, the youngest son was expelled from several local daycares.

Self-determination requires that schools, families, and communities act as equal partners toward a common outcome. Good role models within the family and community may also support young children in this effort, but families often need extra support. Parents may want interventions that result in long-term, socially desirable outcomes that lead to inclusion in their school and community. In addition, parents also want schools to support self-determination for their sons and daughters so they can live, work, and participate in the community as adults. If the goal of the family is to raise self-determined children, then where do we begin and who needs to help?

TABLE 3   Components of Self-Determination
▶ Freedom to live the life you want
▶ Authority over a targeted amount of dollars in a budget
▶ Support to organize resources that you need to live your life
▶ Responsibility for the wise use of public dollars
▶ Confirmation of the important role that individuals play in the system
(Nerney 2003)

Schools are charged with the daunting task of preparing students to successfully enter their communities upon completion of their education. Throughout the educational process, parents want to support the schools but, at the same time, they want to work with teachers, individually, to realize their dreams and desires for their children's futures (Ward & Meyer 1999). It is suggested that teachers should reframe language regarding IQ scores and developmental levels of children in order to be supportive of families seeking self-determination for their sons and daughters. Self-determination begins with individual choice, control, and self-understanding of students' and families' strengths and needs. If teachers increase opportunities for choice, control, and community involvement then students will learn the skills that facilitate a more independent life.

For those parents who want a self-determined life for their child, school-based programs are where the journey should begin. Strategies that support transition and self-determination should start with identifying the likes, dislikes, and subsequent goals as defined by the individual. One certainty, often overlooked, is that children with disabilities will grow up to be adults with disabilities (Held, Thoma, & Thomas 2004). Therefore, the concept of community becomes more and more important as children with disabilities mature and graduate into life outside the structure and security of school and family.

As a concept, "community" should be defined by the skills, strengths, interests, and needs of each individual as well as each family. As part of a community, strategies utilized by disabled persons, their families, and their schools should be geared toward an individual's self-determination and may include the following:

Discovering and Developing Individual Gifts and Strengths

Look to the families for their strengths because children often share the strengths and talents of their family. It is never too early for families and teachers to presume a child's competence and identify their strengths and interests. This will provide sufficient opportunities to enhance the child's gifts through IEP goals and objectives.

Providing Daily Opportunities for Choice and Control

The more opportunities a disabled person has to control their environment the more successful they will become. Making choices is a critical skill to have in a life that is based in a community. Decision-making skills should be taught early, at home and in school. Only when choices are honored and acted upon through appropriate accommodations and services can individuals with disabilities live a self-determined life.

Involving Students in Their Own IEP Processes

Families and teachers should welcome a student into the IEP process. Similarly, students should take an active and age appropriate role in their IEP throughout their school experience. There may be some resistance to the prospect of student involvement but if the focus is on the student at the meeting, this will direct the discussion toward the strengths of, and opportunities for, the student. In a 2004 study, Cameto, Levine, and Wagner found that only one-third of students with autism participated in their IEP or transition planning meetings and only 3 percent of those students led the meetings (Cameto, Levine, & Wagner 2004). As a student with ASD enters high school their curriculum and goals should match their strengths and interests and encompass the dreams and desires of the family. The 2008 article, "Asking Student Input: Students' Opinions Regarding Their Individualized Education Program Involvement," confirms that student involvement in the IEP planning process leads to greater self-determination (Agran and Hughes 2008).

Local, Community-Based Education

Each student should be educated in their neighborhood or community school. Educational opportunities that allow for the maximum amount of inclusion with typical peers will support a student's potential socialization and communication challenges. The relationships that a person develops in a typical environment, such as school, will serve the student for a lifetime. Inclusion may look different for each individual but support should be provided so that each student is on an equal footing with his or her peers. The relationships developed in community schools may lead to opportunities for employment and other community participation.

Person Centered Planning (PCP)

This should occur at major transition points in the school career of each student with a disability. A person centered plan is a process that identifies the skills, strengths, and needs of a student. Ranging from school activities to community involvement, PCPs can help families prioritize their needs and supports while planning for students' futures. Outcomes are developed and rooted in the strength of the family and the student with an emphasis on the student's future living, working, and recreational opportunities. A PCP, followed by an IEP, should include meaningful goals and objectives that serve to unify efforts toward self-determination. School connections to Medicaid and community providers are also critical in order to support the outcomes of the PCP. The outcomes of the PCP may support the services, supports, and accommodations that each individual may need for life in the community. When the families, schools, and communities of students with disabilities work together to plan their future, great things can happen.

Correcting Misconceptions of Guardianship

Often, guardianship takes away all or some of the rights of an individual. Families and uninformed professionals in the school and community are often led to believe that guardianship protects a person from dangerous people and living arrangements. Support from trusted individuals and relationships with family members who are outside of the service system are the key to "protecting" a person from such dangers. People with disabilities need supports, accommodations, jobs, access to family members, and relationships with typical peers, not guardianship, in order to be safe. Guardianship works against the tenets of self-determination but there are alternative options. Legal actions like power of attorney may allow parents, supporters, or siblings to speak for their child in areas such as mental health, housing, or medical care while still allowing for appropriate levels of autonomy. Trusts, which allow families to plan for the future, financial stability, and security of their son or daughter, may also be created. Smart financial planning will provide the services and activities that parents themselves would provide if they were alive.

Parents want their sons and daughters to live a rich and fulfilling life with access to everything their community can offer; disabilities do not change these goals. A systematic approach for providing choices, respect, strong role models, and the opportunity to make mistakes is a crucial part of living a self-determined life. Schools can support families by listening and responding to the dreams that they have for their children. The IEP process is also a great opportunity for schools and families to support the self-determination of each student. Furthermore, schools can foster each family's dreams through person centered planning and planning for the future by securing students' rights.

Chapter 34

The Work of Teachers: What We Can Do

Phil Smith

...special education is not a solution to the "problem" of disability, it *is* the problem. (Linton 2006, 161)

Linton's statement is a pretty provocative one—especially for teachers, and even more so for those who are special educators. Reading it out of context, you might think: "Well, I'm never going to become a special educator. They're all bad people."

That's not what Linton is saying.

What Linton is implying is that the system—the institution—of special education, based on an ideology of ableism, and as it is currently practiced in the United States, does significant, probably irreparable, harm to disabled people. She's not suggesting that special educators who work hard to ensure that people with disabilities are fully included in general education, who make sure that they are included in all communities, are doing the wrong thing. Because she's saying the exact opposite—it's not teachers who are working for inclusion that are doing bad stuff. It's a system of education that, generally speaking, segregates, disenfranchises, and oppresses people with disabilities, that is harmful, that is the problem.

So, what can teachers do? *Is* there anything teachers can do? What can each of us who call ourselves educators do to change what is, essentially, part of our culture—part of ourselves?

Everything.

Can little ol' me really change an entire culture?

Yup.

But where do I start? Where do I begin?

Here:

Start With Yourself

As you've been reading this book, perhaps talking with others about it, maybe looking at it as part of a class, perhaps you've been thinking to yourself:

- ▶ "This doesn't apply to me."
- ▶ "I'm not going into special education—I don't have to worry about any of this."
- ▶ "There won't be any of 'those' students in the classes that I teach or the schools that I work in."
- ▶ "This is all politically correct/liberal baloney, and I don't have to pay attention to it."
- ▶ "I don't know anyone with disabilities—what's this got to do with me?"

- ▶ "I know lots of people with disabilities, and they're not oppressed."
- ▶ "Some of my best friends are people with disabilities, I'm not an ableist."
- ▶ "When I went to school, I knew lots of people in special education, and they didn't seem to have any problems."
- ▶ "Some people are just not as smart as other people—the smart ones will get good jobs, and the ones who can't cut it, well, somebody has to sweep the floors and clean the toilets."

Changing the world starts with yourself, not someplace out there. You don't have to be in Congress, or be the President, to change the world. Change the way you see the world, and you change the world—it literally, not metaphorically, becomes something else.

Teacher Preparation: Advocating for a Different Approach

Inclusive education is the only way to move forward in schools, for both students with and without disabilities— as well as teachers, administrators, parents, and other stakeholders. To do that will require a different approach to the preparation and training of educators (and administrators). Learning about how to implement inclusive approaches in schools is an essential topic, clearly.

But learning about inclusive education cannot happen only for special educators—inclusive education is not a special education thing, it's a school thing. That means that everyone needs to learn about it. And it can't happen in the way we've always prepared teachers—separate programs for general and special educators. Preparing teachers to create schools founded in inclusive education will mean that all teachers need to learn together about how to work with diverse students, diverse communities—that means we'll need to combine departments of special and teacher education in university teacher preparation programs.

What can you do about that? Well, you can attend programs that don't have separate special and teacher education programs. If that's not feasible (the programs are too far away, too expensive, or whatever), then ask the program that you want to attend why they don't change. If you're already in a teacher preparation program, insist that your program change to become the kind of program you want and need.

Students don't realize the power they have over the kind of education they want. Universities will be forced to change if no one comes to the kind of program they offer. And they will also be forced to change if currently enrolled students insist that it happen.

Changing Schools

Schools are communities of students and teachers. Yes, administrators make policy and other decisions. And school boards usually have the final say. Policies and laws are dictated at federal and state levels. But teachers can—must—create the kinds of schools they want to work in.

If you want to work in an inclusive school, seek out the places that are already making that happen. Unfortunately, in many states, they are few and far between. But they do exist. Find those pockets of innovation and excitement, and go work there.

If you're already working in a school that hasn't figured out how to be inclusive, look for allies with whom you might work to make that happen. Don't try to do anything alone—support is critical in doing this kind of work (we *all* need a circle of support).

And, yes, buy-in from administrators for any substantial change initiative (like inclusion) is critical (P. Smith 2010). So convincing them, and establishing ongoing, long-term, positive relationships with them, will be essential to engage them in the process.

Education is Political

We're used to thinking that lots of things that we do or engage in are neutral—that they're not something that is affected by politics, that aren't influenced by people's opinions. One of those areas is education. But it's just not true—everything about education is political.

So what does that mean? It means that teachers need to see themselves as political entities. They—*we*—need to organize, mobilize, and advocate. We can't sit back and hope and pray that things will move in the direction we want them to move. This includes inclusive approaches—inclusion is political. We'll need to work at local, state, and federal levels, in political ways, to implement it in the way that it means to be implemented. We're going to have to drop the belief that there is no way that teachers can be politically active—we have to be. We already are. Doing nothing is itself a political decision, a political activity.

References

ABC News (2008). Autism angel: Carly Fleischmann [Video]. Retrieved from http://www.youtube.com/watch?v=34xoYwLNpvw

Affleck, G., & Tennen, H. (1993). Cognitive adaptation to adversity: Insights from parents of medically fragile infants. In A. P. Turnbull, J. M. Patterson, S. K. Behr, D. L. Murphy, J. G. Marquis, & M. J. Blue-Banning (Eds.), *Cognitive coping, families, and disability* (pp. 135–150). Baltimore: Paul H. Brookes.

Agran, M., & Hughes, C. (2008). Asking student input: Students' opinions regarding their individualized education program involvement. *Career Development for Exceptional Individuals, 31,* 69–76.

Aichroth, S., Carpenter, J., Daniels, K., Grassette, P., Kelly, D., Murray, A., Rice, J., Rivard, B., Smith, C., Smith, P., & Topper, K. (2002). Creating a new system of supports: The Vermont self-determination project. *Rural Special Education Quarterly, 21*(2), 16–28.

Algozzine, B. (2005). Restrictiveness and race in special education: Facts that remain difficult to ignore anymore. *Learning Disabilities: A Contemporary Journal 3*(1), 64–69.

American Association on Intellectual and Developmental Disabilities. (2013). *Definition of Intellectual Disability.* Retrieved from http://www.aaidd.org

American College of Physicians (2010). *Racial and Ethnic Disparities in Health Care, Updated 2010.* Philadelphia: American College of Physicians.

AFB (2007). Attributes of workers with vision loss. Retrieved on December 10, 2007, from http://www.afb.org

American Foundation for the Blind (2012). Explore Careers. Retrieved from afb.org

American Printing House for the Blind (2007). 2007 Annual Report. Retrieved from http://www.aph.org/about

American Printing House for the Blind (2011). Blindness basics. Retrieved from http://www.aph.org/blindness-basics/

American Printing House for the Blind (2012). What is federal quota? Retrieved from www.aph.org

American Psychiatric Association. (2000). *Diagnostic and statistical manual of mental disorders* (4th ed., text rev.). Washington, DC: Author.

American Speech-Language-Hearing Association Ad Hoc Committee on Service Delivery in the Schools (1993). Definitions of communication disorders and variations. *ASHA, 35* (Suppl. 10), 40–41.

Anyon, J. (1997). *Ghetto schooling: A political economy of urban educational reform.* New York: Teachers College Press.

Artiles, A. J., Harry, B., Reschly, D. J., & Chinn, P. C. (2002). Over-identification of students of color in special education: A critical overview. *Multicultural Perspectives, 4*(1), 3–10.

Artiles, A. J., Kozleski, E. B., Trent, S. C., Osher, D., & Ortiz, A. (2010). Justifying and explaining disproportionality 1968–2008: A critique of underlying views of culture. *Exceptional Children, 76*(3), 279–299.

Asperger, H. (1944). Autistic psychopaths in childhood. *Archive for Psychiatry in German. 117:*76–136.

Baglieri, S., & Shapiro, A. (2012). *Disability studies and the inclusive classroom: Critical practices for creating least restrictive attitudes.* NY: Routledge.

Barkley, R. (1997). Behavioral inhibition, sustained attention, and executive functions: Constructing a unifying theory of ADHD. *Psychological Bulletin, 121*(1), 65–94. doi:10.1037/2F0033-2909.121.1.65.

Barnes, C. (1992). *An exploration of the principles for media representations of disabled people.* Halifax, Nova Scotia: The British Council of Organizations of Disabled People and Ryburn Publishing.

Bascom, J., Ed. (2012). *Loud hands: autistic people, speaking* (sic). Autistic Self Advocacy Network.

Battaglia, D. (2010, December 21). Celebrating a milestone in speech-language pathology. *The ASHA Leader.*

Battle, D. (2012). *Communication disorders in multicultural populations (4th ed.)* St. Louis: MO: Elsevier/Mosby.

Baynton, D. (2005). Slaves, immigrants, and suffragists: The uses of disability in citizenship debates. *PMLA, 120*(2), 562–567.

Baynton, D. (2013). Disability and the justification of inequality in American history. In L. Davis (Ed.), *The disability studies reader* (4th ed.) (pp. 17–33).

Beirne-Smith, M., Patton J., & Kim, S. (2006). *Mental Retardation: An Introduction to Intellectual Disabilities.* Upper Saddle River NJ: Pearson Merrill Prentice Hall.

Berger, R. (2013). *Introducing disability studies.* Boulder, CO: Lynne Rienner Publishers.

Bernard, B. (1995). Fostering resiliency in kids: Protective factors in the family, school and community. San Francisco: Far West Laboratory for Educational Research and Development.

Bernstein, D. K., & Tiegerman-Farber, E. (2009). *Language and communication disorders in children* (6th ed.). Boston: Pearson.

Beukelman, D., and Mirenda, P. (2013). (4th ed.) *Augmentative and Alternative Communication: Supporting Children and Adults with Complex Communication Needs.* Baltimore: Brookes.

Biederman, J. (2005). Attention-deficit/hyperactivity disorder: A selective overview. *Biological Psychiatry, 57*(11), 1215–1220. doi:10.1016/j.biopsych.2004.10.020.

Blackorby, J., & Wagner, M. (1996). Longitudinal postschool outcomes of youth with disabilities: Findings from the National Longitudinal Transition Study. *Exceptional Children, 62*(5), 399–413.

Blanchett, W. J., Mumford, V., & Beachum, F. (2005). Urban school failure and disproportionality in a post-Brown era: Benign neglect of the constitutional rights of students of color. *Remedial and Special Education, 26*(2), 70–81.

Blatt, B., & Kaplan, F. (1974). *Christmas in purgatory: A photographic essay on mental retardation.* Syracuse, NY: Human Policy Press.

Bloom, M., & Lahey, M. (1978). *Language development and disorders.* New York: Wiley.

Blumberg, M., Visser, S., Kogan, M., Boyle, C., Boulet, S., Schieve, L, & Cohen, R. (2012). Trends in the prevalence developmental disabilities in US Children from 1997–2008. *Pediatrics, 10*, 2010–2989.

Bower, E. M. (1981). *Early identification of emotionally handicapped children in school (3rd ed.),* Springfield, IL: Charles C. Thomas.

Bower, E. M. (1982). Defining emotional disturbance: Public policy and research. *Psychology in the Schools, 19,* 55–60.

Boyle, C. (2012). Autism and Developmental Disabilities Monitoring Network. Center for Disease Control.

Boyle, C., Boulet, S., Schieve, L., Cohen, R., Blumberg, S., Yeargin-Allsopp, M., Visser, S., & Kogan, M. (2012). Trends in the prevalence of developmental disabilities in US children from 1997–2008. *Pediatrics, 10*(1542), 2010–2989.

Brain Injury Assoication of America (2013). Retrieved from http://www.biausa.org/

Bristol, M. M. (1984). Family resources and successful adaptation to autistic children. In E. Schopler and G. Mesibov (Eds). *The effect of autism on the family.* New York: Plenum Press.

Brown, T. (2006). Executive functions and attention deficit hyperactivity disorder: Implications of two conflicting views. *International Journal of Disability, Development and Education, 53*(1), 35–46. doi:10.1080/2F10349120500510024.

Brown-Chidsey, R., & Steege, M. W. (2005). *Response to intervention: Principles and strategies for effective practice.* New York, NY: Guilford Press.

Bureau of Labor Statistics (2010). *Persons with a disability: Labor force characteristics–2009.* Washington, DC: Bureau of Labor Statistics, U.S. Department of Labor (USDL-10-1172).

Burton, N. (2012). *Living with Schizophrenia*. Acheron Press.

Butler, J. (1990). *Gender trouble: Feminism and the subversion of identity.* NY: Routledge.

Cameto, R., Levine, P., & Wagner, M. (2004). *Transition planning for Students with disabilities: A special topic report of findings from the National Longitudinal Transition Study-2 (NLTS2).* Menlo Park, CA: SRI International.

Carteldge, G. (2005). Restrictiveness and race in special education: The failure to prevent or to return. *Learning Disabilities: A Contemporary Journal 3*(1), 27–32.

Carter, E. W. (2007*). Including people with disabilities in faith communities: A guide for service providers, families and congregations.* Baltimore, MD: Brooks Publishing.

Center for Applied Special Technology (CAST). (n.d.). *About UDL.* Retrieved from http://www.cast.org/research/udl

Center for Applied Special Technology (CAST). (2011). *Universal Design for Learning Guidelines version 2.0.* Wakefield, MA: Author. Retrieved from http://www.udlcenter.org/aboutudl/udlguidelines

Centers for Disease Control and Prevention (2011). *Number of U.S. adults reporting a disability increasing.* Atlanta: Author.

Certo, N., Mautz, D., Smalley, K., Wade, H. A., Luecking, R., Pumpian, I., Saz, C., Noyes, D., Wechsler, J., and Batterman, N. (2003). Review and discussion of a model for seamless transition to adulthood. *Education and Training in Developmental Disabilities, 38*(1), 3–17.

Chadwick, M. (2012) "How Is It that You Move?" Presentation at 2012 conference of Autism National Committee, October 6, 2012, Columbia, MD. Retrieved from www.autcom.org

Child Welfare Information Gateway. (2013). *Long-term consequences of child abuse and neglect.* Washington, DC: U.S. Department of Health and Human Services, Children's Bureau.

Children's Health Act of 2000 (42 U.S.C. § 280i (a)(1) (2000)).

Clarizio, H. F. (1992). Differentiating emotionally impaired from social maladjusted students. *Psychology in the Schools, 24,* 237–242.

Clayton, J., Burdge, M., Dehham, A., Kleinert H., & Kearns, J. (2006). A four-step process for accessing the general curriculum for students with significant cognitive Disabilities. *Teaching Exceptional Children, 38*(5), 20–27.

Collins, B. (2007). *Moderate and Severe Disabilities: A Foundational Approach.* NY: Pearson Merrill Prentice Hall.

Connell, D. (2013). *Clip & save checklist: Learning activities that connect with multiple intelligences.* Retrieved from http://www.scholastic.com/teachers/article/clip-save-checklist-learning-activities-connect-multiple-intelligences

Copeland, S., & Keefe, E. (2009). *Effective Literacy Instruction for Students with Moderate and Severe Disabilities.* Baltimore, MD: Paul H. Brookes.

Corn, A. L., & Lusk, K. E. (2010). Perspectives on low vision. In A. L. Corn & J. N. Erin (Eds.) *Foundations of low vision: Clinical and functional perspectives.* New York: AFB Press.

Crane, L. (2002). *Mental Retardation: A Community Integration Approach.* Belmont, CA: Wadsworth/Thomson Learning.

Crundwell, M. and Killu, K. (2010). Respond to a Student's Depression, *Educational Leadership, 68*(2), 46–51.

Davis, G. A., and Rimm, S. B. (2004). *Education of the Gifted and Talented* (Sixth Ed.). Boston: Allyn and Bacon.

Dennison, E. M. (2003) (Ed.). *Eye conditions in infants and young children that result in visual impairment and syndromes and other conditions that may accompany visual disorders.* North Logan: UT: HOPE, Inc.

Doheny, K. (2012). WebMD. Retrieved from http://www.webmd.com/brain/autism/features/autism-and-family-relationships.

Donnellan, A. (1984). The criterion of the least dangerous assumption. *Behavior Disorders, 9(2),* 141–150.

Donnellan, A., Hill, D. A., & Leary, M. R. (2010). Rethinking autism: Implications of sensory and movement differences. *Disability Studies Quarterly, 30*(1). Retrieved from http://dsq-sds.org/article/view/1060/1225

Donnellan, A., & Leary, M. R. (2012). *Autism: Sensory-movement differences and diversity.* Wisconsin: Cambridge Book Review Press.

Downing, J. (2004). Communication skills. In F. Orelove, D. Sobsey, & R. K. Silberman (Eds.) *Educating children with multiple disabilities: A collaborative approach* (3rd ed.) Baltimore: Paul H. Brookes.

Duchan, J. F. (2002, December 24). What Do You Know About Your Profession's History?: And Why Is It Important? *The ASHA Leader.*

Dunn, L. M. (1968). Special education for the mildly mentally retarded: Is much of it justifiable? *Exceptional Children, 35,* 5–22.

Dunn, R., Denig, S., & Lovelace, M. K. (2001). Multiple intelligences and learning styles: Two sides of the same coin or different strokes for different folks? *Teacher Librarian, 28*(3), 9–15.

Dunn, R., & Dunn, K. (1992). *Teaching elementary students through their individual learning styles.* Boston, MA: Allyn & Bacon.

DuPaul, G., Barkley, R., & Connor, D. (1998). Simulants. In R. Barkley (Ed.) *Attention deficit hyperactivity disorder: A handbook for diagnosis and treatment* (2nd ed., pp. 510–551). New York: Guilford Press.

Duran, J. B., Zhou, Q., Frew, L. A., Kwok, O., & Benz, M. R. (2013). Disciplinary exclusion and students with disabilities: The mediating role of social skills. *Journal of Disability Policy Studies, 24*(1), 15–26.

Dutta, A., Kundu, M., & Schiro-Geist, C. (2009). Coordination of postsecondary transition services for students with disabilities. *Journal of Rehabilitation, 75,* 10–17.

Educational Broadcasting Corporation. (2004). *What is the theory of multiple intelligences (M.I.)?* From the Concept to Classroom workshop, "Tapping into multiple intelligences." Retrieved from http://www.thirteen.org/edonline/concept2class/mi/index.html

Elim Christian Services, & Vander Plaats, D. (2012). *5 Stage: The Journey of Disability Attitudes.* Palos Heights, CA: Author.

Emerson, E. (2011). Health status and health risks of the "hidden majority" of adults with intellectual disability. *Intellectual and Developmental Disabilities, 49,* 155–165. doi:10.1352/1934-9556-49.3.155.

Erickson, W., Lee, C., von Schrader, S. (2012). *Disability statistics from the 2010 American Community Survey (ACS).* Ithaca, NY: Cornell University Rehabilitation Research and Training Center on Disability Demographics and Statistics (StatsRRTC).

Fensham, P. J., & Cumming, J. J. (2013). Which child left behind: Historical issues regarding equity in science assessment. *Education Sciences, 3,* 326–343. doi:10.3390/educsci3030326.

Ferri, B. A., & Connor, D. J. (2005). Tools of exclusion: Race, disability, and (re)segregated education. *Teachers College Record, 107*(3), 453–474.

Fierros, E. G. (2005). Race and restrictiveness in special education: Addressing the problem we know too well. *Learning Disabilities: A Contemporary Journal 3*(1), 75–85.

Fierros, E. G., & Bloomberg, N. A. (2005). Restrictiveness and race in special education placements in for-profit and non-profit charter schools in California. *Learning Disabilities: A Contemporary Journal 3*(1), 1–16.

Fisher, J. L. (2013). *Prosocial student behavior in selected elementary classrooms.* Saarbrucken, Germany: Lambert Academic Publishing.

Florida Department of Education. (2006). *Section 504 online introductory tutorial, module two, collaborative problem solving.* Retrieved from http://www.sss.usf.edu

Forness, S. R. (1996). School children with emotional or behavioral disorders: Perspectives on definition, diagnosis, and treatment. (pp. 84–95) In B. Brooks and D. Sabatino (Eds.), *Personal Perspectives on Emotional or Behavioral Disorders.* Austin, TX: PRO-ED.

Forness, S. R., & Knitzer, J. (1992). A new proposed definition and terminology to replace "serious emotional disturbance" in Individuals with Disabilities Education Act. *School Psychology Review, 21,* 12–20.

Freire, Paulo (1971). *Pedagogy of the oppressed.* New York: Herder and Herder.

Friedman, D. S., O'Colmain, B. J., Munoz, B., et al (2004). Prevalence of age-related macular degeneration in the United States. *Archives of Ophthalmology, 122,* 564–572.

Friend, M., & Cook, L. (1992). *Interactions: Collaboration skills for school professionals.* White Plains, NY: Longman.

Fuchs, D., & Deschler, R. (2007). What we need to know about responsiveness to intervention (and shouldn't be afraid to ask). *Learning Disabilities Research & Practice, 22*(2), 129–136.

Fuchs, L. S. (2007). *NRCLD update on responsiveness to intervention: Research to practice.* [Brochure]. Lawrence, KS: National Research Center on Learning Disabilities.

Gabel, S. (2005). Introduction: Disability studies in education. In S. Gabel (Ed.) *Disability studies in education: Readings in theory and method* (pp. 1–20). NY: Peter Lang.

Gallagher, D. (2010). Educational researchers and the making of normal people. In C. Dudley-Marling and A. Gurn (Eds.) *The myth of the normal curve* (pp. 25–38). NY: Peter Lang.

Garcia, S. B., & Guerra, P. L. (2004). Deconstructing deficit thinking: Working with educators to create more equitable learning environments. *Education and Urban Society, 36,* 150–167.

Gardner, H. (1993). *Frames of mind: The theory of multiple intelligences (2nd ed.).* New York, NY: Basic Books.

Gardner, H. (2000). *Intelligence reframed: Multiple intelligences for the 21st century.* New York, NY: Basic Books.

Gay and Lesbian Alliance Against Defamation (2010). *Media Reference Guide, 8th Edition,* at: http://www.glaad.org/files/MediaReferenceGuide2010.pdf

Gay, G. (2000). *Culturally responsive teaching.* New York: Teachers College Press.

Gerrold, D. (Guest), Champion, J. (Host), Ray, K. (Host, Editor), Roddenberry, E. R. (Producer), & Roth, T. (Producer). (2013, July 11). Supplemental 049a: The one with David Gerrold. *Mission Log: A Roddenberry Star Trek Podcast.* Podcast retrieved from http://www.missionlogpodcast.com/archive/

Gibb, G. S., & Dyches, T. T. (2007). *Guide to writing quality Individual Education Programs* (2nd Ed.). Upper Saddle Brook, NJ: Pearson Education, Inc.

Gillingham, G., & McClennen, S., Eds. (2008). *Sharing our wisdom: A collection of presentations by people within the autism spectrum.* Durham, NH: Autism National Committee.

Glasser, W. (1999). *Choice theory: A new psychology of personal freedom.* New York, NY: Harper Collins Publishers, Inc.

Goffman, E. (1963). *Stigma: Notes on the management of spoiled identity.* Englewood Cliffs, NJ: Prentice-Hall, Inc.

Goldberg, B. (1989). Historic treatments for stuttering: From pebbles to psychoanalysis. Retrieved from http://www.mnsu.edu/comdis/kuster/history/bgoldberg.html

Goodley, D. (2011). *Disability studies: An interdisciplinary introduction.* Los Angeles: Sage.

Gorman, J. (2012). Ancient bones that tell a story of compassion. *New York Times,* December 18, 2012, D1.

Gould, M. (2009). National Council on Disability written remarks. In United States Commission on Civil Rights, *Minorities in special education: Briefing report* (26–34). Washington, DC: U.S. Government Printing Office. Retrieved from http://www.usccr.gov/pubs/MinoritiesinSpecialEducation.pdf

Green, M., Moore, H., & O'Brien, J. (2006). *When people care enough to act: ABCD in action.* Toronto, Canada: Inclusion Press.

Gresham, F. G. (2005). Response to Intervention: An Alternative Means of Identifying Students as Emotionally Disturbed. *Education and Treatment of Children, 28*(4), 328–344.

Griffin, H. C., Williams, S. C., Davis, M. L., & Engleman, M. (2002). Using technology to enhance cues for children with low vision. *Teaching Exceptional Children, 35,* 36–40.

Grimes, J., & Kurns, S. (December, 2003). *An intervention-based system for addressing NCLB and IDEA expectations: A multiple tiered model to ensure every child learns.* Invited paper presented at the National Research Center on Learning Disabilities Response to Intervention Symposium.

Haddad, S., Chen, C. A., Santangelo, S. L., & Seddon, J. M. (2006). The genetics of age-related macular degeneration: A review of progress to date. *Survey of Ophthalmology, 51*(4), 316–363.

Halmhuber, N., & Rocklage, L. (2014). *A century of excellence: The department of special education, Eastern Michigan University.* Ypsilanti, MI: Eastern Michigan University Department of Special Education.

Hallahan, D. P., & Kauffman, J. M. (1977). Labels, categories, behaviors: ED, LD, and EMR reconsidered. *The Journal of Special Education, 11,* 139–149.

Hallowell, E., & Ratey, J. (1994). *Driven to distraction: Recognizing and coping with attention deficit disorder from childhood through adulthood.* New York: Pantheon Books.

Harry, B., & Klingner, J. (2006). *Why are so many minority students in special education? Understanding race and disability in schools.* New York: Teachers College Press.

Harry, B., Klingner, J. K., & Hart, J. (2005). African American families under fire: Ethnographic views of family strengths. *Remedial and Special Education, 26*(2), 101–112.

Hatlen, P. (2000). Historical perspectives. In M. C. Holbrook & A. J. Koenig (Eds.) *Foundations of education: History and theory of teaching children and youths with visual impairments* (Vol. 1). New York: AFB Press.

Heartland Area Education Agency. (2009). *Working together for children: A guide for parents and educators.* Johnston, IA: Author.

Held, M., Thoma, C., & Thomas, K. (2004). "The John Jones Show": How one teacher facilitated self-determined transition planning for a young man with autism. *Focus on Autism and Other Developmental Disabilities, 19,* 177–188. doi:10.1177/10883576040190030501.

Herrnstein, R., & Murray, C. (1994). *The Bell Curve: Intelligence and Class Structure in American Life.* New York: Free Press.

Highwater, J. (1995). The intellectual savage. In N. R. Goldberger & J. B. Veroff (Eds.), *The culture and psychology reader* (pp. 205–215). New York: New York University Press.

Hogan, K., Bullock, L., & Fritsch, E. (2010). Meeting the transition needs of incarcerated youth with disabilities. *The Journal of Correctional Education, 61,* 133–147.

Hollingworth, L. S. (1923). *The psychology of subnormal children.* New York: MacMillan.

Horwitz, S., Kereker, B., Owens, P., & Ziegler, E. (2000). *The health status and needs of individuals with mental retardation.* New Haven, CT: Yale University.

Hubach, S. (2006). *Same lake different boat: Coming alongside people with disabilities.* Phillipsburg, NJ: P & R Publishing.

Hunsaker, S. L. (1995). The gifted metaphor from the perspective of traditional civilizations. *Journal for the Education of the Gifted. 18,* 265–268.

Hurd, W. H. (2009). Racial Discrepancies in Special Education. In United States Commission on Civil Rights, *Minorities in special education: Briefing report* (97–100). Washington, DC: U.S. Government Printing Office. Retrieved from http://www.usccr.gov/pubs/MinoritiesinSpecialEducation.pdf

Individuals with Disability Education Act (IDEA) (2004). Regulations: Part 300 / A / 300.8 / c / 12. Retrieved from http://idea.ed.gov

Institute of Medicine (US) Committee on Health and Behavior: Research, Practice, and Policy (2001). *Health and Behavior: The interplay of biological, behavioral, and societal influences.* Washington, DC: National Academies Press.

Interagency Committee on Learning Disabilities. (1988). *Learning disabilities: A report to the U.S. Congress.* Washington, DC: U.S. Government Printing Office.

International Learning Styles Network. (2010). *About us.* Retrieved from http://www.learningstyles.net/en/

Ivey, J. (2004). What do parents expect? A study of likelihood and importance issues for children with autism spectrum disorders. *Focus on Autism and Other Developmental Disabilities, 19,* 27–33.

Janiszewski, R., Heath-Watson, S. L., Semidey, A. Y., Rosenthal, A. M., & Do, Q. (2006). The low visibility of low vision: Increasing awareness through public health education. *Journal of Visual Impairment & Blindness, 100,* 849–861.

Janus, A. (2009). Disability and the transition to adulthood. *Social Forces, 88,* 99–120.

Johnson, C. (2008). Post-school outcomes for students in the state of Washington, USA, receiving special education services. *Journal of the International Association of Special Education, 9,* 78–88.

Jussim, L., Eccles, J., & Madon, S. (1996). Social perception, social stereotypes, and teacher expectations: Accuracy and the powerful self-fulfilling prophecy. In M. P. Zanna (Ed.), *Advances in experimental social psychology* (Vol. 28, pp. 281–388). San Diego, Academic Press.

Kapperman, G., & Koenig, P. (1996). Integration of visual skills for independent living. In A. L. Corn & A. J. Koenig (Eds.) *Foundations of low vision: Clinical and functional perspectives* (pp. 43–52). New York: AFB Press.

Kauffman, J., & Hallahan, D. (2005). *Special education: What it is and why we need it.* New York: Pearson.

Kavale, K., Forness, S., & Mostert, M. (2005). Defining emotional or behavioral disorders: The quest for affirmation. In P. Clough, P. Garner, J. Pardeck, & F. Yuen (Eds.), *Handbook of emotional & behavioural difficulties.* (pp. 45–59). London: SAGE Publications Ltd.

Kaye, H. S. (2010). Unpublished tabulations of 2005 data from the U.S. Survey of Income and Program Participation in C. Cortiella, *The State of Learning Disabilities 2010.* New York: National Center for Learning Disabilities.

Kelly, E. J. (1993). *Differential test of conduct and emotional problems.* East Aurora, NY: Slosson Educational Publications.

Kessler Foundation/National Organization on Disability (2010). *The ADA, 20 years after: The Kessler Foundation/National Organization of Disabilities survey of Americans with disabilities.* Washington, DC: Author.

Kimmel, M. (2002, November/December). Toward a pedagogy of the oppressor. *Tikkun Magazine.* Retrieved from http://www.fjaz.com/kimmel.html

Kincheloe, J., McLaren, P., & Steinberg, S. (2012). Critical pedagogy and qualitative research: Moving to the bricolage. In S. Steinberg & G. Cannella (Eds.) *Critical qualitative research reader* (pp. 14–32). New York: Peter Lang.

Kirchner, C., & Peterson, R. (1988). Employment: Selected characteristics. In C. Kirchner (Ed.), *Data on blindness and visual impairment in the U.S.* (2nd ed.). New York: American Foundation for the Blind.

Kliewer, C. (1998). *Schooling children with Down syndrome: Toward an understanding of possibility.* New York: Teachers College Press.

Klingner, J. K., Artiles, A. J., Kozleski, E., Harry, B., Zion, S., Tate, W., Durán, G. Z., & Riley, D. (2005). Addressing the disproportionate representation of culturally and linguistically diverse students in special education through culturally responsive educational systems. *Education Policy Analysis Archives, 13*(38). Retrieved from http://epaa.asu.edu/epaa/v13n38/.

Kluth, P. (2010). *"You're going to love this kid!" Teaching students with autism in the inclusive classroom,* (2nd ed.) Baltimore: Paul H. Brookes.

Knoff, H. M. (2009). *Implementing Response-to-Intervention at the school, district, and state levels: Functional assessment, data-based problem solving, and evidence-based academic and behavioral interventions.* Little Rock, AR: Project ACHIEVE Press.

Koenig (Eds.) *Foundations of low vision: Clinical and functional perspectives* (pp. 43–52). New York: AFB Press.

Kornhaber, M. (2004). *Multiple Intelligences: Best Ideas from Research to Practice.* Boston, MA: Allen & Bacon.

Koyanagi, C. (2003). "Failing to Qualify: The First Step to Failure in School?" Issue Brief, Judge David L. Bazelon Center for Mental Health Law, Washington, DC, January 2003, 2. Retrieved from http://www.bazelon.org/

Kraai, R.V., & Snyder, S. (2010). *The church's role in serving people with disabilities.* (unpublished findings).

Kudlick, C. J. (2003, June). Disability history: Why we need another "other." *American Historical Review*, 763–793.

Kunc, N. (2000). Rediscovering the right to belong. In R. Villa & J. Thousand (Eds.) *Restructuring for caring and effective education: Piecing the puzzle together* (2nd ed.) (pp. 77–92). Baltimore, MD: Paul H. Brookes.

Ladner, M. (2009). Minority children and special education: Evidence of racial bias and strategies to avoid misdiagnosis. In United States Commission on Civil Rights, *Minorities in special education: Briefing report* (40–56). Washington, DC: U.S. Government Printing Office. Retrieved from http://www.usccr.gov/pubs/MinoritiesinSpecialEducation.pdf

Larson, S., Lakin, C., Salmi, P., Scott, N., & Webster, A. (2010). Children and youth with intellectual or developmental disabilities living in congregate care settings (1977–2009): Healthy People 2010 Objective 6.7b outcomes. *Intellectual and Developmental Disabilities, 48*, 396–400. doi:10.1352/1934-9556-48.5.396.

Larson, S. A., Salmi, P., Smith, D., Anderson, L., and Hewitt, A. S. (2013). *Residential Services for Persons with Intellectual or Developmental Disabilities: Status and trends through 2011.* Minneapolis: University of Minnesota, Research and Training Center on Community Living, Institute on Community Integration.

Ldonline (2012). Common signs of a learning disability. Retrieved from http://www.ldonline.org.

Learning Disabilities Association of America (2012). For teachers. Retrieved from http://www.ldanatl.org/aboutld/teachers/index.asp

Lerner, J. W., & Johns, B. H. (2012). *Learning disabilities and related mild disabilities.* Belmont, CA: Wadsworth Cengage Learning.

Lerner, M., & Wigal, T. (2008). Long-term safety of stimulant medications used to treat children with ADHD. *Journal of Psychosocial Nursing and Mental Health, 46*(8), 38–48. doi:10.3928/02793695-20080801-06.

LeRoy, B., & Lacey, K. (2010). The inclusion of students with intellectual disabilities in Michigan. In P. Smith (Ed.) *Whatever happened to inclusion? The place of students with intellectual disabilities in education* (pp. 101–116). New York: Peter Lang.

Li, A. (2004). Classroom strategies for improving and enhancing visual skills in students with disabilities. *Teaching Exceptional Children, 36*, 38–42.

Linton, S. (1998). *Claiming disability: Knowledge and identity.* New York: New York University Press.

Linton, S. (2006). *My body politic: A memoir.* Ann Arbor: The University of Michigan Press.

Lowery, Sassafras (2010). *Kicked Out.* Ypsilanti, MI: Homofactus LLC.

Marland, S. (1972). *Education of the Gifted and Talented, Vol. I, Report to Congress of the United States by the U.S. Commissioner of Education.* Washington, D.C.: U.S. Government Printing Office.

Maslow, A., Frager, R. D. (Editor), & Fadiman, J. (Editor). (1997). *Motivation and personality.* (3rd ed.). Upper Saddle River, NJ: Pearson Publishing.

Mayo Clinic (2012). Diseases and conditions. Retrieved from http://www.mayoclinic.com/health/DiseasesIndex/DiseasesIndex

McDonald, A. (2007, June 15). "The other story from a 'Pillow Angel': Been there. Done that. Preferred to grow." *Seattle Post-Intelligencer.* Retrieved from http://www.seattlepi.com/local/opinion/article/The-other-story-from-a-Pillow-Angel-1240555.php

McDonald, A. (2008). Rowing upstream. Retrieved from http://www.annemcdonaldcentre.org.au/rowing-upstream-0

McDowell, R. (n.d.). Federal and state benefits for the legally blind. Retrieved from http://www.ehow.com/list_6808311_federa-state-benfits-legally-blind.html

McLaren, P. (2009). Critical pedagogy: A look at the major concepts. In A. Darder, M. Baltodano, & R. Torres (Eds.), *The critical pedagogy reader* (2nd ed.) (pp. 61–83). NY: Routledge.

Meichenbaum, D. (2008). Bolstering resilience: Benefiting from lessons learned. In D. Brom, R. Pat-Horenczyk, & J. Ford, (Eds.). *Treating traumatized children: Risk, resilience and recovery*. New York: Rutledge.

Merriam-Webster (2013). *Merriam-Webster Online Dictionary*. Available at http://www.merriam-webster.com

Michigan Department of Education (2012). *Michigan administrative rules for special education* (MARSE).

Mondale, S., & Patton, S. (2001). *School: The story of American public education*. Boston: Beacon Press.

Monroe, S. (2009). Minorities and limited English proficient students in special education. In United States Commission on Civil Rights, *Minorities in special education: Briefing report* (21–25). Washington, DC: U.S. Government Printing Office. Retrieved from http://www.usccr.gov/pubs/MinoritiesinSpecialEducation.pdf

Monroe, T. J. (1994). Self-Advocate's Perspective. In President's Committee on Mental Retardation (Ed.), *The national reform agenda and people with mental retardation: Putting people first* (pp. 9–10). Washington, DC: U.S. Government Printing Office.

Moore, J. E., Huebner, K. M., & Maxson, J. H. (1997). Service systems and resources. In J. E. Moore, W. H. Graves, & J. B. Patterson (Eds.) *Foundations of rehabilitation counseling with persons who are blind or visually impaired* (pp. 225–255). New York: American Foundation for the Blind.

Morgan, P. (2009). *Parenting an adult with disabilities or special needs*. New York: AMACOM.

Murphy, R. P. (1986). Age-related macular degeneration. *Ophthalmology, 93*(7), 969–971.

National Advisory Eye Council (1999). Report of the visual impairment and its rehabilitation panel. In *Vision Research—A National Plan: 1999–2003*. NIH Pub # 99-1420. Bethesda, MD: National Eye Institute.

National Association for the Education of African American Children with Learning Disabilities. (2012, July). African American children and learning differences. Retrieved from http://www.aacld.org/images/AACLD_Overview_Fact_Sheet_July_2012.pdf

National Association for the Education of African American Children with Learning Disabilities. (2013, February). Newsletter: February 2013: African American parent leadership. Retrieved from http://archive.constantcontact.com/fs174/1102482301529/archive/1112596520204.html

National Association of State Directors of Developmental Disabilities Services (2010). *Consumer outcomes–Phase XI final report: 2008–2009 data*. Author: Alexandria, VA.

National Center for Education Statistics (2005). Students with disabilities exiting special education. Retrieved from http://nces.ed.gov/programs/digest/d05/tables/dt05_107.asp

National Center for Education Statistics (2007). Status and Trends in the Education of Racial and Ethnic Minorities. Retrieved from http://nces.ed.gov/pubsearch/pubsinfo.asp?pubid=2007039

National Center for Education Statistics (2010). *Status and trends in the education of racial and ethnic minorities*. Retrieved from http://nces.ed.gov/pubs2010/2010015/tables/table_8_1b.asp

National Center for Learning Disabilities (2012). General learning disabilities information. Retrieved from http://www.ncld.org/types-learning-disabilities/what-is-ld.

National Center on Response to Intervention (April, 2010). *Essential components of RTI—A closer look at response to intervention*. Washington, DC: U.S. Department of Education, Office of Special Education Programs, National Center on Response to Intervention. Retrieved from *www.cldinternational.org/articles/rtiessentialcomponents.pdf*

National Dissemination Center for Children with Disabilities (August, 2012). *Response to intervention (RTI)*. Retrieved from http://nichcy.org/schools-administrators/rti

National Eye Institute (2004). April 2004 Archives of Ophthalmology. Retrieved from http://www.nei.nih.gov/eyedata/pvd_data.asp

National Institute for Literacy (2006). *What is scientifically based research? A guide for teachers: Using research and reason in education*. Jessup, MD: Author.

National Organization on Disability (2010). *Survey of Americans with disabilities*. Retrieved from http://nod.org/what_we_do/research/surveys/kessler/

National Research Center on Learning Disabilities (NRCLD). (2007). *Core concepts of RTI.* Retrieved from http://www.nrcld.org/about/research/rti/concepts.html

Nerney, T. (2003) Understanding self-determination. In W. Cohen, L. Nadel, & M. Madnick (Eds.) *Down Syndrome: Visions for the 21st century* (pp. 1–15). Wiley. doi:10.1002/0471227579.

Nerney, T., & Shumway, D. (2003). Giving Clients Freedom to Choose Services Helps People with Severe Mental Disabilities. Robert Woods Johnson National Self-Determination Program.

Newman, L., Wagner, M., Cameto, R., Knokey, A.-M. (2009). *The post-high school outcomes of youth with disabilities up to 4 years after high school: A report from the National Longitudinal Transition Study-2 (NLTS2)* (NCSER 2009–3017). Menlo Park, CA: SRI International.

Nielsen, K. (2012). *A disability history of the United States.* Boston: Beacon Press.

No Child Left Behind (NCLB) Act of 2001, 20 U.S.C.A. § 6301 *et seq.* (West 2003).

Nocella, A. (2012). Defining eco-ability: Social justice and the intersectionality of disability, nonhuman animals, and ecology. In A. Nocella, J. Bentley, & J. Duncan (Eds.) *Earth, animal, and disability liberation: The rise of the eco-ability movement* (pp. 3–21). NY: Peter Lang.

Nutbrown, C. (1996). Wide eyes and open minds—Observing, assessing and respecting children's early achievements. In C. Nutbrown (Ed.) *Respectful educators, capable learners: Children's rights and early education.* London: Chapman.

O'Brien, J., & O'Brien, C. (1996). *Members of each other: Building community in company with people with developmental disabilities.* Toronto, CA: Inclusion Press.

O'Connor, C., & Fernandez, S. D. (2006). Race, class, and Disproportionality: Reevaluating the relationship between poverty and special education placement. *Educational Researcher, 35*(6), 6–11.

Office of Special Education and Rehabilitative Services (2003). *25th annual report to Congress on the implementation of the Individuals with Disabilities Education Act.* Washington, DC: Author.

Ogletree, B. T. and Oren, T. (2006). *How to use augmentative and Alternative Communication.* Austin, TX: PRO-ED.

Osher, D., Woodruff, D., & Sims, A. (2002). Schools make a difference: The overrepresentation of African American youth in special education and the juvenile justice system. In D. Losen & G. Orfield (Eds.) *Racial inequity in special education* (pp. 93–116). Cambridge, MA: Harvard Education Publishing Group.

Parette, P. (2005). Restrictiveness and race in special education: The issue of cultural reciprocity. *Learning Disabilities: A Contemporary Journal, 3*(1), 17–24.

Petreñas, C., Puigdellívol, I., & Campdepadrós, R. (2013). From educational segregation to transformative inclusion. *International Review of Qualitative Research, 6*(2), 210–225.

President's Commission on Excellence in Special Education. (2002). *A new era: Revitalizing special education for children and their families.* Washington, DC: U.S. Department of Education.

Prevent Blindness America (2008). *Vision problems in the U.S.: Prevalence of adult vision impairment and age-related eye disease in America.* Schaumburg, IL: Prevent Blindness America.

Prevent Blindness America (2012). Focus on Eye Health and Culturally Diverse Populations. Retrieved from http://www.eyeresearch.org/eye_fact_center.html

Public Broadcasting Service. (n.d.). *Howard Gardner's multiple intelligences theory.* Retrieved from http://www.pbs.org/wnet/gperf/education/ed_mi_overview.html

Quillman, R. D., & Goodrich, G. (2004). Interventions for adults with visual impairments. In A. H. Lueck (Ed.) *Functional vision: A practitioner's guide to evaluation and intervention* (pp. 423–470). New York: AFB Press.

Quintana, N., Rosenthal, J., Krehely, J. (2010). The Federal Response to Gay and Transgender Homeless Youth. Center for American Progress, at http://www.americanprogress.org/

Reeve, C. (n.d.) Retrieved from http://www.brainyquote.com/quotes/authors/c/christopher_reeve.html

Rehabilitation Research and Training Center on Disability Statistics and Demographics (2009). *Annual compendium of disability statistics: 2009.* New York: Rehabilitation Research and Training Center on Disability Demographics and Statistics, Hunter College.

Reschly, D. J. (2009). Minority special education disproportionality: Findings and misconceptions. In United States Commission on Civil Rights, *Minorities in special education: Briefing report* (57–64). Washington, DC: U.S. Government Printing Office. Retrieved from http://www.usccr.gov/pubs/MinoritiesinSpecial Education.pdf

Riccio, C. A., Ochoa, S. H., Garza S. G., & Nero, C. L. (2003). Referral of African American children for evaluation of emotional or behavioral concerns. *Multiple Voices, 6*(1), 1–12.

Richard, G., & Russell, J. (2001). *The source for ADD/ADHD: Attention deficit disorder and attention deficit/hyperactivity disorder.* Moline, IL: LinguiSystems.

Richardson, J. G., & Powell, J. J. W. (2011). *Comparing special education: Origins to contemporary paradoxes.* Stanford, CA: Stanford University Press.

Rogan, P., & Rinne, S. (2011). National call for organizational change from sheltered to integrated employment. *Intellectual and Developmental Disabilities, 49,* 248–260. doi:10.1352/1934-9556-49.4.248.

Rosenberg, M. S., Westling, D. L., & McLeskey, J. (2011) *Special education for today's teachers: An introduction* (2nd ed.). Upper Saddle River, NJ: Pearson Education, Inc.

Rowjewski, J., Lee, I. H., Gregg, N., & Gemici S. (2012). Development patterns of occupational aspirations in adolescents with high-incidence disabilities. *Exceptional Children, 78*(2), 57–179.

RTI Action Network (n.d.). *What is RTI?* Retrieved from http://rtinetwork.org/learn/what/whatisrti

Rubin, S., Biklen, D., Kasa-Hendrickson, C., Kluth, P., Cardinal, D., & Broderick, A. (2001). Independence, participation, and the meaning of intellectual ability. *Disability & Society, 16*(3), pp. 415–429.

Russell, M., & Stewart, J. (2001). Disablement, Prison, and Historical Segregation. *Monthly Review, 53*(1) 61–75.

Safford, P., & Safford, E. (1996). *A history of childhood and disability.* NY: Teachers College Press.

Saunders, R., Saunders, M., Donnelly, J., Smith, B., Sullivan, D., Guilford, B., & Rondon, M. (2011). Evaluation of an approach to weight loss in adults with intellectual or developmental disabilities. *Intellectual and Developmental Disabilities, 49,* 103–112. doi:10.1352/1934-9556-49.2.103.

Savarese, D. J. (2006) I have a dream. Presentation at Syracuse University Inclusion Imperative Conference, Syracuse, NY. Retrieved from http://tash.org/

Schwartz, D. (1992). *Crossing the river: Creating a conceptual revolution in community and disability.* Boston: Brookline Books.

Schwartz, T. L. (2010). Causes of visual impairment: Pathology and its implications. In A. L. Corn & J. N. Erin (Eds.) *Foundations of low vision: Clinical and functional perspectives.* New York: AFB Press.

Shapiro, J. (1993). *No pity: People with disabilities forging a new civil rights movement.* New York: Times Books.

Shaywitz, S. (2004). *Overcoming dyslexia.* New York: Alfred A. Knopf.

Shelton, H. O. (2009). On the overrepresentation of racial and ethnic minority children and limited English proficient children in special education classes. In United States Commission on Civil Rights, *Minorities in special education: Briefing report* (86–92). Washington, DC: U.S. Government Printing Office. Retrieved from http://www.usccr.gov/pubs/MinoritiesinSpecialEducation.pdf

Siebers, T. (2008). *Disability theory.* Ann Arbor: University of Michigan Press.

Siperstein, G., Kersh, J., & Bardon, J. (2007). *A new generation of research in intellectual disabilities: Charting the course.* Boston, MA: University of Massachusetts—Boston, Special Olympics Global Collaborating Center.

Skiba, R., Albrecht, S., & Losen, D. (2013). CCBD'S position summary on federal policy on disproportionality in special education. *Behavioral Disorders, 38*(2), 108–120.

Skiba, R. J., Poloni-Staudinger, L., Simmons, A. B., Feggins-Azziz, L. R., & Chung, C. (2005). Unproven links: Can poverty explain ethnic disproportionality in special education? *The Journal of Special Education, 39*(3), 130–144.

Skiba, R. J., Simmons, A. B., Ritter, S., Gibb, A. C., Rausch, M. K., Cuadrado, J., & Chung, C. (2008). Achieving equity in special education: History, status, and current challenges. *Exceptional Children, 74*(3), 264–288.

Slenkovitch, J. E. (1986). The behavior disorders as a new EHA category—Pros and cons. *The School Advocate, 1,* 53–55.

Smith, D. (2004). *Introduction to special education: Teaching in an age of opportunity* (5th ed). Boston: Pearson.

Smith, D. (2007). *Introduction to special education: Making a difference* (6th ed.) Boston, MA: Allyn & Bacon.

Smith, P. (1999). Drawing new maps: A radical cartography of developmental disabilities. *Review of Educational Research, 69* (2), 117–144.

Smith, P. (2001). *Invisible voices: People with developmental disabilities tell stories of abuse.* Montpelier, VT: Invisible Victims of Crime Project.

Smith, P. (2004). Whiteness, normal theory, and disability studies. *Disability Studies Quarterly, 24* (2).

Smith, P. (2005). "There is no treatment here": Disability and health needs in a state prison system. *Disability Studies Quarterly, 25* (3), n.p.

Smith, P. (2006). Splitting the ROCK of {speci [ES]al} e.ducat.ion: FLOWers of lang[ue]age in >DIS<ability studies. In S. Danforth and S. Gabel (Eds.), *Vital Questions in Disability Studies in Education,* (pp. 31–58). NY: Peter Lang.

Smith, P. (2008). Cartographies of eugenics and special education: A history of the (ab)normal. In S. Gabel & S. Danforth (Eds.), *Disability and the politics of education: An international reader.* New York: Peter Lang.

Smith, P. (ed.) (2010). *Whatever happened to inclusion? The place of students with intellectual disabilities in education.* New York: Peter Lang.

Snell, M. (2010, March). The 2010 AAIDD Definition Manual and its application to special education. [Video Transcript]. Retrieved from http://www.aaidd.org/snell-transcript.cfm

Sopko, K. M. (April, 2009). *Universal design for learning; Policy challenges and recommendations.* Alexandria, VA: National Association of State Directors of Special Education.

Special Olympics (2001). *Promoting health for persons with mental retardation: A critical journey barely begun.* Washington, D.C.: Author.

Special Olympics (2005). *Changing attitudes, changing the world: Health and health care of people with intellectual disabilities.* Washington, D.C.: Author.

Spencer, T., Biederman, J., Wilens, T., & Farone, S. (2002). Overview and neurobiology of attention-deficit/hyperactivity disorder. *Journal of Clinical Psychiatry, 63* (suppl 12l), 3–9.

Stainback, W., Stainback, S., & Stefanich, G. (1996). Learning together in inclusive classrooms: What about curriculum? *Teaching Exceptional Children, 28*(3), 14–19.

Stevens, L. C. (2011). Chapter 2: Language Acquisition. In R. B. Hoodin (Ed.) *Intervention in child language disorders: A comprehensive handbook.* Boston: Jones and Bartlett.

Subtitle B—Regulations of the Offices of the Department of Education (34 C.F.R. § 300.7 (c)(1) (1999)).

Sugai, G., Horner, R. H., Dunlap, G., Hieneman, M., Lewis, T. J., Nelson, C. M., Scott, T., Liaupsin, C., Sailor, W., Turnbull, A. P., Turnbull III, H. R., Wickham, D., Wilcox. B., & Ruef, M. (2000). Applying positive behavior support and functional behavior assessment in schools. *Journal of Positive Behavior Interventions; 2(3),* 131–143.

Suicide Prevention Resource Center. (2008). Suicide risk and prevention for lesbian, gay, bisexual, and transgender youth. Newton, MA: Education Development Center, Inc.

Sullivan, A., & Bal, A. (2013). Disproportionality in special education: Effects of individual and school variables on disability risk. *Exceptional Children, 79*(4), 475–494.

Swanson, C. B. (2008). *Special education in America: The state of students with disabilities in the nation's high schools.* Bethesda: Editorial Projects in Education. Retrieved from http://www.edweek.org/media/eperc_specialeducationinamerica.pdf

TASH (2003). *TASH resolution on spirituality*. Baltimore, MD: Author.

Taylor, S. V. (2005). Restrictiveness and race in special education: Socio-cultural and linguistic considerations. *Learning Disabilities: A Contemporary Journal 3*(1), 34–43.

The Arc (2013). *Resources, Fact Sheets, Causes and Prevention of Intellectual Disabilities*. Retrieved from http://www.thearc.org/page.aspx?pid=2453

Torres, E. B., Brincker, M., Isenhower, R. W., Yanovich, P., Stigler, K. A., Numberger, J. I., Metaxas, D. M., & Jose, J. V. (2013) Autism: The micro-movement perspective. *Frontiers in Integrative Neuroscience, 7*(32). doi:10.3389/fnint.2013.00032.

Torres, E. B., Yanovich, P., & Metaxas, D. M. (2013). "Give spontaneity and self-discovery a chance in ASD: spontaneous peripheral limb variability as a proxy to evoke centrally driven intentional acts." *Frontiers in Integrative Neuroscience, 7*(46). doi:10.3389/fnint.2013.00046.

Township High School District 214 (2011). *Response to intervention (RtI)*. Elk Grove Village, IL: Elk Grove High School. Retrieved from http://eghs.d214.org/staff_resources/rti_response_to_intervention.aspx

Turnbull, A. P., Summers, J. A., & Brotherson, M. J., (1986). Family life cycle: Theoretical and empirical implications and future directions for families with mentally retarded members. In J. J. Gallagher & P. M. Vietze (Eds.) *Families of handicapped persons: Research, programs and policy issues* (pp. 25–44). Baltimore, MD: Paul H. Brookes.

Turnbull, A. P., & Turnbull, H. R. (1996). Self-determination within a culturally responsive family systems perspective: Balancing the family mobile. In L. Powers, B. Singer, & J. Sowers (Eds.), *Promoting self-competence in children and youth with disabilities: On the road to autonomy* (pp. 195–220). Baltimore: Paul H. Brookes.

Turnbull, A., Turnbull, R., Erwin, E., Soodak, L., & Shogren, K. (2011). *Families, professionals and Exceptionality: Positive outcomes through partnerships and trust*. New York: Pearson Publications.

Underwood, K. (2008). *The construction of disability in our schools: Teacher and parent perspectives on the experience of labeled students*. Rotterdam: Sense Publishers.

U. S. Commission on Civil Rights. (2009). *Minorities in special education: Briefing report*. Washington, DC: U.S. Government Printing Office. Retrieved from http://www.usccr.gov/pubs/MinoritiesinSpecialEducation.pdf

U.S. Department of Agriculture (August, 2012). *National school lunch program fact sheet*. Washington, DC: Author. Retrieved from http://www.fns.usda.gov/cnd/lunch/aboutlunch/NSLPFactSheet.pdf

U.S. Department of Education (1994). *Jacob K. Javits Gifted and Talented Students Education Act of 1988 (P.L. 100-297)*. Washington, D.C.: Author.

U.S. Department of Education (2010). *A blueprint for reform: The reauthorization of the Elementary and Secondary Education Act*. Washington, DC: Author.

U.S. Department of Education (2010). *IDEA Part B child count*. Retrieved from www.IDEAdata.org.

U.S. Department of Education. (2012). *Digest of Education Statistics, 2011 (NCES 2012-001)*. Washington, DC: U.S. Department of Education, National Center for Education Statistics.

U.S. Department of Education, National Center for Education Statistics. (2010). *The condition of education 2010 (NCES 2010-028), Indicator 20*. Retrieved from www.nces.ed.gov.

U.S. Department of Health and Human Services (2008). *Disability and health in the United States, 2001–2005*. Washington, D.C.: Author.

U.S. White House. (2001). *New Freedom Initiative: Fulfilling America's promise to Americans with disabilities*. Washington, DC: Author.

Valencia, R. (1997). Conceptualizing the notion of deficit thinking. In R. Valencia (Ed.), *The evolution of deficit thinking* (pp. 1–12). London, England: Falmer Press.

Van der Klift, E., & Kunc, N. (2002). Beyond benevolence: Supporting genuine friendship in inclusive schools. In J. Thousand, R. Villa, & A. Nevin (Eds.) *Creativity & collaborative learning: The practical guide to empowering students, teachers, and families* (2nd ed.) (pp. 21–28). Baltimore, MD: Paul H. Brookes.

Vermont Department of Corrections (2000). *Facts and Figures.* Waterbury, VT: Author.

Vermont Developmental Disabilities Council (2007). *Choosing words with dignity: Communicating with and about people with disabilities.* Waterbury, VT: Author.

Waber, D. (2010). *Rethinking learning disabilities: Understanding children who struggle in school.* New York: The Guilford Press.

Wagner, M. (1995). Outcomes for youths with serious emotional disturbance in secondary school and early adulthood. The Future of Children: Critical Issues for Children and Youths, 5(4), 90–112.

Wagner, M., Blackorby, J., Cameto, R., Hebbeler, K., & Newman, L. (1993). *The transition experiences of young people with disabilities.* Menlo Park, CA: SRI International.

Wagner, M., D'Amico, R., Marder, C., Newman, L., & Blackorby, J. (1992). *What happens next? Trends in post-school outcomes of youth with disabilities.* Menlo Park, CA: SRI International.

Wagner, M., Marder, C., Blackorby, J., Cameto, R., Newman, L., Levine, P., & Davies-Mercier, E. (with Chorost, M., Garza, N., Guzman, A., & Sumi, C.) (2003). *The achievements of youth with disabilities during secondary school. A report from the National Longitudinal Transition Study-2 (NLTS2).* Menlo Park, CA: SRI International.

Wagner, M., Newman, L., D'Amico, R., Jay, E. D., Butler-Nalin, P., Marder, C., et al. (1991). *Youth with disabilities: How are they doing? The first comprehensive report from the national longitudinal transition study of special education students.* (SRI International Contract 300-87-0054). Washington, DC: U.S. Department of Education, Office of Special Education Programs.

Wallis, C. (2006). "Inside the autistic mind." *Time Magazine,* May 7.

Ward, M., & Meyer, R. (1999). Self-determination for people with developmental disabilities and autism: Two self-advocates perspectives. *Focus on Autism and Other Developmental Disabilities.*

Ware, L. (2006). A look at the way we look at disability. In S. Danforth & S. Gabel (Eds). *Vital questions facing disability studies in education* (pp. 271–287). New York: Peter Lang.

Watkins, S. (1989). *The INSITE model: A model of home intervention for infant, toddler, and preschool aged multihandicapped sensory impaired children,* Volume II. Logan, UT: HOPE, Inc.

Wedl, R. J. (July, 2005). *Response to intervention: An alternative to traditional eligibility criteria for students with disabilities.* St. Paul, MN: Education|Evolving.

Wehman, P., McLaughlin, J., & Wehman, T. (2005). *Intellectual and Developmental Disabilities: Toward Full Community Inclusion.* Austin, TX: Pro-Ed

Wehman, P., & Palmer S. (2003). Adult outcomes for students with cognitive disabilities three years after high school: The impact of self-determination. *Education and Training in Developmental Disabilities, 38(2),* 131–144.

Wheeler, J. P. (n.d.). *Multiple intelligences in the classroom.* Retrieved from http://www.schools.utah.gov/cte.

Whittaker, R. (2001). *Mad in America: Bad science, bad medicine, and the enduring mistreatment of the mentally ill.* Perseus Publishing.

Whittaker, R. (2010). *Anatomy of an epidemic: Magic bullets, psychiatric drugs, and the astonishing rise of mental illness in America.* Crown.

Wilens, T.E., Faraone, S.V., Biederman, J., & Gunawardene, S. (2003). Does stimulant therapy of attention-deficit/hyperactivity disorder beget later substance abuse? Retrieved from http://www.ncbi.nlm.nih.gov/.

Wilkinson, M. E., & Trantham, C. S. (2004). Characteristics of children evaluated at a pediatric low vision clinic: 1981–2003, *Journal of Low Vision and Blindness, 98,* 693–702.

Willcutt, E., Doyle, A., Nigg, J., Faraone, S., & Pennington, B. (2006). Validity of the executive function theory of attention-deficit/hyperactivity disorder: A meta-analytic review. *Biological Psychiatry, 57*(11), 1336–1346. doi:10.1016/j.biopsych.2005.02.006.

Williams, J. L., Pazey, B., Shelby, L., & Yates, J. R. (2013). The enemy among us: Do school administrators perceive students with disabilities as a threat? *NASSP Bulletin, 97*(2), 139–165.

Winzer, M. (1993). *The history of special education: From isolation to integration.* Washington, D.C.: Gallaudet University Press.

Wolfensberger, W. (1975). *The origin and nature of our institutional models.* Syracuse, NY: Human Policy Press.

World Health Organization (2011). *World report on disability.* Geneva, Switzerland: Author.

Young, S. R. (2011). *Real people, regular lives: Autism, communication & quality of life.* www.autcom.org. Durham, NH: Autism National Committee.

Zamora, P. (2009). Minorities in special education. In United States Commission on Civil Rights, *Minorities in special education: Briefing report* (86–92). Washington, DC: U.S. Government Printing Office. Retrieved from http://www.usccr.gov/pubs/MinoritiesinSpecialEducation.pdf

Contributors

Sally Burton-Hoyle: Dr. Sally Burton-Hoyle, sister to a person on the autism spectrum, serves on the Interagency Autism Coordinating Committee (IACC) at the federal level and has focused her life and career on improving the education and lives of people with autism and other challenging behaviors. She developed the Masters of Autism Spectrum Disorders program at Eastern Michigan University (EMU) and is currently faculty in this program. This program is based on Positive Behavioral Supports and family/community involvement. Dr. Burton-Hoyle has been at EMU since 2006 and was Executive Director of the Autism Society of Michigan from 1994–2006 prior to coming to EMU. In addition, she has classroom experience as a special education teacher in Kansas, Missouri, and Illinois. Dr. Burton-Hoyle holds a doctorate in counseling psychology and special education from the University of Idaho and a master's degree in special education from the University of Kansas.

Deon Chaneyfield: Deon is 26 years old, and lives in Ypsilanti, Michigan. He is a student at the Washtenaw Intermediate School District Young Adult Transition Program. He has three different jobs. He likes to play basketball and football and just hang out. He loves to go out to eat.

Pamela Colton: Pamela earned her bachelor's degree in Anthropology & History and the Maize and Blue award from the University of Michigan. After graduation she had a son, David, who was later diagnosed with autism. Pamela's second degree from the University of Michigan was a master's in American Culture, with concentrations in race and disability studies. For the past 15 years Pamela has lived and worked in urban communities. She was employed for several years as a long-term substitute teacher by the Flint Community School district, while completing her master's degree, and eventually earning her teaching certifications in Special Education and History, and then the Brehm Scholar Award at Eastern Michigan University. She now lives in Flint, Michigan, and teaches in Pontiac, Michigan.

Jennifer Desiderio: Jennifer Desiderio received her B.A. in Psychology from Skidmore College (New York), subsequently pursuing a graduate concentration in School Psychology from Miami University (Ohio). Emerging with both M.S. and Ed.S. (Educational Specialist) degrees, she served for almost fifteen years in public schools as a school psychologist, educational trainer, and consultant. Most of that time was spent in southwestern Ohio, where she was immersed in the Response to Intervention model of service delivery. Jennifer has worked directly with K-12 students certified with a wide variety of disabilities as well as presented workshops in the areas of collaborative teaming and problem solving, scientifically-based academic and behavioral interventions, curriculum-based assessment, IEP goal writing, Attention Deficit Hyperactivity Disorder, Universal Design for Learning, and learning styles. Currently an associate professor at Eastern Michigan University, Jennifer teaches classes in assessment, classroom and behavior management, and writing for special education.

Janet Fisher: Dr. Janet Fisher teaches courses in autism and classroom management as a Professor at Eastern Michigan University. Janet also instructs teachers throughout the country regarding powerful strategies that improve student behavior and academics as a Director and Trainer for the Center for Teacher Effectiveness. She has worked for over 20 years in the educational trenches of public schools as a teacher and administrator in general and special education developing evidence-based behavior strategies. She currently helps teachers to engage in a systematized approach that builds relationships, supports students, and helps them to understand then change their behavior. Janet has presented at numerous conferences throughout the country and has authored manuscripts that effectively address challenging behavior. She is in the process of publishing a manual that will assist educators and parents with positive behavior support strategies to successfully include students who are challenged by syndromes and disorders in general education settings.

Megan Hoorn: Megan has a BA in speech-language pathology with minors in human biology and human sexuality. She is the College Buddy Director for Best Buddies at Eastern Michigan University. Best Buddies is an international non-profit organization that works to create opportunities for one-to-one friendships, leadership development, and integrated employment for people with intellectual and developmental disabilities. In her free time, she enjoys knitting, running, reading, and spending time with her family.

Lisa Jordan: Lisa lives with her fiancée in Ann Arbor, Michigan, although she is originally a native of the cold, snowy tundra called Minnesota. She has a bachelor's degree in chemistry and works as an analytical chemist for a public health company. She has a strong interest in public health and environmental science. She enjoys spending time with friends and family—particularly the growing gaggle of nieces and nephews, outdoor winter sports, traveling, craft beer, and ultimate frisbee.

James Kleimola: James is a student at the Washtenaw Intermediate School District Young Adult Transition Program. He lives in an apartment on Eastern Michigan University's campus with a roommate. He works with the EMU football team, carrying balls and equipment. He is the Buddy Director for Best Buddies at Eastern Michigan University. He works for the EMU Echo Newspaper where he deliver papers to the office buildings around campus. He is also a part of the RAP project at EMU. He goes to church and plays his guitar there.

Rhonda Vander Laan Kraai: Rhonda Vander Laan Kraai, Ed.D., CCC-SLP is an assistant professor of special education at Eastern Michigan University in Ypsilanti, Michigan. Dr. Kraai earned a doctoral degree in Special Education and Reading from Ball State University, an M.S. from Marquette University in Communication Disorders, and a B.S. in Speech Pathology and Audiology and Elementary Education from Western Michigan University. Her research interests are in the areas of religion and disabilities, metacognitive strategy use in spelling, and academic service learning for preservice teachers. She is a member of the American Speech Language Hearing Association and the Council for Exceptional Children. Dr. Kraai is married to Dr. James Kraai, a professor, and they have three children and four grandchildren.

Alicia Li: Dr. Alicia Li is currently a professor in the Department of Special Education at the Eastern Michigan University. Prior to pursuing advanced degrees in the U.S., Dr. Li had an interdisciplinary educational and employment background in nursing and education. As a registered nurse, and certified teacher in general education and special education, Dr. Li primarily worked with students with physical impairments and other health impairments in Taiwan, especially children with cerebral palsy. Following her master's study in education for students with intellectual disabilities, doctoral degree in education for students with visual impairments, and a certificate in orientation & mobility (O & M) for the blind, Dr. Li worked as an itinerant teacher and O & M specialist for students and adults with visual impairments including those with other disabilities. In addition to her teaching students of all ages for nearly three decades, Dr. Li has published and researched work on vision programs, Brain Gym in students with visual impairments, autism, print and braille letter reversals, and math and science learning in students with visual impairments.

Sandra McClennen: Sandra McClennen is Professor Emerita of Special Education at Eastern Michigan University, a certified teacher and a Licensed Psychologist. She has taught autism endorsement courses online for EMU, is psychological consultant to community mental health agencies serving people with developmental disabilities, and has a private practice. Her entire career has been devoted to helping parents and teachers provide the best possible learning and living environments for individuals with cognitive, neurological, and physical disabilities. She looks for and focuses on people's gifts rather than deficits. Access to communication for those who do not speak is an essential part of good environments. When facilitated communication was first introduced in the United States, she immediately saw its importance. Since then, she has used the technique successfully with many individuals of all ages, including those diagnosed as having intellectual disability as well as those experiencing autism.

Jackie McGinnis: Jackie McGinnis has spent 30 years working in various capacities in the field of special education. She began her career in Omaha, Nebraska, as a physical therapy assistant, eventually teaching students with multiple disabilities in the Lincoln Nebraska Public School System. She received her Ph.D. from the University of Nebraska-Lincoln with an emphasis in Augmentative Communication. She worked for the Ministry of Health in Ontario, Canada, providing assistive technology services. Before beginning her position as a teacher trainer at Eastern Michigan University, she provided contract services for augmentative communication to persons with developmental disabilities in Livingston and Washtenaw Counties in Michigan. She is currently an associate professor in the Department of Special Education at EMU.

William Milburn: William Milburn is a special educator in Oregon. His student population consists of students with emotional and behavioral disorders, learning disabilities, as well as students on the autism spectrum. William is a former recipient of the Delores Soderquist-Brehm scholarship from Eastern Michigan University. He has researched, published, and presented work involving school climate for lesbian, gay, bisexual, transgender, and queer/questioning students and the social, emotional, and academic implications of anti-gay bullying. He has researched and spoken on the willingness and ability of teachers to effectively address anti-gay bullying in their schools.

Ann Orr: Ann Orr, Professor in Special Education at Eastern Michigan University, received her doctorate in Educational Studies from the University of Michigan. She teaches undergraduate and graduate courses in assistive technology, special education, and human development. Before coming to EMU, Dr. Orr taught in a residential facility for adolescents with serious emotional impairment and as a K-5th grade teacher consultant. Her higher education teaching includes adjunct positions at the University of Michigan and Madonna University. Dr. Orr has been a co-author/co-primary investigator on several research projects, including the Michigan Department of Education's "Project Success: Assisting Students with Disabilities to Succeed in Mathematics." Her research agenda currently focuses on using iPads and apps in special education. She has published a number of articles in scholarly journals such as *Learning Disabilities Quarterly* and the *Journal for Ethnographic and Qualitative Research*. Dr. Orr is the recipient of EMU's Distinguished Faculty Award for Teaching.

Loreena Parks: Professor Parks is an associate professor in the special education department at Eastern Michigan University. She has degrees from Wayne State University and Eastern Michigan University and attended the University of Western Ontario. She has acquired a SpA in Curriculum, a M.A. in Learning Disabilities, a B.B.A. in Marketing and a B.S. in Hearing Impairment (K-12) and General Education (K-8). Prior to joining the faculty at Eastern Michigan University, Professor Parks taught and consulted in public and private schools, at the Kindergarten through University level in Michigan and Ontario, Canada.

Michael Peacock: Michael is currently an educator for at-risk youth in the Detroit area. He was named a College of Education Scholar of Excellence in 2012, a Delores Soderquist Brehm Scholar in 2011, and the first recipient of the Brehm Fellowship at Eastern Michigan University, where he studied elementary and special education for students with emotional impairments. He also holds a degree in humanities from the University of Michigan-Dearborn, where he was named the Honors Scholar in Humanities in 2007. Michael was a contributing author to the *Brehm Scholar Research Monograph, Volume 2* (2012) and *Both Sides of the Table: Autoethnographies of Educators Learning and Teaching With/In [Dis]ability* (2013). He has presented on topics such as intersectionality, autoethnography, performativity, democratic education, and interdisciplinary teaching, both nationally and internationally.

Linda Polter: Linda Polter is currently an Associate Professor in the Department of Special Education at Eastern Michigan University. Her focus is on preparing students to be teachers of students who are deaf or hard-of-hearing, utilizing an approach that emphasizes listening and spoken language. Before coming to EMU, Linda taught in the public school system for over 30 years. She worked as a classroom teacher of students who were deaf or hard-of-hearing and had experiences working not only with students at all levels (pre-school through high school), but also working with families and general education teachers. Linda also worked as an itinerant teacher consultant for six years, supporting students with hearing loss who were included in general education settings and collaborating with their teachers. Linda concluded her career in public schools as a supervisor of a center program for students who were deaf or hard-of-hearing.

Ruth Salles: Ruth has completed her master's degree coursework for a special education certification (K-12) and teaching certificate (K-5) at Eastern Michigan University. She worked for the Student Advocacy Center of Michigan as an advocate, implementing and facilitating a drop out prevention program for at-risk high school students, known as Check & Connect, and currently is a special educator in Ypsilanti. In her free time, Ruth does yard work and loves spending time with her two dogs. A Jill of all trades, Ruth is also musically and artistically inclined and enjoys taking on any opportunity to keep up on those talents. She is working on a novel of her own, which she hopes to someday see published.

Karen Schulte: Karen Schulte worked in the public schools for almost 30 years as a special education teacher consultant and as a professional development consultant. She received her Bachelor of Science degree in Special Education for Students with Emotional Impairments, her Master of Arts degree in Special Education for Students with Learning Disabilities and her Specialist degree in Special Education Administration and Supervision all from Eastern Michigan University. She is currently an Associate Professor in the Department of Special Education at EMU, specializing in the area of learning disabilities.

Phil Smith: Phil describes himself as being post-everything and after boundaries. He received the Emerging Scholar Award in Disability Studies in Education in 2009, and has had papers published in a variety of journals, as well as several book chapters. He's published several books, including *Whatever Happened to Inclusion? The Place of Students with Intellectual Disabilities in Education* (2010) and *Both Sides of the Table: Autoethnographies of Educators Learning and Teaching With/In [Dis]ability* (2013). He is also a published poet, playwright, novelist, and visual artist. For more than 25 years he has worked as a disability rights activist, and served on the boards of directors of a number of national and state organizations, including as Treasurer of the Society for Disability Studies. He identifies as a person with a disability, rides his bicycle to work, and tries to remember to wear his socks. Phil owns Flamingo Farm, where he makes maple syrup; and he spends lots of time beside Lake Superior, where wolves, moose, and bald eagles peek into his cabin.

Lizbeth Curme Stevens: Lizbeth Curme Stevens is a licensed speech-language pathologist and professor in the Department of Special Education at Eastern Michigan University. She worked in the public schools in Michigan for over 20 years providing services to children and adolescents with diverse communication disorders. She holds the Certificate of Clinical Competence (CCC) from the American Speech-Language-Hearing Association (ASHA) and now teaches and writes about language acquisition and disorders. Publications include book chapters and articles in various professional journals. As a current reviewer for the ASHA publication, *Perspectives on Language, Learning, and Education*, she keeps abreast of the latest research in the field. Stevens who was awarded ASHA Fellow in 2007 has long employed academic service-learning in her classes and frequently presents and writes about this as well as other topics related to the scholarship of teaching and learning.

Gilbert Stiefel: Gil is an associate professor at Eastern Michigan University in the Department of Special Education. He is the program coordinator for the emotional impairment program area. He completed his Ph.D in psychology and education at the University of Michigan in 1985. He had approximately 30 years experience as a school psychologist and served as an adjunct instructor in the Psychology Department at Eastern prior to his full-time appointment to the Department of Special Education. He teaches courses in assessment and research methods as well as the introductory course in emotional impairments.

David C. Winters: Dr. Winters is an associate professor in the Department of Special Education at Eastern Michigan University. He has been a classroom teacher, tutor, diagnostician, administrator, and tutor/teacher trainer for over 30 years. He currently teaches courses introducing special education to preservice teachers as well as instructional and assistive technology, writing, and assessment in special education for preservice special educators and speech language pathologists.

CPSIA information can be obtained
at www.ICGtesting.com
Printed in the USA
FSHW012342260719
60443FS

9 781465 272591